LANGUAGE AND LOVE

William Mallard

LANGUAGE AND LOVE

Introducing
Augustine's Religious Thought
Through the
Confessions Story

The Pennsylvania State University Press
University Park, Pennsylvania

Library of Congress Cataloging-in-Publication Data

Mallard, William.
    Language and love : introducing Augustine's religious thought
through the Confessions story / William Mallard.

        p.   cm.
    Includes bibliographical references and index.
    ISBN 0-271-01037-1 — ISBN 0-271-01038-X (pbk.)
    1. Augustine, Saint, Bishop of Hippo.   Confessiones.   I. Title.
BR65.A62M35   1994
270.2′092—dc20   93-9070
                                                                        CIP

Published by The Pennsylvania State University Press,
University Park, PA 16802-1003

It is the policy of The Pennsylvania State University Press to use acid-free paper for the
first printing of all clothbound books. Publications on uncoated stock satisfy the mini-
mum requirements of American National Standard for Information Sciences—Perma-
nence of Paper for Printed Library Materials, ANSI Z39.48–1984.

Contents

Preface

The purpose of this book is to introduce Augustine's *Confessions*, and also the larger outline of his mature theology, with both of these tasks woven into one project.

Can the larger outline of his thought in fact fairly emerge through a study of *Confessions* I–IX? Of course extensions and additions become necessary. Also, his thought evolves through thirty years following the *Confessions'* composition, in many and subtle ways. Still, some important cornerstones are in place by *Confessions* time (397–399 C.E.). His affirming the good of creation (against the Manichaeans—with Neoplatonist support); his describing the struggles of the human will and the freedom given by God's grace through Christ (anticipating his debate with Pelagius a dozen years later); his sense of the Christian people's identity—universal, open, yet strangers in the world (in opposition to the Donatists, and to polytheism, anticipating his *City of God*); his view of reason in relation to authority (looking forward to his *The Trinity*): all are substantively present in the *Confessions* narrative. Beyond that narrative (I–IX) are the reflective materials of *Confessions* X–XIII. Except for occasional references, these chapters do not play a part here; unfortunately, they would extend this project beyond manageable bounds. Hopefully, readers will investigate them on their own.

In any case, the intent of this book is in no way to serve as a substitute for reading the *Confessions* itself. Rather, the book is a kind of theological meditation on the *Confessions* and its major topics. The invitation is to read it before, or after, or along with the *Confessions*, as seems helpful. The

Introduction gives an interpretive survey of the rest of the book, to be read at the outset or returned to as an appendage. All quotations, unless otherwise indicated, are from the *Confessions*.

One possible reading of the *Confessions* unfolds here. Countless others are possible, as well. The aim is hardly to be definitive, but to introduce the rich potential of the text. All translations from the *Confessions* are the author's (and from Augustine's works generally, unless otherwise noted), so that the translations inevitably constitute part of the interpretation. My search has been for a clear, distinct English that nevertheless retains some of the rhythm and elevation of the original. My hope has been to avoid both the archaic and the prosaically flat.

The theme of "language" in fact serves as an entry into the account as a whole. Augustine, whose first career was to teach rhetoric, is an ancestor of those today who offer rhetoric and language as keys to the human situation. At a time when drastic change has undermined trusted cornerstones of life (both in his century and ours!), persuasive, communicative language may be able to rally the general imagination and point people toward new hopes and intentions.

On the one hand, Augustine found such language only frustrating: he wanted to get beyond words to the eternal things themselves. Yet again, he knew that language is an unavoidable medium and even let himself be fascinated with its powers. The rhetorician in him knew that even very common words, spoken well, can flame upward into the human heart (*Christian Doctrine* IV, xviii). The theologian in him knew that the very Incarnation of God's Word in Christ parallels the everyday human event of speaking up and saying what we have in mind (*Christian Doctrine* I, xiii). The Incarnation empowered mere human language. The plain rhetoric of New Testament stories carried the force of God's truth, God's Word, incarnate in simple words. So the Incarnation brought truth (philosophy) and language (rhetoric) remarkably together. God had honored language. So Augustine wanted to dedicate rhetoric to truth-telling (*Christian Doctrine* IV, ii).

I have tried to deal with his concerns by speaking of Augustine's language "worlds"—family, school, government, church—a terminology not his, but contemporary. Yet I think my usage is true to his struggle to leave behind vain, empty speaking and find language whole, as he held that God intended it.

In retelling the *Confessions* narrative, the question of historical accuracy must arise. How well did Augustine remember, across a dozen years, the events that shaped his conversion? Regardless of that question, the primary goal here has been to explore the richness of that memory and see where it leads. If Augustine's later reflections have been selective toward the past and interlaced it with interpretation, the results are nevertheless of high significance. Thus my main concern is: Where was his mind in 397–399 C.E., when he wrote the *Confessions?* Analysis is subsequently more literary than historical. At the same time, I admit to believing that his ability to recall is trustworthy.

The greatness of Augustine and his works are not making the impact they should now on religious belief. Many find the material difficult or diffuse; the scholarship is immense and varied. A starting point is therefore not easy to find. I hope that this book may be a good starting point for some.

Many persons have been essential in bringing this project together, though I take full responsibility for its final form. Roberta Bondi, Karen Carter, and Gregor Sebba read carefully and gave invaluable early encouragement, while David Pacini and John Hayes made crucial suggestions concerning theme and structure. More recently Patout Burns was encouraging and illuminating, and I am indebted for thorough and essential critical readings to Robert J. O'Connell and Rowan Greer. Suggestions also came from Brooks Holifield and Charles Gerkin. I am indebted to successive deans of the Candler School of Theology, Jim L. Waits and R. Kevin LaGree, for released time, and to the Association of Theological Schools for grant support, moving the work to completion. Gatra, Rob, and Cole Mallard helped with reading, technical work, and suggestions, as did Norma Ware; and Vivian Pollard was faithful to a demanding typing task. Finally, thanks to Philip Winsor of the Penn State Press.

*For the students
in my classes,
past and present*

A Note on the *Confessions*

Augustinian scholarship through the ages has mounted an awesome monument of editing and comment, of which the *Confessions* has called forth a significant part. The pursuit of a sound, critical edition of the *Confessions'* Latin text has been in itself a complex story. After more than a thousand years of intensive use of his works in scattered centers, the Maurist Fathers (Benedictine) of the seventeenth century determined to bring together a wide collection of manuscripts of his works, including the *Confessions*, and produced from them a collected edition (Paris, 1679). This edition was reprinted by J.-P. Migne in his foundational source collection of the Latin Fathers (*Patrologia Latina*, Paris, 1845). It was this Maurist text, used by Migne, that E. B. Pusey followed in preparing his famous English translation of the *Confessions* (London, 1838) for the *Library of the Fathers*, a project of the Tractarian movement, of which John Henry Newman was a part.

The twentieth century has seen marked strides in critical, scientific pursuit of an authentic Latin text. During the decade 1925–1935, not only the number of surviving *Confessions* MSS was carefully reviewed (288 complete, 35 incomplete), but the comparative validity of the various MS families was judged through the pains and skill of Dom B. Capelle, who thereby provided the principles of a new scientific edition. Martin Skutella then followed these principles in revising an edition by P. Knoll (then almost forty years old) to produce what has been called the Skutella edition (Leipzig, 1934). The *Confessions* found in the *Oeuvres de Saint Augustin*, 2d series, vols. 13–14 (Paris, 1962) in the *Bibliothèque Augustinienne*, employs the Skutella text, generously amplified with introduction, notes, and French translation, and has been the text consulted in preparing this book.

Several English translations of the *Confessions* are available. The nineteenth-century Pusey translation remains a careful and vigorous text; yet its language is heavily archaic to the late twentieth-century ear. Two mid-century series of translated sources have included the *Confessions* in English: Vernon Bourke, noted Augustinian scholar, has offered a 1953 translation in the extensive *Fathers of the Church* series; Albert Outler, more recently a welcome authority on John Wesley, produced a 1955 translation in the *Library of Christian Classics*, vol. 7. The Bourke translation is a clear, literal rendering. The Outler includes helpful footnotes from time to time on major points of Augustinian thought. R. S. Pine-Coffin offers a paraphrase-translation in Penguin Books, valuable for rapid, initial reading. Comparable to Pine-Coffin is the Rex Warner translation of 1963 (Mentor Books); yet Pine-Coffin is superior in introduction and notes, and in the adept use of English, especially the striking phrase. J. K. Ryan's translation for Image Books (1960) is a careful, close reading, yet contemporary in expression, with valuable notes, references, and introduction. Henry Chadwick has provided a new translation (1991) through Oxford University Press with especially helpful, knowledgeable footnotes, introduction, and index.

Though not a full translation, a commentary on Books I–IX by Colin Starnes (Wilfrid Laurier University Press, 1990) has recently come into my hands, promising great usefulness.

Introduction

One of the reasons the religious thought of Augustine wins attention is because it comes out of a story. His *Confessions* tells that story in the form of a long conversation with God. Why do twentieth-century people fifteen hundred years later continue to find the story compelling? Mostly it is because his struggles with his own life, expressed directly to God, remind us of ourselves.

The gist of what he says still sounds very familiar: God, I've had to search for you; I didn't know how to find you. There's still so much I don't understand. I made so many mistakes in my life, not only in my actions, but in my thinking. When I grew up, many things in my parents' house were not right. When I was a teenager I felt like I wanted to die. Later I was a success at the university, and I attracted women, but I didn't know how to love anyone—certainly not you, God. And I didn't understand you: I thought the sun, moon, and stars were part of you! Later I decided I was one of the wisest people on earth. Yet somehow, God, through all this wandering and misery, you were working for me in ways I didn't even know. You helped me by keeping me frustrated with my own wrong-headedness. You also helped me by letting me meet some wonderful people in your church. I'm glad beyond anything I can say that you brought me from being my own worst enemy to peace and understanding. Help me to tell my story.

"my story"—yet he is not telling a private story. He writes in order that everyone else may overhear what he says to God and take heart. His most famous line includes everyone:

> You have made us for yourself, and our heart is restless until it rests in you. (I, 1, 1)

Two Worlds

Augustine started out in childhood with a restless heart because he had to live in two different worlds: the world of his mother's religious faith, and the world of everything else.[1] The two worlds had two different ways of talking that seemed to contradict each other. In his mother's world, talk was about Christ the Savior and about the mighty God who helps us, especially to go to heaven. In the other world, talk was about winning and achieving: get an education, win a prize, be a great speaker and debater, rule over others, be wealthy and honored, satisfy your parents who did so much for you. Augustine's father cared only for the "winning" world. Augustine's mother loved the "God" world and taught it to her children carefully, though she wanted Augustine to succeed in the second world as well.

To live in two worlds and talk two ways about life disturbed Augustine as a child and a youth. Even his mother, Monica, added to the confusion in some ways. She taught him that nothing and no one was as important as his Father in heaven. Yet she did not have him baptized. Even when he was sick and almost dying (at age eleven), Monica did not call a priest to baptize him. She feared that later, as he grew up, he would commit sins, and then could not cleanse himself by baptism because he had already used it! Yet the eleven-year-old had cried for baptism. Which world was he living in? The world of God and baptism? Or the world of school, and lessons, and jealousy, and cheating to get ahead? Which way of talking told the truth?

When he was sixteen, the money keeping him in school ran out for a time. Yet back at home his parents had no plan for his everyday good behavior, for he was not baptized and they felt he could not learn good Christian behavior until later on. Both his worlds, religion and school, hung suspended, and he fell between them. He had nothing to do from day

---

1. Augustine of Hippo was born a North African, of North African descent, in 354 c.e. during the time of the late Roman Empire. His father, and then his mother, were small landowners in the inland town of Thagaste and provided his education at the University of Carthage in rhetoric. He was a teacher and later the emperor's rhetorician in Milan, Italy. At length he converted to the Catholic Christianity of his childhood, returned to North Africa, and served many years as the bishop of Hippo until his death in 430 c.e.

to day or week to week. During that time he and some others damaged someone's pear tree down the road. He remembered this small incident years later because of how he felt at the time—not about the pear tree, but about his life. Really, he wanted to die. His mother expected great religious things from him, but he was unbaptized and not even qualified to try. Both parents expected great learning from him, but there was no money and therefore no way to progress in school. It was bad enough to try living in two worlds. It was worse as a teenager to have neither world and to belong nowhere.

Augustine later realized that belonging to two ways of doing always ends in belonging to nothing and being nobody. Outwardly, he went on to succeed. He put on a tough, Roman discipline, finished the university, wrote speeches for the emperor, became learned and philosophical. Yet inwardly, two worlds and two ways of talking still pained him and gave him no happiness. He took a concubine, and they had a son, whom he greatly loved; but he could never belong fully to the concubine because she was part of his world of convenience and advantage. He taught students fine speaking (rhetoric), but not how to tell the truth. He joined a religious sect, but one that taught that God is only a gentle light, whose home is far away, while everything besides God is evil and accursed.

In the sect he had one very special friend, but the friend died, and the God of gentle light could not comfort him in the evil world of death. Later he had other close friends who wanted, with him, to live for God, but even together they could not find a way to leave the world of lies, pride, and deceit. Later under his mother's influence, he dismissed his concubine to prepare for marriage in the world of God and religion; but he found himself engaged to someone of acceptable class and proper family, who was only ten years old!

At length he found philosophers that were masters of learning and schooltalk, who could nevertheless speak of God. The two worlds of school and religion linked! Yet he then began to think of himself as an expert on God and pulled the new philosophy back into his world of personal achievement and puffed-up ego.

One World

Through all of this something was deeply wrong with him and with the life around him. It wasn't simply the case that the world of God and heaven was good, and the world of everyday life and struggle, bad. Something worse was going on. In fact, there were not really two worlds, even if there were two ways of talking. Such talk was a symptom of a deeper problem, as if a person were sick and feverish and talking out of his head. What he came to realize is that after all there is only one world, and that world belongs to God, even if it is different from God. Since there is one world, both religion and getting-on-in-life have to fit together, even if they seem not to. Even if the Christian Bible has Christ saying, "My kingdom is not of this world" (John 18:36),[2] it does not mean that there are two worlds, one good and belonging to God, one evil and belonging to the Devil. The same Christ had said, "God so loved the world . . ." (John 3:16). That means that there is one world, one God, and really only one way of talking.

Then how did people get into living and speaking as if there were two? What is the deeper problem? Augustine concluded that people *create* two worlds in their imaginations (with two ways of talking about them) so that they can keep God in God's heaven, on the one hand, and then take over the world of power and advantage for themselves. People want to seclude God within religious affairs, then control the get-ahead world by lying, cheating, and stealing to become powerful. The deeper problem is the human desire to control everything.

The world is good. Everything in it is good. But evil moves in when people decide to carve the world in two, put God in the first and seize the second. Or they may pretend to be God's representatives from the first, yet still actually want the second for themselves. This move is variously called hypocrisy, duplicity, double-dealing, and injustice. The aim is not only to control the world of personal advantage, but really to restrict God's world by keeping God in God's place. In fact, attempting to restrict God was really how it all started. Adam and Eve (in whom Augustine believed literally and historically) decided to take the serpent's advice and "be like God" (Genesis 3:5), that is, take control of their own life rather than obeying God's approach to it, which seemed long and tedious. Even religion for them became a way of taking over God's authority. They decided to become like God at once, set their own religious rules, and be free to play with the rest of the world as they wished. The world went wrong through the human attempt to assume God's spiritual rule (become as gods) before

---

2. Biblical translations throughout (except directly from Augustine's Latin) are from the Authorized Version, the Revised Standard, or the New Revised Standard, depending on helpfulness in context.

any lying and stealing and blaming ever took place. The worst evil, and the first evil, was religious evil.

Augustine had to admit that his mother had tried to control him religiously to bring him to God, even in ways that God would not approve. Even good people, like his mother, could slip into a two-world approach; she also wanted him to be a winner in the deceitful world, even before baptism. The problem was very deep and serious. All humanity seemed caught in a tangle of religious and everyday power plays and ways of speaking. All persons felt the tug of the two worlds inside themselves. Religious people still wanted to dominate others. Profane people, looking for power, wanted to ignore God, yet could not entirely, since "our heart is restless until it rests in you." One way or another, by religion or by everyday aggression, all people wanted, first, to divide the world, then to conquer it. Whole peoples, governments, and institutions used two ways of talking as if there were really two worlds. Augustine was convinced that holding to two worlds actually meant having no world at all.

A Solution

I began by saying that Augustine had experiences that people today can recognize. Much of the above two-world problem is recognizable now in personal life, in communities, in governments, and institutions. Augustine held also to what he considered a solution to the two-world, two-talk problem. Looking at his solution raises the question whether it works today, as he felt it did for him then.

The solution begins by supposing there is one world and one consistent way of talking. Simple enough. Yet it turns out to be very difficult to hold to that simple approach.

If there is one world, a single creation under the rule of one Creator God, then it can be only a wise move to honor and please that Creator, to live by the Creator's rules, so that things turn out well. The Creator wants human care for the creation, including care both for the earth and for other fellow human beings: friends, family, community, world. At the same time, one has to protect and advance oneself in a world of danger and competition where all others are likewise advancing themselves. To please the Creator could mean being overwhelmed in the world's great rush for advantage. (Augustine's first boyhood prayers for help in school did not relieve his harsh situation.) Yet to fight to preserve oneself can quickly divide the world, manipulate God, and dominate others.

Augustine came to believe in one essential key to living in God's good, but dangerous, created world: learn to do it gradually. There has to be steady practice, day by day and year by year, which starts small and patiently lives in one world, hoping to grow. Augustine was horrified that he did not have an introduction to such growth as a child and youth. Yet someone objects: How is it possible to start small? What situation will allow it? How can I resist the temptation to break my world apart?

One answer is that the child or adult needs some place safe enough to experiment with life, with keeping God and world together, yes, even with "getting ahead," but also with caring and being cared for—in small ways at first, then in greater and greater ways. But what place? One answer is the family. The family offers safe boundaries and life experiences that are guarded and close. Yet Augustine's family was divided and inadequate. If the foundation of the family is in creation and the Creator God, then the family needs God's clear support to stay on track. Therefore the Creator is present in the Creator's church, as if in a large family, to offer life once again in one world.

For the Creator of all things, everywhere, to be in a particular place, a particular church, seemed impossible. Yet a particular place, a safe shelter, was just what humanity had to have. To begin to live in one world there had to be beginner's rules, reasonable safety, and step-by-step progress. To solve everything at once would mean collapsing in two. To become both someone strong, and yet someone caring, took time. The Creator's church, then, was like a family, a family Augustine did not experience in his early life, but discovered after much struggle. This family offered closeness and warmth, personal nurture, as well as discipline. Augustine finally held that the Creator actually had appeared on earth to provide what the family needed: authority, teaching, self-giving, trust. That seemed like a mythological tale, and it was a long while before he could grasp it. Yet mythology deals in a two-world outlook, the immortal gods and mortal humanity; while the Creator's appearance was God uniting with humanity, in Christ, even dying, to accomplish a one-world outlook. This appearance as a human being, and the onset of the Creator's church, were local and particular; they had to be if they responded to humanity's need for a place to start again. Yet people of every nation and race on earth were invited to participate.

The Creator had started over with humanity, not only to heal the two-world outlook, but also to remedy the two ways of talking and bring them into one. Philosophical school language had spoken of God, but Augustine had discovered that it led him only to puffed-up conceit as a "wise" man. Talk of God, therefore, like everything else, had to start simple and grow. When he had first looked at the scriptures of the church, he had found them crude. Later he realized that this direct plainness concealed deeper meaning, forced beginners to be humble until they were ready for subtle truth. There is one way of talking, but it operates at different levels. The plain level humbles those whom philosophy would make conceited; the philosophical level keeps plain readers searching, who might become complacent. Both levels tell about one Creator, one truth, one world, one hope. The creator appeared on earth partly to join the simple language of religion and the rigorous language of philosophy. Such joining was an act of compassion: the Creator brought language and love.

The Creator also brought justice. The desire to make the world two was the drive to be unjust. Exile God to heaven and run the earth as you please. Or pretend to be God's religious representative and nevertheless dominate unjustly. Two-world people put aside God's care for the whole creation and all people equally, and seize power for themselves and their cronies. Augustine saw so much embedded two-world living and thinking around him that he did not hope to see just societies on earth. The best that could be done, he thought, was for government (even unjust government!) to hold the lid on violence. The real society of justice and care was growing meanwhile inside the Creator's church.

Still someone objects: What about two-world thinking in the church itself? The church is no exception. The church can be just as bad as any other part of humanity. Augustine knew that. He saw failure in whole sections of the church. But finally the good elements in the church belonged to the Creator, not to people. He saw no other plan.

Does the Solution Still Work?

The problem of separated worlds has gone on for centuries. Is Augustine's remedy still convincing? For one thing, Augustine and his age presupposed without question some kind of rule across the universe: the Creator's rule, or some all-governing principle, or design. The modern world has not always presupposed a rule across all things. The human being may be a limited survivor in a world that has no design or meaning. Modern folk sometimes believe that the only order to things is the order they themselves temporarily create. Augustine held that there is an order to the world. His question, then, was how he would ever find what it is and play a part in it. Another way of saying this is that Augustine was convinced of his own soul; it has some place in the universe, and he needed to find what that place is. In the modern world the *soul* has often become a *self*, and whether the self has any recognized place in the world has become a question. Is it just a short-term survivor?

One of the dilemmas of the modern self is its many ways of talking (not just two). These are not simply different levels of one inclusive way of speaking, as with Augustine, but different, independent ways, for example, physics, chemistry, biology, sociology, and psychology, as well as religion. Is it plausible still to speak of one world and one way of talking, according to the rule of one Creator?

This book takes the position that the core of Augustine's solution is right, though modern people must struggle with him at many points. I hope the book itself will help the reader find whether he or she agrees.

PART I

THE PATTERN OF HIS
EMERGING THOUGHT

1

Childhood: Lost Language, Lost Baptism

(*Confessions* I)

Great are you, O Lord, and greatly to be praised. Your power is exceeding, your wisdom finds no measure. And humankind wishes to praise you, [this human] particle of your creation . . . wishes to praise you!

Indeed, you arouse this human creature to take delight in praising you, for you have made us for yourself and our heart is restless until it rests in you.

Give me, O Lord, to know and to understand whether first to call upon you, or to praise you; and whether first to know you, or to call upon you. (I, 1, 1)

How was he to begin? How was Augustine, in 397 c.e. a mature Catholic bishop of the Mediterranean coasttown, North African Hippo, to begin to tell in his *Confessions* the story of all that had brought him to that time and place? Should he not begin with birth (354 c.e.), hometown, parents, childhood? In Book I of the *Confessions* he does treat these, but not first; he chooses to begin with God. "Great are *you*, O Lord . . ." He does not begin his story in the past; he begins it in the present, with an exaltation that points away from himself to God. His beginning is God, the beginning and origin of all things. Later, when he does deal with his birth, infancy, childhood, and parents (I, 6ff.), he does not do it in the modern, autobiographical way, but tells of his emerging birth out of mystery (I, 6, 7) and spends considerable time on how he learned to express himself and speak (I, 6, 8; 7, 11; 8, 13). He then bypasses details of his home and traces his way into his early schooling, especially reading, writing, and theater (I, 9–10). There follows a significant intrusion, a focused account of his parental home and its religious character (I, 11). Then almost the complete remainder of the book (I, 12–19) returns intensively to the topic of school and learning—certainly not the balanced modern approach to an author's earliest years. What overriding concerns are selectively shaping his account? What is Augustine's chosen entranceway into his life's story?

In a manner quite different from a modern biographical or psychological description, Augustine weaves together in Book I two major preoccupations: God and language. The greatness of God brought him into being. On the other hand, his stumbling, initial efforts to speak began the long quest for a language to praise this Creator God. So the book opens: "Great are you, O Lord . . ." God is the final object, ". . . and greatly to be praised." Praise requires toward God a full, right, and glorious language. The whole of his account tells in many various ways his search for God and for a language that is true and right toward God. The *Confessions* itself, written as a prayer, is his powerful attempt to speak that language. Further, language has two sides to it: the language of religious truth and the language of rhetorical expression. He was the powerful rhetorician, writer, and orator, who became Western Christianity's greatest thinker and truth-seeker. He loved the truth of God and the praise of God. Therefore, his life-story, the *Confessions*, is not an autobiography but in fact, as the title proclaims, a confession—a confession in the language of both truth and praise. For a confession in the early church meant confessing the glory and wonder of God, and only secondarily confessing one's sin. Autobiography, as modern writing has developed it, follows the progress of a self-relation, that is, shows the unfolding of self and world through one another, with an I-centered reference point. Confession follows the progress rather of a God-relation, that is, shows the unfolding of a relation between God and one's soul with a God-centered reference point.

Even when he recalls his infancy and the good gift of life given him by God, his attention is caught by language. "Thus I was casting about my limbs and [uttering] the sounds of my voice as best I could, [making] signs (the few signs I had) something like my wants, for [these signs] were not really true to my wants" (I, 6, 8). The road is long to a language that leads to God. Not only so, the untutored signs used by an infant can take a damaging direction: "to get by crying even what, if it were given, would be hurtful" (I, 7, 11). The uses of language are ambiguous from the start. He is intrigued by learning to talk, listening to words spoken by adults, and attaching these words to the things they signify. In this way, he grew to be "a boy, talking" (I, 8, 13). With boyhood came school. With school came the transition from naturally learning to speak at home, in order to express desires, to the far-flung arena of disciplined public speech (I, 9, 14).

A whole world of language opened up, which he was expected to master. Language was not only personal, but public, an immense and variable struc- *lang.* ture, a medium of shared public life and tradition, and structure of common-*as public* ality. At the same time, language was an expression of the innermost thoughts and feelings of the individual. Augustine's story of his search for a language of praise is the story of his search for a faith both private and public. At school the strain and pressure of dealing with language, a vast public structure, bore down upon him. How would his rich, inner intensity, his personal language, deal with that structure?

Distortions of Language; The Loss of God's Ordering

He recalls in the *Confessions* the terrible severities children suffered at school under the burden of their studies, including the basics of language (I, 9, 14–15). From his adult perspective years later, that of the *Confessions* author, he views language as intended to express, not human whims, but → *OT –* rather God's vast ordering of all things. A Psalm could glorify God in the *Genesis* wonders of creation. In his boyhood school, to the contrary, the work of *Psalms* language and the realm of God's true ordering became divided. A severe *Babel Tower /* gap opened between God and the uses of language. Language served ends other than God's truth; God's ordering appeared in a niggardly, partial, and distorted form. Indeed, without language as a means of praising God, distortions took place both of language and of God's ordering. So he sees the stated goal of his boyhood schooling as deceitful.

> God, my God, what misery and ludicrous pretense I experienced there [in school] whenever it was put to me that for a boy to live rightly [meant] to obey his teachers so that I would flourish in this world, and excel in linguistic arts to be honored by humanity, and to serve empty riches. (I, 9, 14)

In school the goal of language became not praise, but vanity. He recalls his

↳ lang → vanity Not praise

delight in winning awards for declaiming Virgil, though the performances aroused emotions whimsically and pointlessly (I, 13, 20–22; 15, 24; 17, 27).

Not only so, the school taught basic language arts by a brutal discipline. Failure meant severe beatings (I, 9, 14). He recalls with painful dismay his parents' laughing at the thrashings he received.

> Can any generous-spirited person, Lord, cleaving to you with great feeling—I should say, can anyone at all, for even some of the stupid can [feel sympathy!]—Then, all the more, can anyone devoutly loyal to you be so caught up in devotion that racks and hooks and the whole range of tortures mean nothing—especially when loved ones are bitterly afraid?—when everywhere on earth folk, hideously fearful, cry out to you, and flee such instruments?
>
> Can any such a one laugh at the tortures our teachers inflicted on us boys, the way our parents laughed? (I, 9, 15)

Decades beyond his schooldays Augustine will distress many readers with the comment, "If one were asked either to endure death or childhood again, who would not be aghast and choose to die?" (*City of God*, XXI, 14; cf. XXII, 22).

He recalls that under these circumstances he first attempted as a child to pray: "and as a little one with no little feeling, I entreated you that I would not be beaten in school" (I, 9, 14). Yet the beatings continued. In such crying out to God, Augustine says, "I broke the knots [that tied] my tongue" (ibid.). Nevertheless, in light of the whole of Book I, a significant split separates the language of school from the language of prayer, undoubtedly learned at home. The discipline of school language is ruthless and offers an empty human glory. The language of prayer is a child's desperate plea that doesn't work. The breadth and power of language in school misrepresents God's true ordering. The language of prayer, of God's rule, is earnest but limited, lacking the authority to deal with life's agonies. The damage is done of separating the language of God learned at home from the power of language in the world. He begins to live in two separated discourses.

In fact, Augustine cannot finally accept the separation. He determines that God used even the distortions and deceits of school to a good end. He was forced to learn, and he deserved the punishment (I, 12, 19). The boys' behavior was unacceptable: "We sinned in writing, reading, and thinking about our lessons less than was required of us" (I, 9, 15). So eager is the mind that the world should make sense, that suffering have some justification, that language be a link to God, that Augustine came to accept the role of the harsh schoolmaster. He affirms "your laws, O God, your laws, from the rod of the schoolmaster to the testing of martyrs, having the power to mingle the healthful with the bitter" (I, 14, 23).

His fateful childhood experience of the schoolmaster's rod will influence his thinking later as a mature leader of the North African church, when he adopts religious coercion. The order of school discipline represents a part of God's true ordering in its most severe mode.

On the other hand, as a boy he loved (not surprisingly) games and play. He loved to win, with great pride in his victories; he would tell lies to conceal his play habits, and cheat to win, if necessary (I, 19, 30). He later saw such cheating and games as models of the deadly games played by adults in business, politics, and war. Therefore, children, who would rather play, cheat, and lie, had to toil agonizingly over their books in order to become powerful and established adults—who would in turn play, cheat, and lie. Expectations were terrifying; the mark of success was hypocrisy (cf. I, 10, 16).

Therefore, the boy Augustine, thrust into a world where the two most important realities were God and right language about God, found only partial or distorted versions of both. This outcome dominates Book I. From there, the story will pursue the young Augustine in search of a true language of authority that teaches one how to know and praise God truly and well. His Christian conversion, the climax of the entire account, will be a conversion to that authority and that language.

Only when in Book I this large and definitive theme of God and language is firmly established does Augustine focus, in a secondary way, the picture of his early home and of his parents.

> . . . I had been told, when I was still a boy, about the eternal life promised us through the humility of the Lord our God, who descended to our pride. . . . I was then regularly signed with the sign of his cross, and I was regularly seasoned with his salt, from my mother's womb, for she had great hope in you, God. . . . Thus, at that time, I was a believer, as my mother was, and our entire household, except my father only. (I, 11, 17)

"I had been told" introduces for the first time in the Confessions a reference to the language of his early religious instruction, which took place predominantly (as best we know) at home. Yet his mother and his father were divided over the matter of religion and religious training. "I was a believer, as my mother was, and our entire household, except my father only." Here was an ominous gap, setting up a division in goals and expectations. His father, Patricius, expected success in vocation, marriage, and social status. His mother, Monica, expected all that, plus spiritual and moral well-being before God. This difference between the parents concerning their son was complicated by severe tensions between themselves. The household was not at peace.

His Father

Patricius was a struggling, small landowner, undoubtedly of African background rather than Roman,[1] striving for upward mobility, dead—probably of overwork—by the time Augustine was seventeen. His life exploded on occasion into harsh fits of frustration and anger against Monica. Augustine hints that he could burst into sudden moments of generosity, as well. The most detailed picture he gives of his father is not wholly unattractive:

> No one had anything but praise for my father who, despite his slender resources, was ready to provide his son with all that was needed to enable him to travel so far [i.e., to Carthage] for the purpose of study. Many of our townsmen, far richer than my father, went to no such trouble for their children's sake. Yet this same father of mine took no trouble at all to see how I was growing in your sight or whether I was chaste or not. . . .
>
> One day at the public baths he saw the signs of active virility coming to life in me and this was enough to make him relish the thought of having grandchildren. He was happy to tell my mother about it. (II, 3, 5–6)

Patricius could freely tell his wife his delight in the boy's puberty; Monica could only hide her dismay at the news. Yet the father was rough and raucous, ambitious and frustrated. He had climbed to the position of a town councillor, but this itself was a hazardous post. Councillors had to entertain officials from Rome out of their own pockets and likewise make up shortages

---

1. V. J. Bourke, "Perler's Contribution to Augustine Biography," in *Augustinian Studies* (Villanova: Villanova University Press, 1971), 2:234.

in taxation. Such councillors had occasionally fled, perhaps to monasteries, only to be returned to their duties by the police.[2] Irascible, driven, an African struggling to rise in a Roman system, a hearty, laughing, hot-tempered, and crude man, Patricius was no easy father to encounter.

Patricius expected of his son—and here Monica joined him—excellent performance in school. The pressure of study, especially language study, has already been considered above. Thus Augustine's life mirrored in miniature that of his father, whose existence was divided between bone-crushing demands and raucous liberties. Just so, Augustine's burdensome dull good, with its beatings, was split away from games and play, with its lying, cheating, and winning. Augustine was thus a childish version of his father's lot. Yet the Augustine of the *Confessions* remembers no real relationship between himself and Patricius. He feels that Patricius focused on his son as an object or category, relative to his own schemes.

> He cared only that I should have a fertile tongue, leaving my heart to bear none of your fruits, my God. . . . [Indeed] both parents (as I knew) wanted [my education] too much: my father because he gave almost no thought to you, and only empty thoughts to me. (II, 3, 5; 3, 8)

Augustine's lack of feeling for Patricius nowhere betrays itself more clearly than in the recollection of his father's death—only a secondary phrase in a sentence concerned with other matters: "The allowance which my mother paid me was supposed to be spent on putting an edge on my tongue. I was now [eighteen] and she supported me, because my father had died two years before" (III, 4, 7).

Thus Patricius urged the learning of school language distorted in its aim and method. With this distortion, the vast ordering of all things by God, which language existed to articulate, appeared in a corrupted form. What commanded attention was the skewed and deceptive order of ambition, prestige, riches, and personal vanity, a caricature of the delights of the Creator's cosmos. Rhetoric, like child's play, was a game to be won.

His Mother

At the same time, he had a different kind of opportunity for absorbing the language of faith and religious instruction through his mother. Monica's

2. J. J. O'Meara, *The Young Augustine* (London: Longmans, Green, 1954), 25.

zeal and commitment never faltered; indeed, she has been called "relent-less."[3] She wanted social and educational success for her son, but ultimately she counted only on the kingdom of heaven and spiritual strength, to which she saw even his studies at school contributing (II, 3, 8). Hers was an impassioned, self-demanding spirituality, emotionally disciplined, learned from childhood.

In part, her devoted rigor was a response to the plight of women in Roman North African communities. Augustine tells us that she served her husband "as her lord": poised and patient, she never confronted him with his known infidelities against their marriage (IX, 9, 19). When his temper flashed, she remained silent and only later, when he was in a reasonable mood, attempted to explain her actions. The faces of other wives in the community showed blows and bruises; never Monica's. She chided her fel-low wives for their gossiping tongues and recommended patient obedience to their husbands, like her own. Augustine tells us that as a child she was cared for, not usually by her parents, but by an aged and respected servant. This person let her have no water to drink except sparingly at mealtimes, in order to allay adult desire for wine. In response, Monica became a childhood alcoholic! or nearly so, sipping wine her parents entrusted her to bring up from the cellar. She was shocked out of drinking one day by accusations from a household servant girl (IX, 8, 17–18). Clearly, she carried inner tension into adulthood: subservience with determination, lofty standards of personal performance, and an anxious fascination with misbehavior.

Toward Augustine, she determined to prosecute his welfare in every way open to her: "For she always loved to have me close with her, as mothers will, but far more than many mothers" (V, 8, 15). Her teaching him North Africa's Christian faith and warning him concerning his father combined into one: "She was constantly seeing to it that you, my God, should be a father to me, rather than he. And in this you supported her" (I, 11, 17). Admittedly, he learned the language and doctrines of the Christian faith, in a fashion deeply colored by his mother's emotional commitments. The remainder of the above passage adds a further touch:

> . . . that you, my God, should be a father to me, rather than he. And in this you supported her, so that she would prevail against her husband, whom she always obeyed, because in doing this she was certainly obeying your law, and therefore more virtuous than he.

3. Peter Brown, *Augustine of Hippo: a Biography* (Berkeley and Los Angeles: University of California Press, 1969), 30, 208.

Monica's quiet obedience not only saved her from physical blows on earth, but caused her to outrank Patricius in heaven. In any case, Augustine clearly learned that membership with God in heaven ultimately matters, even though one may not savor outward material benefits here and now. As noted above, his earliest remembered prayers were to be spared school beatings—and they did not work (I, 9, 14). The world of belief and everlasting life lay markedly separate from this world, undermining here the pleasures of games, cheating, and prizes, and failing to ease daily burdens. Only the immense personal authority of Monica made religion real ("at that time, I was a believer, as my mother was"). Indeed, the radiant world of his mother's aspirations stayed with Augustine all his life. He had drunk in the name of Christ "with my mother's milk" (III, 4, 8).[4] *biblical phrase?*

Monica, for her part, determined to save her son for God. Admittedly she wanted him close to herself ("close with her . . . far more than many mothers"). Her intent, however, was that he would be in touch with the best she knew, as the church taught her through doctrine and ritual. A twofold problem nevertheless affected her religious instruction. For the child, the sweet name of Christ within his heart produced no ease and joy of outward circumstances in life, only strict demands and abstract promise. Further, the power of the faith was indistinguishable, in practice, from Monica's own personal power. "[My father] did not conquer in me *my mother's piety*, which rightly *held sway*" (I, 11, 17; emphasis mine). Once *family as allegory?* again, the language of religious devotion (life with Monica) stood limited and separate from the wide language of academic disciplines and public affairs. God's true ordering was heavily reflected as Monica's own ordering, both in her understanding and her enterprising commitments. The language of the larger world remained the language of vain self-seeking. This strain of separation between otherworldly piety and everyday realities became intensified by a critical event during Augustine's later childhood.

The Cry for Baptism   *{what do we make of diff here — was delay typical of age + Mom's relig or was it unusual?*

You saw it, Lord—when I was still a boy—one day, stomach pains.
Suddenly I burned with fever, almost at the point of death—you

4. There are numerous psychological interpretations of the *Confessions*, though this study does not mean to take that special approach. Compare, for example, D. Capps and J. E. Dittes, eds., *The Hunger of the Heart: Reflections on the Confessions of Augustine* (Purdue University: Society for the Social and Scientific Study of Religion Monograph Series 8, 1990).

saw it, my God, because you were my keeper then! I begged, burning, with all my soul, in faith for baptism—the baptism of your Christ, my God and Lord—I begged it by my mother's devotional duty and the duty of your church, the mother of us all!

And the mother of my flesh was dismayed, for she was then in labor more dearly than when I was born—but now laboring in her chaste heart through your faith, for my eternal salvation! Right then she would have seen to it at once that I was admitted to your saving sacraments and washed clean, confessing you, Lord Jesus, to the remission of my sins—except that I immediately recovered. Thus my cleansing was delayed, for it was deemed a certainty that if I lived on, I could get defiled again; and such captivity to criminal filth is stronger and more dangerous, after baptism . . .

I ask you, my God, I wish to know (if it be your will), for what purpose was I held back and not baptized then? Was it for my own good that the reins on my sinning were as if relaxed? Or did the delay of my baptism not relax those reins? [If not,] how is it that even today, again and again, we hear ringing in our ears: "Let him alone. Let him do it. He is not baptized yet!" (But we do not say, concerning bodily health, "Let him get worse. He's not well yet.") (I, 11, 17–18)

The child Augustine had learned from his mother an otherworldly faith under God, in Christ's name. God did not ease a child's burdens now or encourage zest for life; rather, faith promised greater strictures and burdens in order to guarantee blessedness on the other side of death. Obviously, this kind of faith exactly fit the case of a frightening illness. The child's explicit belief in the doctrines meant to him that now, if ever, was the time for baptism. The issue was survival, not on earth, but in heaven. Dying children have cried for medicine; this one cried for the sacrament. Monica's teaching had taken hold.

Yet she withheld the cleansing act. The boy responded in fierce dismay: "I begged, burning, with all my soul, in faith for baptism. . . . I begged it by my mother's devotional duty and the duty of your church . . .!" Of course Monica had her reasons for not complying, reasons not clear to the ill youngster. Much of ancient Christianity held that sins after baptism had no forgiveness. Therefore, baptism often came far on in life, even at its end. Baptism meant a point of maximum assurance concerning oneself, for

Images of Family or Saints in Early Xian Church?
Images from African Xianty? Maps.

Childhood, Lost Language, Lost Baptism   21

if its cleansing powers were lost through further sin, it could never be repeated. If baptism were lost, only a later, once-only, public penance through the church could avail.[5] For Monica his extreme youth prohibited his baptism at that time, lest he survive the illness and live in peril. As he says, "the waves of future temptation hanging over me seemed [to Monica] so many and so great" she could not believe he would keep his baptism intact in years to come, were it used so early (I, 11, 18).

All of this was lost on the boy Augustine. He urgently entreated. Why withhold the act of salvation at this critical time? Why was the rule of God absent on the very occasion for which it was designed? Monica's strong authority halted in the dilemma. His careful defense of her behavior in the *Confessions* suggests that in the small boy's eyes, as well, she had needed defending: Her intent was pure, if not her judgment; she was laboring for his salvation as if in second pangs of birth. She *would* have had him baptized, had she seen him really about to die. Her commitment never came to the test because of his recovery; and the statement of his recovery is ambivalent at best, a final dangling clause ("except I immediately recovered")—almost as if the chance for his mother's vindication, and for his cleansing, were lost, plunging them all back into bleak inconclusiveness. Her defense by Augustine, the adult, confirms the incomprehending dismay of Augustine, the child.

Even more important, the adult Augustine *still* disagrees with her decision not to baptize. He defends her good intent, but not her understanding of Christian teaching. He looks back and sees the loss of the childhood baptism as a blow.

> . . . how much better if I had been healed [i.e., baptized] right away and that were followed by your continuing guardianship of my soul's salvation—guardianship by you, who gave the gift of that salvation, through the diligence of myself and those close to me. Indeed how much better! But the waves of future temptation hanging over me seemed so many and so great, as she, my mother, certainly knew, that she was willing to commit to those waves the clay, out of which I would later be formed, rather than my actual baptized image. (I, 11, 18)

5. F. Van der Meer, *Augustine the Bishop*, trans. B. Battershaw and G. R. Lamb (London: Sheed and Ward, 1961), 382–87.

Note the author's horror in the figure of unformed clay committed to the waves (a hint of living burial at sea), with its suggestion of eroding identity. Through much of the *Confessions,* distress is with the unformed and un-shapen, the inconclusive, the uncertainty concerning what counts in one's favor, and what surely counts against (e.g., V, 14, 25; VII, 21, 27).

The adult author of the *Confessions* not only still disagrees with her decision, he mourns the results of it in the sort of nurture that followed after his recovery. Note again the lines:

> . . . for what purpose was I held back and not baptized then? Was it for my own good that the reins on my sinning were as if relaxed? Or did the delay of my baptism not relax those reins? [If not,] how is it that even today, again and again, we hear ringing in our ears: "Let him alone. Let him do it. He is not baptized yet!"

The delay of baptism meant in his home a relaxed attitude toward his wayward behavior. The logic was: Don't worry too much about his behavior now; that will all be cleaned up later when he is baptized. The adult Augustine found this view appalling. Accountability astonishingly rests on Monica, the only member of the household really concerned with his behavior. Perhaps she had the interest, but not the authority, while Patricius had the authority to correct, but no interest in doing so. In any event, Augustine grew up too much at liberty. His nurture, for all its spiritual doctrine, related only distantly to the burdens of school, not at all to the relaxed "reins on my sinning."

The problem of the language of God (expressing otherworldly concerns) as separate from the language of education and the public arena thereby intensified. The crisis over baptism and the consequent lack of "reins on my sinning" meant that a whole area of the child's religious formation was given up. The limited language of religion at home did not include a child's full religious nurture; it lacked spiritual integrity. That religious discourse lay even further apart from everyday practical demands, including school-ing, moral, and vocational formation, household discipline, and even life-threatening illness. The separation confronted the child with accountability to two fathers: In the language of affairs and ambitions, he was accountable to his father Patricius; in the language of religious belief he was accountable to his Father God. Monica's dominance in the latter and involvement in the former did not bridge the two areas so much as they added an element of ambivalence to her own posture (as *Confessions* II will increasingly indicate).

Playing games, lying, cheating, and winning, the counterpart of bleak schoolwork, remained a lively discourse. Now a disturbing religious sanction arose for this behavior: "Let him do it. He is not baptized yet!" Again the two language worlds drifted further apart, with the name of God in the limited, religious one, and volumes of God's everyday language of creation in the vain, public one, with only the barest connection. The world of work—and play!—had virtually no grounding in faith.

Had the baptism taken place, Augustine tells us it would have introduced a "guardianship by you [O God] . . . through the diligence of myself and those close to me," especially Monica. That is, the boy would have been more accountable in behavior, more directly under God, being formed in his own life and faith. He would have made a step forward in growing up, in knowing God and the language of God. He would have prospered more wholesomely in the area of religion and thereby in all areas. How is that area of religion to be understood for him, in the fourth century? In his treatise *True Religion*, written in his mid-thirties, Augustine associates religion first with sacramental rites; but if it is *true* religion, then he proposes that rites must join with philosophy so that the one, all-embracing truth of God will inform both doctrines and rites (i, 1; v, 8). True religion meant for him, then, participation in the total ordering of all things by God through embracing the languages of belief, worship, and truth.

Such participation was blocked for him as a child by the divided horizon of his experience, the separation of God, and language about God, from the vast ordering of the world, the language of his studies. Any slender connection between the two lay in Monica's hint that study and educational prominence would somehow be pleasing to God, but that was weakened by his lack of baptism and accompanying nurture in the life of faith. What recourse did a child have whose languages of work, play, and worship were so at odds? He simply alternated practicing the different languages outwardly on demand. The core of his soul became increasingly withdrawn as the mouthing of speech in different areas was required of him.

He knew of school and street play, and he knew at home about God, but he did not know how to relate God to school and street. The relation was not an order, but a disorder (he sensed this without knowing how to conceive it). Much later he realized such disordering was the nature of evil. That is, he came to see evil as a disorder in things that were in and of themselves good (language, school, street), but that people had thrown into disarray by their warped intentions. He knew something of God and of religion, but in a twisted form that actually participated in evil. To know only a limited, separated language about God meant that religion itself participated in the disorder and division of languages, and thereby participated in evil.

Lang —
Adam?

2

Sin: Love of Evil, the Pear Tree

(*Confessions* II)

> There was a pear tree in the neighborhood of our vineyard loaded
> with fruit, not really good to look at or to taste. One night, past
> any decent hour—we had the sick habit of playing that late in the
> streets—a crowd of us no-good youth went off to shake down and
> carry off that fruit; and we made away with great sacks of it, not to
> eat, but to dump it to the pigs. Or perhaps we ate some, but the
> point that caught our fancy was that we had violated something . . .
> we were tickled to laughter through and through to think we were
> tricking the owners unawares and that they were totally outdone
> with it. (II, 4, 9; 9, 17)

Augustine knew evil, not as natural evil (earthquakes, disease), nor as
metaphysical evil (reality is flawed), but as sin. Or at least he later came
to see evil in this way: Evil is either sin or the penalty for sin—a sweeping
principle to which he admitted no exceptions (*True Religion*, xii, 23).[1] And
sin is itself a specific form of evil, and not simply a general condemnation
of behavior. Sin is distinguishable from guilt and from ritual uncleanness,
all three of which are metaphors attempting to give some shape to evil.[2]
Ritual uncleanness or taboo borrows the metaphor of stain; evil in this case
is a taint or exterior soiling. Guilt borrows the metaphor of burden; evil in
this case is an interior weight that one is forced to carry. Sin, by contrast,

---

1. Also, xx, 39; xl, 76; cf. xvi, 32; xxiii, 44.
2. Paul Ricoeur, *The Symbolism of Evil* (New York: Harper and Row, 1967), part I, passim.

borrows the metaphor of wandering or losing one's way. Evil in the form
of sin (if evil can be said to have a form) is missing the path, being cut off
from one's destination, lost in the woods, or in a maze. Not simply exterior
or interior (like taboo, or guilt), evil as sin is a relation between oneself
and one's world, a skewed relation that disrupts all productive flow.

Evil came to the young Augustine as sin, losing his way, falling into
dysfunction with his world. Chapter 1 has already noted how "the reins on
my sinning were . . . relaxed" by the delay of his baptism. "Let him alone.
Let him do it. He is not baptized yet!" The ordering of his behavior, when
clear, was excessive (beaten in school); otherwise, it was absent. Outside
school the guidelines sagged, the moral mapwork blurred. He had no path
he had to follow; therefore he missed the path. Evil came as sin. Monica
urged and cautioned, but it was not the same as if he had been baptized—
or as if the parents had enjoyed a firm unity between themselves in dealing
with his behavior.

The climax came when he was sixteen. His earlier teen years had found
direction in studying literature and public speaking at nearby Madaura.
Then finances failed at home. He had to return home to Thagaste, while his
father struggled for the means to send him on to the university at Carthage.

> . . . in my sixteenth year my studies lapsed out of financial necessity,
> and I took up an [idle] life away from school with my parents. Then
> the brambles of desire began to grow thick about my head, with no
> hand to root them out—certainly not my father's . . .
>
> But in my mother's heart you had already begun to build your
> temple, the foundation of your holy habitation . . . and I remember
> that in private she warned me with uncommon anxiety against forni-
> cation and, most of all, against adultery with someone's wife. All
> this seemed to me a womanish warning which I would blush to heed.
> Yet all of it was from you, and I did not know it. (II, 3, 6–7)

Thus far the picture is much as one would expect. In the new crisis of
adolescence, father stands one way; mother identifies with God, and stands
another. The adult Augustine gives her credit; her warnings coincided with
God's. The problem, of course, was awakening sexuality. The dilemma of
random behavior in childhood now intensified.

Then Augustine moves surprisingly to bring his mother once again into
a questionable light. As the earlier issue had been that of baptism, so the
new issue also arose as a ritual and moral one: whether he should marry.

Monica struggled with the question, since marriage would channel sexuality *Sexually*
within honorable bounds. Looking back, Augustine seems to hold that
marriage would have been an appropriate bridle on his activity (II, 2, 3),
and notes that his parents failed to pursue it (II, 2, 4). He remembers
himself, meanwhile, as rushing about the "streets of Babylon" (II, 3, 8).

The mention of Babylon sets off a strange literary move. He immediately
thinks of the wicked city under the image of a mother, then states that his
own mother was not free of Babylon herself. "In her navel [i.e., of Babylon] *merger*
. . . I tenaciously fastened myself." The image of Babylon and the figure of *mother*
Monica then merge to a degree. He says of her:
Babylon +

> Not even indeed she—the mother of my flesh, who had fled from
> the center of Babylon, but was making less progress in other parts
> of it—who had warned me about unchastity, and so was concerned
> about what she had heard of me from her husband [i.e., signs of
> puberty], and now was thinking of restraining my sexual sickness
> and its perils-to-come within the bonds of married love (if it could
> not be cut back to the root): No, she did not carry through on this,
> because of the fear that my hope would be obstructed by the shackles
> of a wife. Not the hope of the world to come, which my mother
> already hoped for in you, but the hopes for my education, which (as
> I knew) both parents wanted too much; my father, because he gave
> almost no thought to you, and only empty thoughts to me; and my
> mother, because she saw in the usual course of studies not only no
> detriment, but indeed no small help in attaining to you. Looking
> back as best I can, I believe these were the basic attitudes of my
> parents. Indeed, the reins on me were relaxed, to play myself out
> beyond any sure, decent way of doing and into destructive random
> relations. (II, 3, 8)

mom doesn't want her marriage because disrupt education (prioritizes over God?)

Once again, the reins are relaxed. Once again, Monica struggles with her
conscience: Should he receive the sacrament, this time matrimony? Yet,
this time, unlike baptism, the boy does not plead for it; he is beyond that.
Matters have grown absurd. Baptism and nurture of the child, once an
option, have deteriorated into the paltriness of an adolescent wedding, a
technical morality. Yet the Augustine of the *Confessions* regrets that marriage was not invoked, shows more disturbance with Monica on this count
than he did on her withholding of baptism: "She . . . had fled from the

center of Babylon, but was making less progress in other parts of it," he wryly observes. The prominent and commanding negatives,

> *Not* even, indeed, she . . .
> . . . if it could *not* be cut back . . .
> *No*, she did *not* carry through . . .

tell rhythmically his unease over Monica's inaction. Yet surely her options were increasingly tight; the situation, more desperate. Patricius had but another year to live. Monica's religious controls had faltered; yet her desire for his education was real. Augustine admits that his studies, for Monica, were to be a "help in . . . attaining to you." Her womanish warning on sex had actually been God's counsel, unrecognized. She meant well, and he strives to be fair, "looking back as best I can" to assess accurately "the basic attitudes of my parents."

Yet, while his parents placed their hopes for the future upon his bright promise, they did not succeed with his life at the time. They continued to treat him as the property of their designs and fears. On the one hand, he was wonderful, their promise and solution; on the other, he was unworthy of decent guidance, or so the message came. They lived only in the future: when he will be masterful, when he will be successful, when he will be baptized and finally be with God—but not now.

Therefore the boy perceived their presence as harsh, dry, and boringly external. Patricius laughingly cited his prospects for grandchildren and wrestled finances; Monica gave sexual advice; but for his present energies and hungers they provided little.

The phrase that nevertheless captures the entire passage above (II, 3, 8) is the parenthetical "as I knew": "my education, which (as I knew) both parents wanted too much." He recalls knowing, at the time, the excesses of their determination. He had gained an independent vantage point and along with it, surely a resentment. How does such a one respond, who feels the hollow straining within parental ambitions? He knows that something is wrong, and that he is to be the solution; but something is wrong with him. He is very special indeed, yet not tended to; preparing to win great victories, but not worthy to grow up; prized, but abused: the family champion, who cannot be trusted with the elemental rite of baptism, or trusted beyond his mother's protection; but if not trusted, simply let loose into the winds, to scatter and to wander. The agony of contradiction set in; adolescence stood between impossibly bright and dark alternatives (they think

I'm wonderful; they think I'm nothing). The consequence was rebellion. He reversed all the heavy expectations into chaotic behavior.

reverse expect. in chaotic behavior

The Pear Tree

His famous instance of his own chaos is the pillaging of a pear tree. For seven sections of *Confessions* II he ponders the wildness of the act, to a chorus of yawns across the centuries (his guilt over a few pears when he was sixteen is a confounded bore!). Yet, to look only at the factual event is to miss the image and its power. Augustine himself is caught up, not by the specifics, but by the love of evil inherent in the actual deed. His full account of the event (quoted at the head of this chapter) includes the following:

bonus

love of evil a problem

> . . . a crowd of us no-good youth went off to shake down and carry off that fruit; and we made away with great sacks of it, not to eat, but to dump it to the pigs. Or perhaps we ate some, but the point that caught our fancy was that we had violated something. (II, 4, 9)

The deed was mild enough, compared to real adolescent crime and to his own hints at sexual exploits. The image, for him, nevertheless clings. He cries out with surprising pain:

> Look there at my heart, God [i.e., in the pear tree story], look there at my heart! which you had mercy on in the depths of the abyss. Let it tell you now—yes, my heart—what it was looking for in the pit: Why was I gratuitously evil? Why was there no cause of my malice except malice? It was foul, and I passionately wanted it. I loved it. I loved—I wanted—to perish! I loved my own failing— not something I was failing *for*—but I loved my own failing itself. My twisted soul was plunging from your solid ground into outer chaos, hungering—not for something disgraceful, but for disgrace. (II, 4, 9)

More is involved than a tree-load of pears. For six more sections, to the end of Book II, the author worries this knot: What is the love of evil as such? He considers that his love of evil was an attempt to imitate God,

what is the love of evil

that he was enjoying an illusion of power, that doing it in a crowd gave it its zest. He never successfully penetrates the blackness of the love of evil; nor does he feel still trapped by it. Yet the pear tree lingers and lingers. What is it? Why is it?

The focus of an image is more than its rational, literal play in context. Its fitness rests on more than deliberate decision. At the levels of genre, of subject matter, and of style, the image lives. Certainly the pear tree recalls the tree of knowledge of good and evil in the garden of Eden. At the same time, the subject matter here is the hollow rage of an adolescent, strung between the family's expectation and casual disregard (neither of which accords with who he really is): feeling the intense emotions of his parents but unable to get their attention; confident that he is nothing of what they expect; the scruffy ground where they put him to pasture proves it. The genre and style, moreover, are those of lyrical confession; the pear tree is a confessional image. The pear tree is therefore his own soul: fruit not of the best, there in the darkness, green, disappointing, fit for pigs; yet highly prized, highly desired by someone. Now show them! Make them listen now. The wonderful joke is on them! Show them they are fools! Shake it, shake it down! Show them it is no good! Destroy it—now!

> Look there at my heart! . . . I loved—I wanted—to perish! . . . My twisted soul . . . into outer chaos, hungering . . .

Here the critical element has been added to the notion of evil as sin, or losing one's way. An individual lost in the woods likely has no appetite for it. An individual who has lost the path of a good and happy life may increasingly delight in aimless crashing and plunging. Evil in the form of sin may be frightening, but it is loved. Twisted love enhances the obvious suicide motif. Losing one's way is not a bewilderment, but a passion.

If evil as sin is loved, and sin is losing one's way, then the shock is that one may love one's own failure, yearn for it, run toward it. Thus the pattern of Augustine's theology has one of its primary themes in the problem of human loves. He did not say about the human person, but he could have: "One is as one loves." Therefore, in his thought, human love is not simply a "good thing." Love is varied, subtle, and treacherous. One may love well, and then all is well. On the other hand, one may love ill, and then all is lost. To depart from well-being is not simply to stop loving. It is to love destructively. I may love the evil of my own dissolution. The mystery of this bemused him. The minor pear-tree incident captured its essence for a fleeting glimpse. Love is a yearning to unite. Love of evil is a yearning to unite with nothing, to disassemble, to scatter, to vanish away nameless.

The Search for Integrity

Such love of destruction is a mystery; yet the situation of language in which the sixteen-year-old Augustine found himself provides a setting for the mystery, if it does not explain it. As indicated in chapter I, he lived within two intense realms of discourse: the severe language of school, and the language of Monica's religious devotion. His mother's religious language told of a powerful God over all things and a merciful savior Christ; it carried the tone of Monica's own personal intimacy and fervor. Yet it seemed ineffective in meeting the demands of the wider world, especially school, where a language of rigor, competition, and survival dominated. Yet his mother supported both languages, one for his soul, the other for his personal advancement, and also his soul.

Yet, his soul (quite literally, the *animus* or intelligent soul of his *Confessions* language) was divided, since it belonged to, and was identified within, the fragmented languages of his experience. Those languages, the religious and the academic, spoke of a vast, rational ordering of things, in heavenly kingdom and earthly empire, that his soul could believe in. Yet, either the languages were false (there was no order), or they presented the order in a skewed fashion (which he later concluded was the case). Therefore, he looks back in *Confessions* II and sees his soul as a teenager broken and fragmented within language as he knew it.

A broken spirit, by the Augustinian anthropology, nevertheless does not cease to will and to love. That dynamism continues as long as life lasts. Therefore, the sixteen-year-old Augustine, broken in soul, loved that brokenness, especially his own brokenness, as articulated for him in separated languages. The continuing movement of the heart turned to love of evil, to verify and unite with the broken situation. He desired to plunge himself into the void between languages.

Only a spark of integrity remained, in that frightful situation. He recalls a moment of linguistic strength in the turbulence, articulate in two small words: *ut nossem* (as I knew; II, 3, 8). That is, he made a conscious judgment that his parents wanted his education too much, "as I knew."

On the one hand, this knowing simply fed his wild behavior. Knowing the linguistic brokenness does not solve it, but simply empties all things. Objects, experiences, colors, sounds, and scenery tumble into oneself, consumed with desperate determination: "I was looking for you out there. Unlovely, I rushed heedlessly among the lovely creatures you have made" (X, 27, 38). Then all creatures become fantasies of what they really are, so that they plunge into the gaping self-emptiness, wasted and gone.

On the other hand, verbalizing his parents' error, though it led to random rebellion, was a linguistic island of good judgment. His response was not a blind response. From somewhere a spark of independent thought came to him that enabled him to say no to the forces arrayed against him. The first move of philosophy is a negative move, a no-saying to blind custom and dreaming acquiescence. In a rough and untutored manner the boy Augustine made the negative move, saw the wrongness in his household, and tried by his actions to speak it out. That negative was so strong it could include the love of destruction, even his own destruction. Yet it was based on an accurate piece of knowledge about his parents' ambition.

That bit of independent judgment also foretold a further element in the pattern of his thought: Any religious view, to be acceptable, would have to satisfy his own reason, experience, and understanding in some significant way. He would never be able to render blind obedience to a doctrine or system. His youthful search for an identity and a belief became of necessity a search for integrity, including the satisfaction of his own rational judgment. Oddly, the intrusion of evil into his respected household served to wake him up. He discerned that something was wrong. Such power of personal judgment, once aroused, never left him, but demanded a hearing for the rest of his life. He knew that the response to evil could never be blind adherence to good, but must call forth the individual's best mental powers.

The emerging religious philosophy of Augustine therefore included the mystery of sin, the love of evil, able to invade even the process of Catholic nurture. And genuine Catholic nurture is distinguishable from false because it encourages and promotes rational integrity. That is, Catholic faith respects the experience and reason of the individual. Even in the midst of religious authority, the individual has confidence that honest questions will find an answer. A wholeness of language must occur in which articulations of religious authority and of wide, public reason harmonize and grow fruitfully. The youthful Augustine knew that his parents were too ambitious. This independent, adolescent insight anticipated the powerful, rational integrity of all his later thought. Truth given by authority must ultimately coincide with truth sought out by reason, since God's truth is one.

3

Happiness: Love of Wisdom, Cicero

(*Confessions* III, 1–5)

[handwritten: are we reading anything by Cicero?]

. . . in the usual course of study I came across a book by a certain Cicero, whose tongue almost everyone admires, but not his heart. That book contains an exhortation to philosophy and is called the *Hortensius*. Truly, the book changed what I set my heart on! and towards you yourself, Lord, it changed my prayers; it shifted all my wishes and desires. All my empty ambitions became repulsive to me, and I found myself yearning for deathless wisdom with unbelievable zeal of heart; I started to pull myself up to move back towards you. (III, 4, 7)

[handwritten margin: Power of BKS]

The direction and redirection of one's loves became the whole of the Augustinian religious outlook in miniature. Love should not be love of evil. When love reaches out vainly and destructively, how does it turn and become fruitful and nourishing? Augustine searched for the answer. Love, the direction of the heart, became a vital theological key.[1] Other theologies in Christian history have seen differently: For Origen, the parallel to Augustine's emphasis was intellectual enlightenment. For Luther, it was self-abandoning trust at the Cross. For Schleiermacher, the father of modern theology, it was a feeling of ultimate dependence. For Augustine, it was love. The movements of the human heart are subtle and profound, its

[handwritten margin: how turn so love is fruitful + nourishing]

---

1. A theological key, that is, on the human side of the God–human relation. On the God side, the key was of course God's grace, God's unmerited help and favor, the foundation of any hope at all. The human side had to do with the key to human nature and to the character of human responsiveness to God.

[handwritten: love or direction of the heart = vital theological key]

desires complex. One human individual in a single lifetime exercises many, many loves. How can they be a pattern of harmony and not a jungle of destruction? "Our heart is restless . . ." is his famous saying, ". . . until it rests in you [O God]" (I, 1, 1). Augustine struggled to find some single prior love that would orchestrate all loves into peaceful exercise. How can all loves come into a vital and fruitful order? Only by getting their priorities clear. Which love comes first is crucial to which comes second, third, and fourth. The first love, he decided, for harmony of the whole, must be the love for God.

That priority was difficult to find. In his sixteenth year, his spark of hope evidently lay in rational integrity, the possibility of intellectual independence, clear-headed reflection (see Chapter 2). What did this have to do with love of God? Would love of God not, in fact, confuse clear thinking, in favor of some grand emotion? How did love find order? How did it relate to honest thinking?

The answer to much of this came compactly, yet forcefully, in his discovery of the Roman orator, Cicero. As the above passage states, "the book changed what I set my heart on!" Offhand, Cicero seems an unlikely source for the love of God. Yet the discovery was a major turning point for the future theologian. Throughout the rest of his life as a Christian leader and teacher, he never abandoned the framework of thought that came clear to him in first reading Cicero. "Towards you yourself, Lord, [the book] changed my prayers . . . I started to pull myself up to move back towards you." The book redirected his confused loves: "It shifted all my wishes and desires." It also motivated him toward intellectual clarity: "I found myself yearning for deathless wisdom." How was all this accomplished in a single impact?

The story of the renewal of his love by Cicero begins with his coming to the university at Carthage at age seventeen. He was now to pursue the study of rhetoric at a high level. Apart from this curriculum Cicero would never have come to his attention. He came to train his mind; the result was renewal of heart. Nevertheless, his early experiences at Carthage were hardly promising with respect to heart and love. Initially, his personal life and feeling were a desert.

The University Student

> I came to Carthage, a Carthage roaring about me like a hot vessel
> of burning, demanding loves. I was empty of passion, yet I longed

to feel passion, and with a deeper yearning hated myself as yearning for little. I was seeking what I would long for; I was longing for—longing! and I despised serenity, and being free, unentangled. I was famished within for want of food—I mean want of yourself, my God; yet in this hunger, I was not hungering! I felt no desire for enduring food—not because I was filled; rather, the more I lay starving, the more tasteless food became. Thus my soul sickened and was casting about outside itself, ulcerous, miserably to be scraped by covetous contact with sensuous things, things without soul, which can never know love. For to love and receive love were of greatest sweetness to me, enjoying, bodily, someone loving me.

I defiled, then, the heart's blood of friendship with the stain of concupiscence; I dulled over its brightness with the hell of lust. With towering vanity, mean and dishonest, I postured myself as elegant, urbane. I fell in love—I yearned for it to seize me. And you, O my God, my mercy, you were good! You laced all that sweetness with so much gall: for I was loved in return and I darkly won through to the bondage of love's pleasure consummate. Then joy and pain at once bound me up; I was whipped down, burning, with metallic stings of jealousy, suspicion, fear, anger, quarreling. (III, 1, 1)

He had solved nothing at home in Thagaste. He brought the bruised problem with him. In effect, he submerged conflict with his parents into numbness. "I was empty of passion . . ." The point was to find new, fascinating emotions to fill the void, to distract from old issues hard as stone. Carthage roared like a dry furnace with a variety of loves.

If his inner vacuity remained, his outward life changed sharply. Suddenly, he was no longer the physical juvenile of the streets. He was a professional candidate, and he assumed the role. His childhood fascination with achieving and winning, his youthful prowess at declaiming, had made him ambitious. As a boy he had had a distaste for studies and a fear of beatings; he had sought play and mischief. Now studies became advanced play: find preeminence in public speech, oratory, law, theater. Win the prize. Become renowned within circles of leisure and learning. Be welcomed by powerful and literate friends, in settings of country estates, of marble houses and gardens. Still, he balanced on the line between ambition and rebellion. Thus he makes peculiar reference to a group called the "Overturners" or "Wreckers."

I already stood first in the school of rhetoric. I disported my haughtiness, tall with conceit—although I was far more restrained (Lord, you know this!) than the Overturners [*eversores*]; in no way was I into their outrages. For that name "Overturner" is cruel, devilish; it labels the dregs of city life. I did live among them (shockingly ashamed not to be like them!). I kept their company. Sometimes I savored their friendship. But I was horrified at their actions, their perversities [*eversiones*]. They shamelessly tracked down the shy new students, banged their way into them, for nothing! Made a mockery of them, glutting their evil pleasure. Nothing was more demonic. (III, 3, 6)

The previous Augustine of "us no-good youth" at the pear tree was still there, drawn toward the Overturners. Secretly, his inhibitions chafed at him for not joining. "Shockingly ashamed not to be like them!" Ironically, their name coincided with his ravages at home, the overturning of his loves into waste and turmoil. He lived around them and found friendship with them, but he did not join.

The inconclusiveness weighed upon him: emptiness within and tension between ambition and rebellion without. Nothingness at the center was a dry fear; and by contrast, restless inquiry, and the darting eye, sought a way out: "Thus my soul . . . was casting about outside itself, ulcerous, miserably to be scraped by covetous contact with sensuous things. . . . I defiled, then, the heart's blood of friendship with the stain of concupiscence." Here the word "concupiscence" embraces more than sexuality, indeed, does not at all damn sexuality as such. *Concupiscentia* is not merely physical desire, but *endless* desire, the problem of desire that cannot be satisfied. One combats the brokenness by enlarging it. The world is reduced to fodder; the fathomless hunger swallows it up and is not eased. Then hearty, graphic success (stepping forward to receive the prize) shields the restlessness. One goes to the theater to live disguised sorrow through tragic action (III, 2, 2 and 4), but matters are unrelieved. The flatness, the restless grasping, continue.

Kafka refers, in the twentieth century, to qualities of laziness and impatience: because of impatience humankind was driven out of paradise, and because of laziness, was unable to return.[2] The two together were the origi-

---

2. Aphorism 3, in *Hochzeitsvorbereitungen auf dem Lande und andere Prosa aus dem Nachlass*, ed. M. Brod (New York: Schocken Books, 1953), 39. Cf. W. A. Strauss, "Franz Kafka," *Centennial Review*, 5, no. 2 (Spring 1961): 214.

nal sin. Augustine, the university student, who some twenty years later began to write his own views on original sin, unknowingly at Carthage actualized Kafka's saying. He strove impatiently, seizing his world; he languished helplessly, generating nothing.

The Concubine

Augustine's relation to his mistress focuses the problem of restless loves, in at least part of its complexity. He evidently was not long in Carthage before he began his life with the concubine, an arrangement that lasted for some thirteen years. Such an arrangement, in late antique Rome, was no degradation or disgrace. Countless young men kept a concubine until their circumstances permitted them to marry. What he specifically says about the contract is brief:

> In those years I had someone, not as if lawfully married. I had tracked her by my wandering passion, not out of good sense. Still, she was the only one; I kept a faithful marriage with her. During this experience the difference occurred to me between a marital agreement (a union favoring the birth of children) and a pact of sexual desire, where a child is born unwanted—though once born, knows that it is loved! (IV, 2, 2)

Child

Another line may refer to their finding of one another. On the other hand, it may refer to some other kind of pursuit:

> I dared even in the celebration of your solemn mysteries, within the walls of your church, to desire and to carry out an arranged business of deathly fruition. (III, 3, 5)

The first passage above reveals a distinction between two kinds of relationships, a distinction he says occurred to him during those years of concubinage: the difference between a relationship based on sexual desire and one based on religious law. He feels the two are at bottom opposed to each other (sexual desire within holy matrimony will be controlled and dedicated to procreation). The one does not want children, the other does. It is not open to him to dignify or understand the kind of love that wants to include

diff types of relationship

→ vs. Hosea ≠ ~ sexual desire for God
or Psalms

both. Just so, in a later passage, he finds it a wonder that marriage can be both honorable and sexually exciting at the same time (VI, 12, 22).

In the above passages he keeps finding the stiff contrast: passion versus good sense, concubinage that is surprisingly faithful, attraction to a woman versus the church's solemn prayers. The choice between the two, offered by church and society, was a poor choice by modern standards. One could not love his concubine honorably, or enjoy her child. Yet Augustine's capacity for love surprises his own analysis: By his rule, a concubine's child is not wanted, "though once born, knows that it is loved!" Not necessarily. The unwanted child does not necessarily win a father's love. Augustine had the "unwanted" son by his concubine, named him Adeodatus ("given by God"), and loved him greatly. One of his early dialogues, The Teacher (389 C.E.), recorded a conversation with Adeodatus when he was just sixteen. Augustine greatly wondered at the intelligence of the boy; not long after, the young man suddenly died, with what agony for his father we can only imagine (IX, 6, 14). In any case, Adeodatus was much beloved. Augustine's ranging heart knew more possibilities for love than the custom of concubinage deigned to allow.

His relationship with the concubine herself was accordingly complex. When scholars comment that modern readers make more of his concubine than any of his contemporaries would (the Roman attitude was thoroughly matter-of-fact),[3] they forget what Augustine himself tells us of his feelings when he lost her: "My heart, where it clung [to her] was cut through, wounded and springing with blood" (VI, 15, 25). The wound was partly loss of status, violation of privacy; but clearly, some personal, emotional bond took the blow. What was the bond? To say that he loved her raises modern associations that are not warranted. Modern romantic love includes an idealizing and a peer companionship not fostered in fourth-century concubinage. Nevertheless, some sharp emotional claim and security was there. For one thing, he came to Carthage wanting to be "in love": "I fell in love—I yearned for it to seize me. . . . I was loved in return . . . with metallic stings of jealousy, suspicion." Was the concubine a bland exception to this love-quest, a reversion to settled expediency? No, since "I had tracked her by my wandering passion, not out of good sense." For her part, the concubine disclosed something of her feelings when years later she was forced to give up the relationship, leave Augustine, and return to her home.

---

3. Brown, Augustine, 39, 61–63. On 88–90, Brown allows for more feeling, but without explanation.

In that unhappy moment she did not bewail a general injustice on principle, but rather left "vowing to you [O God] that she would never know another man" (VI, 15, 25)—a vow of intended monastic continence, certainly; but also clearly a confession that the bond with Augustine was singular, unique.

The relation was admittedly a "pact of sexual desire" (IV, 2, 2), and Augustine later told a friend that he was captive to the "habit of satisfying an insatiable desire" (IV, 12, 22). Yet he remembers that the wound he felt in losing her could not be healed by another woman, but became more chilling and desperate (VI, 15, 25). Physical craving was not all.

Some important attachment was there; yet whole segments of his being could not be touched by it. Outwardly, the relationship was conventional and even respectable. Many a young man during his schooling maintained a concubine, only to dismiss her when he married (for socially she was not marriageable above her class). Both church and society saw dismissal as moral improvement(!) Then high above concubinage loomed matrimony, the law of God, with elaborate series of conditions to be fulfilled, social, economic, legal, religious. Augustine found himself in one arrangement, presuming to prepare for the other, and finding the promise of satisfaction in neither. Marriage was far distant and undoubtedly burdensome. Could he ever happily achieve that higher estate?

On the other hand, his link of feeling with the concubine was classified "inferior" by religious and civil authorities. If indeed the pair did meet in church, the setting ironically did not sanctify, but only denigrated their relationship. Here was the problem: A level of respectful commitment developed in their thirteen-year, loyal pact of sexual love; but no existing religious views acknowledged that commitment. He had no standard by which to dignify his relation to her. The relationship fell between the two linguistic regions of discourse that had troubled his childhood. On one side, Monica's language of God included law, prayers, wedlock, "good sense," faithfulness, children. On the other, the language of school and general experience included sexual attraction, desire, "arranged business," concubinage of convenience, "wandering passion," no children. The relation between Augustine and the concubine included something of both, yet was not either. It had no name; it hovered in the awkward space between available discourses. His problem of language as a child and schoolboy persisted, intensified. (His odd link to the Overturners had suffered the same anomaly.)

Readers have differed regarding Augustine's concubinage. Each has tried to construe it simply, conclusively, as love-story, convention, tragedy, power-play, victory, defeat. None of those discourses can define the relation-ship because it had no discourse of its own. By the jumbled fragments of it he recalls, it belongs to his same unfolding account: He was becalmed between linguistic worlds.

She was more than physical satisfaction, but she represented his chaos, his uncommittedness. She fell short of honor, but he faithfully sought satis-faction only in her. He claimed her, but he could *not* claim her. He married her; he could not marry her. Lost among dry definitions of righteousness, his sense of her found no home.

By belonging to his language dilemma, the account of her also belongs to his love dilemma. The priority for love, the axis of all other loves, rested high above him in language of God, righteousness, matrimony, spiritual discipline. These were oppressive; how could he love them? He loved suc-cess, but this was a sophisticated and likely dishonest game. He loved friendship, but the Overturners reminded him of the bleak love of destruc-tion that he brought from Thagaste. The bond with the concubine and their son was none of these, not matrimony, or success, or friendship, or destruction, or home. His loves were empty, uneasy.

Cicero

One day a surprise: The fist of his mind closed on something new. The passage at the head of this chapter tells of his discovery of Cicero. The particular book that so moved him, the *Hortensius*, has survived today only in fragments, some of them, indeed, Augustine's quotations from it.[4] Hundreds of students in rhetoric evidently studied it, a textbook case of powerful Latin speech. It awakened in Augustine a commitment to its message rather than to its style. "For I did not use that book to sharpen my tongue . . . nor did it convince me by its eloquence, but by its substance" (III, 4, 7).

At just this point, Augustine made a discovery that for the first time gave him insight into language and the grave disordering of language that had burdened his childhood. Cicero caused him to distinguish eloquence from substance. That is, language may embellish and flatter, yet seduce. Polished,

4. Albertus Grilli, ed., *Hortensius* (Milano: Istituto Editoriale Cisalpino, 1962) is a thor-oughly documented collection of the fragments available.

academic language boasts fine form, but can be turned to private, corrupt ends. The point was obvious, yet so struck the young student that he differentiated the rest of his life between the outward sounds and arrangements of speech that can deceive, and the ideal meanings those sounds, rightly employed, can convey. He had thus discovered one means of describing the separation of discourses that had troubled him for so long. Substance, or ideal meanings meant language as it expressed God's true ordering of things. Eloquence without substance meant the ordering of language as it served, not God's ordering, but the private interest and dominance of some party or group. The eloquent language of partisan dominance was separating, divisive language.

Cicero showed him ideal meanings in the *Hortensius*. For the first time, he saw how sophisticated academic language could express the possibility of a wide, true philosophy of life rather than be just a tool of political advantage. The seed of his own sense of truth and integrity, glimpsed previously in the parenthetic "as I knew" of his sixteenth year (see Chapter 2), responded to this discovery of Cicero. His fractured world of language, in which his own soul had been broken, shifted to hopeful possibility.

> I found myself yearning for deathless wisdom with unbelievable zeal of heart. . . . How I felt myself on fire, my God, on fire to turn back from mundane things towards you, not knowing what you would do with me! For [to be] with you *is* wisdom. The Greek word *philosophia* means love of wisdom, and Cicero's world enflamed me with that love. (III, 4, 7–8)

The reading caused him to reach toward God. Yet he had learned of God only seriously through Monica, a God in a realm beyond chaos, in a place of strength, rightness, and hope, who had sent his son. That language had been contradicted by the language of everyday life, especially of school. Now this wonder: at the heart of university studies in rhetoric, apparently empty and pretentious, a book appears that in learned language nevertheless recalls a hope in God. A link connects for him some of the qualities of Monica's teaching with Cicero's polished words on wisdom and truth. Perhaps there is, after all, a language both learned *and* devout, both sophisticated *and* truthful. Such a language might bring together Monica's ideal spirituality plus his own education and experience that went beyond both parents. Such a language could articulate an order of belonging for his soul, and for its restoration. It could bring hope to his broken and abused world.

Such a language was now promised in philosophy, Cicero's *philosophia*. It was a language of the search for truth unchanging, therefore of hope for happiness in a violently changing world, and of the wisdom of finding that truth. The promising student of rhetoric saw the language of simple faith and the language of advanced learning touching upon one another, and was excited.

This moment in the young student's life was important for the history of the West. Rhetoric and philosophy had long had opposing reputations. Ever since Socrates, seeking to know the truth, battled the Sophists (those ready to use language for personal advantage), the two had seemed opposed. Now Augustine, guided by Cicero, moves toward a rhetoric, the art of persuasion, that is nevertheless dedicated to philosophy and truth. He will become the towering Western figure uniting power in speech with dedication to truth, the love of wisdom.[5]

Also both love of heart and enlightenment of mind came together in this "love of wisdom." In the conclusion of Chapter 2 above, integrity of reason made the crucial difference between valid and perverse Christian nurture. Yet love, not reason, has emerged as the key to his theology. Both are correct. For Augustine, rational integrity meant a kind of love, the love of truth. Likewise, love of God meant a kind of enlightenment, that special understanding called wisdom. Indeed, "love of wisdom" was the goal that captured both heart and mind, the true meaning of *philosophia*. This love of truth was no dry, intellectual compulsion or drivenness, but an ardent lover's yearning for God, a flaming passion that came alive in him ("zeal of heart . . . on fire . . . on fire to turn back . . . towards you"). Cicero remarkably renewed Augustine's love; his love-priority became love of wisdom (later, of course, Wisdom, the second person of the Trinity). He would love first of all *God's truth* and all other things would find their place and proportion. The goal of his ardor he came to see as happiness, *beatitudo*, true blessedness. His theology became a theology of love pursuing truth.

Yet what happened in this discovery to the importance of Catholic Christian teaching? If Cicero solved the problem of the heart's love, did Christian doctrine become unnecessary? Did his liberal education in the classics enable him to leave behind the narrow restrictions of his early Catholic training? Is he now fortunately liberated by Cicero from the burden of Christian belief? To the contrary, from the first Cicero recalled qualities and hopes

5. H. I. Marrou, *Saint Augustin et la Fin de la Culture Antique* (Paris: Editions E. de Boccard, 1958), 8–9, 169–73, 509.

he had attached to God in childhood. He later realized that Cicero enhanced his Christian legacy even more widely. Not Christianity, but the
clutter of false, sectarian philosophies throughout the empire fell prey to
Cicero's critique:

> There are those who seductively color and adorn their errors under
> the excellent, winning, and honest name of philosophy. This book
> [the *Hortensius*] considers and casts in their true light almost all such
> teachers, from Cicero's time and before. And clearly the substance
> is here [in Cicero] of that wholesome warning by your Spirit, through
> your good and devoted servant [Paul]:
> "Watch out! that no one deceives you through 'philosophy': really
> empty seductions, long-standing human contrivances, the premise
> of the world as self-sufficient; that is, 'philosophy' not grounded in
> Christ, because in him, a bodily piece of the world is the habitation
> of true Godhead" (Colossians 2:8–9). (III, 4, 8)

Cicero's book gave him the *substance* of a passage in Paul, of a piece of
inspired Scripture, before he ever read Paul for himself! Are Christ and the
Holy Spirit found in Cicero? In one sense, yes:

> . . . you know this is true, you Light of my heart, because Paul was
> not yet known to me! I nevertheless was delighted with this one
> thing in Cicero's exhortation: that I should love, not this or that
> sect, but wisdom itself, whatever it might be; and that I should seek
> it and follow it, hold it and bravely embrace it; and I was excited
> by that reading, kindled and ablaze with enthusiasm. (III, 4, 8)

"Wisdom itself," not this or that sect, meant the one true order of the
world, by which everything coheres. Augustine later saw this order as God's
truth, God's Word (John 1:1), by which the Creator made all things; and
that Word or wisdom came into the world as Christ. Cicero's wisdom coincided with the universal Christ, sought and worshiped by all Christians, in
another sense sought by all genuine inquirers after truth. Cicero's philosophy was not vain philosophy; it illumined what clearheaded Christianity
truly affirmed. It presented truth as a blissful object, beloved of the seeker,
whose heart burned with longing to embrace the wise God ("excited . . .
kindled . . . ablaze"). If only Cicero had known the actual name of Christ,
so that he could have included it!

And in so much flaming ardor, for Cicero's book, I was checked by only this one thing: that the name of Christ was not there. For my tender heart had devotedly, in my very mother's milk, drunk in that name and long retained it. Whatever was lacking this name, no matter how literate, polished, and valid, did not completely take hold of me. (III, 4, 8)

That is, the Incarnation was not there. Cicero described the one true way upward to God as philosophy; he did not include God's way downward into human affairs (the Incarnation) as a help with the philosophical search. Cicero and Paul shared the same goal (love of wisdom, or love of God); yet Paul knew the coming of wisdom, the lover, into the world, in the Word made flesh.

Nevertheless, at one point Cicero coincided with the New Testament, namely, love of the one, final truth. Something Monica had meant by "God" could be articulate in the language of the schools, and could point through that language to the one beloved God of world-embracing wisdom. Cicero offered a link between separated discourses.

Was it possible, then, to be at once biblically faithful and broadly philosophical? How could this be? In the modern West biblically "conservative" and theologically "liberal" (or philosophical) are invariably opposed. But in Augustine's day Cicero's philosophy was no easy optimism about liberal values; it was a sharp criticism of culture, of pagan polytheism and sectarian strife. Augustine's discovery of Cicero came to mean that one need not give up the Bible to be broadly philosophical, and certainly not give up rich, philosophical wisdom to be biblical.

Did Augustine see this at the time? No. He tells us (III, 5, 9) that since the name of Christ was not in Cicero, he turned to the Scriptures. He was disappointed. The humble style he found there did not compare with Cicero's nobility, or so he felt. A long way lay ahead before he would actually grasp the relation of scriptural material to the wisdom of philosophy.

He did become convinced that all humankind (as he knew it) was seeking this wisdom, the single truth of God. Is that too lofty a view of humanity? No, he decided, since all humankind is certainly seeking happiness. And what is happiness but to rest in an immortal wisdom, a deathless good, the passionate love of truth? Truth alone endures and provides a happiness that cannot be lost. Admittedly, most people do not realize that in seeking happiness, God's wisdom is actually what they seek. Yet happiness in other things will disappoint them; then they may realize their error and turn their love. His theology therefore became a theology of happiness, blessedness, and humanity's unremitting quest to find it.

Cicero, then, not only caught and focused Augustine's love. He encouraged the young student's honest seeking. He redeemed sophisticated, rhetorical language into an instrument of truth. Cicero provided an intellectual passion that promised, not to sever Augustine's early religious roots, but to reconceive them.

PART II

HIS MATURE
POSITION UNFOLDS

Section 1

Creation . . . (anti-Manichaean)

4

The Manichaean Life

(*Confessions* III, 6–12 through IV)

. . . O Truth, Truth, how sensitively the very quick of my mind
yearned for you [O God], while [the Manichaeans] were dinning
your name at me over and over ["Truth! Truth!"], more and more,
now with their voices, now in their countless, ponderous books.
Those were the deadly vessels in which they served up to my hungering for you, as if they *were* you, the sun and the moon! your beautiful
works—but still your works, not you. . . . How much better to love
the sun itself, which is at least true to our eyes, than to love the
glittering fantasies in those [Manichaean] vessels, which use the eyes
to deceive the mind. But I thought those false images were you. I
fed upon them—not eagerly, for I could not savor you there as you
really are. You were not those empty figments, nor did they nourish
me. I was only more exhausted. (italics added) (III, 6, 10)

After his encounter with Cicero and his newfound love for truth, Augustine surprisingly became for nine years a follower of the Manichaean
religion. Such a practice seemed to go squarely against what he had just
discovered. Manichaean belief was not a rational philosophy, but a myth.
The Manichaean movement was not a universal way of wisdom for all, but
a sect. Their language departed from Cicero's language of philosophy. The
very passages he quoted from Cicero had warned him against just such a
sectarian group. Why, then, did he almost immediately turn to them? For
one thing, though the religion was mythological, its adherents insisted
that they followed only the most enlightened scientific reason and could

demonstrate all their claims: "[They] were dinning your name at me over and over, ['Truth! Truth!']." For another, though they were sectarian and elitist, they claimed to be universal, weaving together the best elements from several major historic religions. Also, they included the name of Christ, which touched Augustine at the level of his childhood loyalty.

Most important, the Manichaeans' special interest was the problem of evil. Why is there evil in the world and how shall we respond to it? The Manichaeans powerfully attracted many to their movement because they seemed to have the answer. Obviously the young Augustine was a prime candidate for such a lure. He knew the pressure and complexity of evil in his own life. Here was a group that presumably could both account for evil and show him a way out of it.

In addition, Cicero was but the beginning, not the end, of his pilgrimage. In Part I (above) the pattern of Augustine's theology as a whole has been surveyed, from early religious teaching, through destructive error, to the renewal of Christian intent via Cicero and the heart's love of truth. Yet to say that Augustine grasped this pattern by the time he was nineteen is far from saying that he had executed it in his own life. He saw the pattern and the goal and loved the ideal, but he did not know how to apply these to daily choices and directions. The task of a lifetime was only beginning. Just as Dante, centuries later, found himself lost in a wood and turned to climb up a small mount where he saw the sun rising; found his climb obstructed, and found himself forced the long way around through hell and purgatory;[1] so Augustine had much purgation and hell to experience on a long, round-about journey before the Ciceronian-Christian goal could be his. He especially did not know, when he was eighteen, that the Christian church could be a home to him once again in the future.

He had experienced evil, and he had turned toward wisdom; but he had no insight into the *nature* of evil and therefore, as yet, no reliable wisdom. The pattern of his theology, already glimpsed, had yet to be disclosed concretely from day to day. His first move, like Dante's, was to lunge upward after truth. He joined the Manichaeans. Yet he found himself in a greater tangle of error: "So I fell in with a wild, proud group, fleshly minded, glib of speech" (III, 6, 10).

1. Dante Alighieri, *The Divine Comedy*, "Hell," canto I, trans. C. E. Norton (Boston: Houghton Mifflin, 1941), 1–8.

The Manichaeans

Because the problem of evil has always preoccupied the Western world, and since the Manichaeans made it their focus, the history of religion has vividly remembered the Manichaean religion. The term "manichaean" has become a common technical term in theodicy, that part of theology concerned with evil in an essentially good world. The problem for theodicy, and for Augustine, has always been this: Either evil is an unaccountable mystery in an otherwise good world, or evil turns out to be a particular *part* of the world that needs to be suppressed: human appetites, physical nature, customary institutions, wealth, or simply the "other"—other tribes, other peoples, other types than ourselves. The former solution (evil as mystery) denigrates no one, but is really no solution at all. The Manichaeans there-fore chose the latter. Let part of the world suffer the blame; then the righteous have a target to shoot at—always a popular option. The term "manichaean" has thus become synonymous with splitting the world into two parts, of which one is the source and substance of evil. The term has endured because the practice has endured. A phenomenal variety of scapegoats, split-off parts of the world, have carried the blame for evil through the centuries: Hate the earth, hate sexuality, hate organized society, hate dark-skinned people, or Jews, or orientals, or finally hate ourselves. Augustine struggled for nine years, and indeed throughout his life, with the tenacious and often subtle appeal of this option.

The Manichaeans, the followers of the third-century Persian prophet, Mani, spoke of truth like philosophers, of the cosmos like scientists, and proposed to combine in religion the best of Christ, Buddha, and Zoroaster.[2] As religious philosophers, they began with Zoroaster's notion of two great realities, the light and the dark, the primal constituents of all things. The world as we know it, caught between the two, is largely dark and evil, but includes particles of light. In such a situation the whole of reality is split (metaphysical dualism); yet, as will appear, the Manichaeans found ele-ments of purity both within themselves and within the special company of their saints.

In Manichaean mythology, the forces of darkness once attempted to at-tack the Father of Light and his kingdom, and sparkles of light were trapped

2. A fine introduction is J. J. O'Meara, *The Young Augustine* (New York: Longmans, Green, 1954), chapter 4. Cf. Brown, *Augustine,* chapter 5. For primary source selections, cf. Hans Jonas, *The Gnostic Religion,* 2d ed., revised (Boston: Beacon, 1963), 213ff.

in the battleground, known to humanity as the world. Indeed, the world is still such a battleground, where elements of light yearn to find their way to the Kingdom of Light and strain against the heaviness of gross material things surrounding them. This light-dark tension obviously governs the whole human situation. Each individual experiences physical light in the world with the physical eye: sunlight, fire, electricity, moonlight, starlight. The individual also has "light" feelings within: gentleness, loneliness, nostalgia, the longing for truth, peace, and love. For Mani, the two kinds of light—physical without and spiritual within—are substantively the same: not modern "matter" but "corporeal fantasies," as Augustine called them (III, 6, 10). One's longing for spiritual peace thus arises from an inner corporeal light, not different in kind from Mani's fantasies of outward electricity or fire. That inner light is caught within the gross functions of the flesh and longs to be with the Father, yet is unable to escape its imprisonment.

The factors borrowed from Buddha and Christ then logically follow. From Buddha, Mani learned ascetic self-denial of all fleshly desire. One who lives a quiescent, vegetarian life and does not reproduce (having children is more serious a violation than sexual intercourse as such, since birth perpetuates the entanglement of light with darkness)—that person moves toward releasing the gentle light within so that in time it may slip loose from all fleshly drives and ascend beyond the world to the Father. Christ, for Mani, contributed hope for such a blessed end through his preaching of the coming Kingdom. His preaching, skillfully interpreted, points actually to the return of all light substance to its home country, beyond the cosmos, beyond all human striving. If blessed disengagement from the flesh should take more than one lifetime of rigor, transmigration of the light spark, born in a new body, gives further opportunity. A good Manichaean may be reborn in the life and body of a Manichaean saint, near the goal. A murderer, however, will be reborn as an elephant, which has almost no possibility of progress. In no case shall fruits and vegetables, which contain light, be given to a starving yet impure human being, in whom the light may be trapped by eating—a moral protection of fruit over starving neighbor that later scandalized Augustine as he thought back upon it (III, 10, 18).

The reader may have difficulty working imaginatively into Manichaean mythology, but the attempt to do so is important. In the first place, the entire cosmos is like a vast room, alive at every point with the light-dark struggle. The sky testifies to the side of things that is light; the earth, to the side that is dark. Historical time is of little consequence since it carries no promise; only cosmic cyclical time provides the setting for release. The immense room is closed, without a transcendent governor or principle ruling over it. Rather, the room holds only two impersonal opposing forces, which everywhere flash a brilliant display of dark-light encounter. Divinity is light within; divinity is sunlight, fire, and stars, and sparkling matter within vegetables. Perdition is flesh, blood, sexual passion, earth, rock, beast and bird, human striving, history, and government. The outlook is all-consuming: Things are not what they seem and have no free identity of their own; they are forces of either dark or light, or points of clash between the two. Even "the body of the air . . . thin and subtle . . . [the Manichaeans] imagine to be a malignant mind stealing through the earth" (V, 10, 20).

In some Manichaean teaching, the daily release of light particles from earth was proved by the phases of the moon: A waxing moon showed gathering particles from earth; a waning moon showed those particles passing on to the beyond. For one's imagination to live in such a world meant surrendering the common identity of things. The sun is not simply the sun, nor the moon, the moon, but rather collections of divine light. Reason's everyday order of things collapses into a metaphysical struggle, always happening, always the same: "How much better to love the sun itself, which is at least true to our eyes, than to love the glittering fantasies in those [Manichaean] vessels, which use the eyes to deceive the mind." In this outlook, God is simply the total collection of all sparkles of light everywhere, inward and outward, including the heavenly bodies.

> . . . they served up to my hungering for you, as if they *were* you, the sun and the moon! your beautiful works—but still your works, not you. . . . But I thought those false images were you. I fed upon them—not eagerly, for I could not savor you there as you really are.

The myth of the Manichaeans was a myth of monotony, offering everywhere the same, drab metaphysical standoff.

Mani and the Soul

As he tells us, Augustine likely never gave his full assent to Manichaean doctrine (*The Happy Life* I, 4). His involvement nevertheless tested him severely at least at one particular point: Manichaean mythology blocked any strong, individual integrity. All things, one's own soul included, were divided into two impersonal, corporeal elements. Such an arrangement split any tough, personal sense of "I as a person will do thus-and-so." The soul divided against itself became its own prison, certainly in the wider range of life's critical affairs. The conscious "I" had no steady rational order, either within or without, to count on or refer to.

"How sensitively the very quick of my mind yearned for you," yearned, that is, to be in touch with a reasonable order of things, some knowledge that the world makes sense. Manichaean quasi-science offered no such knowledge. Furthermore, the splitting of the soul between two forces meant that doing evil was not the work of one's own accountable, unified person.

> For . . . I thought it was not we who sin, but some other nature in us (I don't know what) that sins; so I took prideful delight in being blameless and in not confessing any evil doing. . . . Rather I loved to excuse myself and to accuse this unknown thing, which was with me, but which I was not. But in fact, I was one whole being, and my own ungodliness against myself had divided me. That was the more irrecoverable sin: that I thought myself no sinner! (V, 10, 18)

Thus, Augustine became a spectator at his own wrongdoing. Dark substances within executed destructive acts that seemed to happen willy-nilly.

At least one might suppose that his sense of integrity remained intact as regards virtue. If some other force in him did evil, then he at least did the good, and could give himself credit for it. To the contrary, the affirmative side collapsed, also. If there was no free choice to do evil (something does it in us), then there was no free choice to do good. No personal dignity actually decided, one way or the other. The "light" sense within had its inclination and tendency (to live gently, pacifically), but remained at the mercy of heavy irrational powers. Augustine affirmed an oasis of purity within himself ("I took prideful delight in being blameless"), but at a deadly price: giving up his nature as "one whole being." The "good" soul thinned out into passive yearning. Then evil activity claimed the more vigorous features of the person as ransom for the purity of the tenuous light within. There was no full and competent "I myself will . . ."

The Manichaean notion of Christ also echoed the same problem. In Mani's account, the Father of lights had sent his offspring, the Primal Man (Christ) with his weapons of light to halt the invading darkness. The Primal Man had stopped the darkness by allowing its demonic forces to eat himself and his light weapons, thus damaging the dark ones severely, even though allowing himself to be trapped and benumbed. The fragments of his weapons became human souls, caught in dark bodies, while the Primal Man remained statically imprisoned in the structures of creation, stretched out wounded across earth and sky in the form of sun, moon, and stars. Mani held, of course, to no historic crucifixion since Christ could have no flesh. He saw the story of Jesus' crucifixion as a crude symbol of the Primal Man's metaphysical plight, crucified throughout the cosmos. Christ lay caught in the heavenly sphere. There this suffering Christ awaited his homecoming in glory in some distant eon; so the good Manichaean waited patiently, refining a life of rigor. Christ, separate and pure, yet nostalgically caught within the world, reflected the Manichaeans' personal sense of self, but writ large across creation.

Why did Augustine adhere to so bizarre a mythology for nine young-adult years? Certainly his own background bristled with dualities: his mother's tough, passive devotionalism versus his father's raucous and lively abandon; the antagonism within their marriage; his father's world versus the world of his Father, God; the world of his mother's spirituality versus the world of her ambition for his career; harsh beatings, the slow burden of the good versus the liberty of playing, stealing; one's own tender status as praiseworthy, full of hope, versus the beaten child, laughed at, undisciplined; random drives versus ideal aspirations; ambitions versus truth; sexuality versus continence; flesh versus spirit.

Yet why did he turn away from the promising language of philosophy learned with Cicero? Certainly he had the mentality to see through the Manichaeans' constructs. What held him? Their preoccupation with evil, like his, has already been noted. Also, they promised truth and reason to him, sufficient to attract a recent convert to Cicero's ideal of truth and wisdom. Not only so, they promised to overcome the dilemma of the separated discourses, to heal them into one, within the unity of a mythological narrative. Their one widely symbolic tale, presumably profound, accounted for a known discourse of gentleness and love, on the one hand (the merciful Father), and a known discourse of raucous strife (the violent father), on the other. Mythology could relate disparate elements within a story, when ordinary reason found great difficulty doing so. Inspired by Cicero, Augustine reached out for wisdom with the Manichaeans, hoping that more substance lay in their myths than appeared on the surface (*The Happy Life* I, 4). As for philosophy's passionate quest, he and his friends yearned to be free and devote themselves to this glory, yet could not loosen the ties that bound them to their everyday obligations (VI, 14, 24). The Manichaeans well understood the binding heaviness of ordinary obligations. They promised to explain it—mythologically—but their way out of it, realistically, seemed interminable.

Later, he discovered that the Manichaean mythic language had composed a unified outlook on the world falsely. The account was irreconcilable within itself. A mythic saga loses credibility in attempting to describe the warfare between two natures that are markedly different, that could never meet, as if an orangutan wrestled a moonbeam. Or if they do meet, then the character of God must be falsified (VII, 2, 3). The breakdown had already begun when the famed Manichaean teacher, Faustus, came to Carthage. Augustine, as a Manichaean, had eagerly reserved troublesome questions to raise with the renowned teacher, only to discover that his smooth eloquence disguised an actual lack of knowledge in critical areas (V, 3, 3; 6, 10–13). Once again, language had deceived and broken down, had fallen short of truth and wisdom! Augustine later discovered that he had deserted the rational, coherent terms of *philosophia* for pretentious accounts, the tools of a religious elitism.

Manichaeanism and Grief: The Death of a Friend

Augustine records not only Manichaean theory, but an emotional crisis in which the practice of Manichaeanism came vividly to life. When still relatively new in the sect, he suffered the death of a close friend. His account offers not only a classic description of grief, but also an exceptional entranceway, not into Manichaeanism as myth or system, but into personal Manichaean existence.

> In those years when for the first time I began to teach in my native town, I found a friend exceedingly dear, with much in common between us. He was my age, and we were wonderfully young together and flourishing. He grew up with me as a boy: We were in school together, we played together. But he was not then such a friend. . . . Nevertheless, it [became now] a sweet friendship, mellowing in our warm, shared interests. (IV, 4, 7)

Augustine recalls that he influenced his friend away from the Catholic faith into Manichaean views (his ability to make, and then to lead friends, was powerful).

> That man (along with me) was now wandering in error, in his mind; and I could not go on without him, in my soul. And look! you [God] drawing close behind your fugitives . . . look there! you took the man out of this life, my friend for hardly a year, sweeter to me than any pleasure I knew. (IV, 4, 7)

Augustine recalls a remarkably detailed account of his grief.

> My heart was plunged into black sorrow; whatever I looked upon was death. My home country was torture to me, and my father's house a shocking misery. Whatever I had shared with him, now without him, became a frightful cross to bear. My eyes looked for him everywhere, but nothing produced him. And I hated everything that did not have him and gave no signal to me, "Look, he's coming" . . . as things used to when for a little he would be away. I became a great inquiry into myself and interrogated my soul why it was sad and why it disturbed me so greatly, and my soul knew nothing to answer me. If I said, "Hope in God," it rightly did not obey. For the human being was truer and better, that dearest one that my soul had lost, than the phantom I commanded it to hope in. Tears alone were sweet . . . (IV, 4, 9)

That tears alone were sweet fascinated him. At one point, attempting to reason it through, he recalls:

> I wept most bitterly, and I rested in bitterness. So I was pitiable; yet that miserable mere life was more dear to me than was my friend. No matter how keenly I longed to relieve my plight, I shrank from losing life more than I shrank from losing him. And I doubt that I would have died for him—even for him. . . . In me a most contrary feeling—I don't know what—had arisen: I was too heavy with loathing to live life, yet too fearful to die.
>
> I believe that the more I loved him, the more I hated this vicious enemy, death, that had taken him from me. I fantasized death suddenly consuming all living folk, since it could consume him. This was my state, as I remember.

Look at my heart, O my God, look within, see these things I have remembered. . . . For I marveled that other mortals were living, since the one I loved as deathless, was dead. And I wondered even more at my own life, to live with that one dead, for I was himself, his "other." Therefore, life was a horror to me; I refused to live by half.

But therefore also, I powerfully feared dying, for then he would wholly die, whom I so loved.

. . . So I burned, I sighed, I wept, I was in tumult; there was no rest or reason. I carried about my crushed and bleeding soul, rebellious at being forced about by me, and I could find nowhere to lay it down. Not in pleasant woods, not in games and singing, nor in sweet fragrant places, nor in feasts finely laid, nor in the pleasures of love, not even in books and poetry did my soul yield. Everything was horrible, even the daylight, and whatever was not what he was, all flat and hateful—except groans and tears; in these alone was there a little rest. . . .

Towards you, Lord, my soul needed to be lifted up for cure, I knew that! but I did not will to do it, nor could I, all the more because I saw you as nothing substantial and sure, as I conceived you. You were only an empty phantom. My error was my God. If I tried to lay my soul there, it fell through the emptiness and came down again on me. I remained an unhappy place, where I could not stay, and I could not go. Where could my heart flee from my heart? Where could I flee from myself? Where would I not follow myself?

Yet actually I did flee: from my homeland.

My eyes searched for him less in a place they were not used to. So I left the town of Thagaste and came to Carthage. (IV, 6, 11–7, 12)

The world of love and death was acutely subjective; his soul's heartbreak therefore transformed his entire world into ashes. He looked at his own feelings when he looked at the outside world.

My country was torture . . . my father's house a . . . misery. . . . Whatever I had shared with [my friend] . . . became a frightful cross. . . . Everything was horrible, even the daylight . . . all flat and hateful. . . . So I was pitiable.

Many have noted the poisonous qualities of pity. With Augustine, the pity for himself effected a chaos of narcissistic pleasure and agony. In this condition the drama of being the world's deepest wound oddly heightened life, right at the point where there was no use going on. Suicide beckoned, but the romantic engagement of life would not let go. "That miserable mere life was more dear to me than was my friend. . . . I shrank from losing life."

The impulses to overcome and to succumb, to live and to die, hung in irresolution: "I wept most bitterly, and I rested in bitterness." Therefore, the linchpin of his situation was stalemate. This stalemate, his "rest in bitterness," grotesquely parodied the rest he sought throughout the whole *Confessions* story ("our heart is restless until it rests in you" [I, 1, 1]). The result was the repulsive parody of rest in his clearest statement of it: "I was too heavy with loathing to live life, yet too fearful to die."

His experience of friendship and loss had plunged him into the world defenseless. That world was a balanced question mark; he could not endure it, but he could not let go of it. Love seemed a trap, a means of drawing him out of fragile safety into the infinitely unresolved riddle of things. Such a world could only waste itself. ("I . . . an unhappy place, where I could not stay, and I could not go.") He hung, suspended, a paradigm of the cosmos.

What he was experiencing in naked directness was of course the world of Mani, suspended forever in irresolution with no conqueror. To taste love and death was to taste the Manichaean light and dark, direct and unvarnished. The light was evil as much as the dark, for the light exquisitely completed the suspension. Just as in grief, where everything became pain, so with Mani: the cosmos was one's own anguish writ large, and one's individual existence was the horror of the cosmos focused. Integrity of world or person collapsed into the same dreary condition everywhere, without end.

Assuredly, if he tried to lay his soul on God, "it fell through the emptiness and came down again on me"—since God *was* his soul, plus countless other souls and sparkles. Augustine's piercing love and grief were his part in the cosmic crucifixion of Christ. His crushed soul was Christ in agony; his inability to escape from himself was the Son of God engrained through the earth. His pain was his real baptism into Mani's world. For the only consoling baptism for the Manichaean, as Augustine found, was his tears. Why were they alone sweet? They were tears for himself (as in that sect one could be baptized only by oneself); tears of love, because one had found love and become precious to oneself; tears of despair, because the moment of finding love was the moment of dying and of boundless anguish. In the twentieth century, certain plays of Eugene O'Neill offer the same outlook in which love becomes only a lure into personal and metaphysical entrapment.[3]

Mani could only reflect the world; he could not change it. To permit oneself to love was to follow Mani into the heart of his morass, where the stalemate of good and evil was itself the true evil, the darkest evil of all.

3. For example, *Strange Interlude* (New York: Horace Liveright, 1928), especially acts 4–6. Cf. *The Iceman Cometh* (New York: Random House, 1946), especially the characters Parritt and Slade, act 2 (from the middle) and act 4.

5

Reality of God, Reality of Soul

(*Confessions* V through VII, 10)

When I wished to think of my God, I did not know what to think except a bodily mass. . . . I was driven to think of you as something bodily through all space and location, either infused into the world or even diffused outside the world through infinity. . . . for whatever I deprived of such physical space seemed to me nothing at all, absolutely nothing, not even emptiness. . . . The mass of air . . . above the earth does not resist the sun's light or keep it from passing through. The light penetrates the air without disrupting or breaking it; indeed the light completely fills it. Just so I reckoned the body of the sky, air, and sea and even of the earth, was passible and penetrable [by you] through all its parts, great and small, and received your presence. Then by a secret inspiration you inwardly and outwardly governed everything, which you had created—or so I thought because I could not think otherwise. But it was all wrong: . . . the body of an elephant would receive more of your presence than the body of a sparrow! (V, 10, 19; VII, 1, 2)

The problem of evil turned out to be the problem of God. In Manichaean thinking, both evil and God were fantastic corporeal stuff of one kind or another. If evil was part of the corporeal world-stuff, then the good God turned out to be the other part of that stuff. Then no single God or ruling principle governed all things; God was only a part. No single set of rules or expectations applied everywhere equally and truly. No consistent nature of things linked all minds and bodies. Rather, everything was unnegotiably divided, including one's soul. God could not pervade the scene.

Augustine's steps forward in learning to think of God were painful and slow. In the passage above, he has come to think of God as a kind of boundless ether or electromagnetic field. Still, this was progress of a sort. He tells us in one passage: "I had not thought of you, O God, in the shape of a human body since I began to grasp something of philosophy" (VII, 1, 1). He began to grasp some philosophy at eighteen, when he first read Cicero. By implication, he had thought of God in bodily human form (an old man on a mountain?) until he was eighteen years old! A bright North African youngster had been culturally deprived. (How skewed was Christian instruction for a child in Thagaste?) Even Mani had been a step beyond this, conceiving the "old man" as a fantastic light substance on one side of reality. Now Augustine had moved from God, the old man, and God, the light substance, to God, the ether. Could he make the final step, to God as spiritual substance?

That step forward would be intellectually arduous and personally painful. Through Cicero, he had come to love wisdom, but he had skewed the love and intellectually failed the wisdom. The move forward to recover his hopes was personally painful because it was a move toward himself, toward the real nature of his soul, as well as toward God. His progress tested him severely each step of the way.

The Natural Philosophers

Thinking the truth about God began for him in a limited, ordinary manner. Something small and persistent can embarrass a monumental mythology, like a weed through cracked pavement. For Augustine, the first step came through an item of natural science. Previously, Cicero called him to a quest for truth. Prior to that, the boy Augustine had raised a lonely question about the expectations of his parents. Yet the first focused test of truth itself concerned, of all things, the sun and moon. What about eclipses? Did the Manichaean light-dark struggle deal with them? What about the fact that the natural philosophers (scientists) could predict them?

> For using their own minds and ingenuity—given them by you, [Lord]—they looked into such things and discovered a remarkable

lot, and foretold years in advance eclipses of the great lights, the sun and the moon: the day, the hour, and what the extent of those eclipses would be. And their calculations did not fail them! . . . I held on to many true points made by these people about the crea- tion. For their reasoning came clear to me: their mathematics, the order of the seasons, the clear evidence of the constellations.

And I compared them with assertions of Mani: in his raving way he set down reams of material on all the same matters, and *no* reasoning was clear to me, not on the solstices, or the equinoxes, or eclipses—indeed, not on anything, not as I had read it in those books of secular learning. (V, 3, 4; 3, 6)

With such an element of realism via astronomy, his suspicions of Mani- chaeanism, long entertained, pressed him severely. The point here is not an appeal to natural theology, the position that the Christian God can be inferred from plain, scientific evidences. Augustine wants it very clear that the astronomers had not, by pondering their results, come to acknowledge God. That required lowliness of heart (V, 3, 4–5). His benefits from the astronomers contrasted sharply with his determination not to grant them any religious authority.

The matter was not one of natural theology, but of a kind of language. These early astronomers had a reasoned language of measure that unveiled one strand of order in natural events. If there is an order greater than oneself that can be known, where may it appear? In an eclipse? Possibly. No matter what the exact basis for knowing the order, or its relation to God, some signal of order is there, if an eclipse is predictable. That glimmer of order may lead finally to atheism (no god is needed to explain it). It may lead to pantheism, the view that the order of the world is itself divine. It may lead to the Christian God, incarnate in Christ. Augustine later became convinced that the order of nature and the order of faith do join, that the order of nature is "graced," that a link of reason lies between creatures and Creator: "that our souls may rise up into yourself, leaving their weariness, supporting themselves on the creatures you have made, and going on to- wards you, who wonderfully made them all" (V, 1, 1). That was a later reflection. For the moment, he learned that the sun had a set of appoint- ments and an identity as sun, not simply a mythic role in an alien Man- ichaean drama. And if the sun had an identity, and the moon, and each known object, then perhaps Augustine also had an identity and some reasonable order in which to exercise it. If so, could one simply begin to live by that identity? Dare I test out who I am?

Departure from Monica

The intellectual side of seeking the one God thus emerged by reading astronomy. The personally painful side, the move toward himself, as well as toward God, emerged in leaving his mother to take a new job. The point is important since rational consideration of God, in theory, could never for him be separated from personal, painful freedom and accountability in relation to that God. To suppose God's reasonable order even in the slightest, meant to begin experimenting with a possible life in that order, a life of reasonableness and integrity. Seeking a new career opportunity, and increasingly doubtful of Manichaeanism, he determined to go to Rome. Monica despaired that he was still unbaptized, still in Mani's sect, and blocked his departure in every way she could.

> [My mother] in a paroxysm of protest . . . followed me all the way down to the sea. She physically held onto me, until either I would cancel the trip or take her with me. But I tricked her; I fabricated a supposed friend: I would not leave until the wind favored my friend's own sailing. So I lied to my mother, even to that mother! (—and escaped!)
>
> . . . Still, she refused to turn back without me, and I barely persuaded her to spend the night in a shrine to St. Cyprian close by our ship.
>
> But that night, secretly, I set out without her; she was left behind praying and weeping. And what did she pray for, God, with so many tears, but that you would not let me sail! But you, with deeper wisdom, . . . you took no heed of this asking (—essentially to do for me, in the long run, what she really wanted). So the wind blew and the sails filled, and the shore line faded from view.
>
> On that shore the next morning she was insane with grief and filled your ears with complaints and groans, because you had despised her pleas. But just as you took me away through my own schemes (to make an end of my scheming!) so you arranged that her hunger for closeness to me justly should feel the whip-sting of grief. For she

always loved to have me close with her, as mothers will, but far more than many mothers.

She had no idea what joyous things you were going to create for her out of my absence. She had no idea; therefore she wept and wailed. . . . Nevertheless, after denouncing my deceitfulness and my cruelty, she turned once again to praying for me, and went back home, and I on to Rome. (V, 8, 15).

Here the drama has elements of the comic. Monica's wrong judgment is not devastating, but contained. She will become a power to be reckoned with once again later on, but in this scene she is a frenzied figure, not in control, forgiven her excesses because in a distant way she genuinely desires his well-being (compare his lifelong indebtedness to her eloquent prayers in V, 9, 16–17). Also, the identification of Monica's way with God's way is broken up. A gap opens between what Monica wanted for her son and what God wanted, that is, as regards the *way* to the good life. Therefore, God rebukes her "hunger for closeness" to her son, so that it "justly should feel the whip-sting of grief." Her emotional strategies for directing him come to the end of their tether.

Here an insight emerges concerning the old separation of languages. To separate off an arena of discourse is to domesticate part of God's ordering as a region of private control. Monica's discourse, when Augustine was a child, had pointed to the one and only God, creator and keeper of all. But her discourse had domesticated part of God's language and ordering as her region of control—to survive her circumstances, to prosecute her son's welfare. She had determined to govern his future and thereby had narrowed the meaning of God, whom she had intended to proclaim.

Yet with the dismissal of Monica's feverish control, Monica's God does not have to be dismissed. That God turns out to be significantly other than Monica's version of him. The God of her religion does not have to fall away with the failure of her designs, but can still be rediscovered by Augustine for himself. Such a rediscovery required great strength, patience, and searching on his part. What were the channels of grace that provided that strength? Was there a sturdy deposit within all the distortion of his early home life, a gift within the twisted package? Monica herself showed great strength. The God of her strength was not exactly what she thought, but she bequeathed to Augustine the strength to find that out himself. Monica's temptation, her disciplined power, was also her bequest, even though it came in a rough-hewn form. The great strength she gave her son was the strength to resist herself and to find her God in his own way, a surprising gift. She is always credited with giving him the piety to follow her example; she also gave him the strength and courage to hold herself at arm's length and work out his own faith.

In his later theology, Augustine held the notion that evil is good, fallen into disorder. He learned some of this in dealing with Monica. The error of her controlling way was a deeper good, forced into distortion. His life became an exercise in sorting out, beyond distortion, that deeper good.

Thus no reasoned progress was possible in finding God apart from the painful progress of finding his own soul. Both intellectual and emotional vitality engaged him.

Milan, Ambrose

The venture toward himself, and God, took him into strange horizons and surroundings. His new circumstances, the job in Rome, were darkness compared to all his old familiar lights. Perhaps his desperate illness upon arriving in Rome was a signal of that darkness (V, 9, 16–17). The new bid for freedom, intellectual and personal, involved much that was dulling and uncertain. He faced setting up shop, claiming new associates, settling his concubine and child, silently agonizing over his Manichaeanism, dealing with a different clime, a different race, a different accent in speech (critical for a professional rhetorician).

Furthermore, all this was to be but for one year in Rome. A post opened in Milan as teacher of rhetoric and public orator, requiring readjustment again. Since the Western emperor's court was in Milan (not Rome), the appointment raised Augustine to a kind of minister of propaganda, offering oratory in support of government policies and programs.[1] He had been recommended by Symmachus, senator and prefect of Rome, a former proconsul of Carthage, a man who had risen by virtue of his literary talents, member of a conservative pagan elite. Symmachus and his group were deeply suspicious of the Catholic church and had formed a link to the anti-Catholic, heretical Manichaeans. Augustine, known as Manichaean, must have seemed to Symmachus an ideal appointment in rhetoric to Milan, to resist the strong Catholic influence there.

1. Suggested in Brown, *Augustine*, 69. Cf. generally 70–72.

The atmosphere in this northern Italian city of Milan was once again a marked change. The cooler, often gray climate must have struck the African, never before north of the Tiber. Likewise, the bustle of the court: Barbarian troops from across the Alps kept guard. Most of all, Ambrose, bishop of the Christian city, and its former governor (oddly, cousin to the pagan Symmachus), ruled his churches and indeed the community with strength, learning, and finesse.

> That man of God received me like a father. . . . I began to love him, not at first as a teacher of truth (I completely despaired of your church, Lord!) but simply as a man who was kind to me. (V, 13, 23)

The meeting was a gracious formality for Ambrose, though not insincere. The government's new professor of rhetoric was someone to be concerned about.

> I gave [Ambrose] rapt attention when he was speaking among the people, not for the reasons I should; rather I was sensing out his style and whether it matched his reputation. I was intent, hanging on his words. As for *what* he said, I was indifferent and aloof, but I was delighted with the harmony of his speech. . . . This empty concern, for *how* he was saying what he said, was all I had left—because of my despair of finding any way toward you [Lord] open to a human being.
>
> Admittedly, his topics, which I disdained, reached my soul along with the words, which I loved. . . . And while my heart stood wide open to catch his eloquence, into me came also—gradually—the truth.
>
> For the first time, what he said began to seem defensible: the Catholic faith! I had thought nothing could be said for it, against the Manichaeans' attacks; now I saw that affirming it was no shame, especially when this or that passage of the ancient Scriptures was solved by allegorical mystery. . . . When Ambrose interpreted passages spiritually, I precisely could not believe my own despair. . . . Consider the passage on the human being created by you *in your image* [Genesis 1:26–27]. Your spiritual sons and daughters . . . never understood that passage to mean—never believed and thought— that you [O God] were cast in the form of a human body! What a spiritual substance in fact *is* I had no idea, uncertain or mysterious.

> But I rejoiced. I blushed, remembering all those years I had ranted, not against the Catholic faith, but against their supposed fantasies of materialistic thinking. (italics added) (V, 13, 23–14, 24; VI, 3, 4)

His early discovery of Cicero was repeated long after, in his discovery of Ambrose. He attended church to listen to Ambrose's oratorical style, but began to heed the substance, as he had previously with Cicero. Here was eloquence *with* substance, no mere partisan instrument. In addition, Ambrose described an approach to language that permitted glimpses of ideal truth through ordinary words, namely, allegory. Allegory, distinguished from myth and parable, presupposes a known order of abstract truth lying behind a literal account. The language of allegory is a code for abstract truths, as in the quotation above; "the image of God" (a physical symbol) stands for the human capacity to think intelligently, like God. Once again, Cicero's ideal object of language, called wisdom, came through Ambrose, along with instruction on how that language works.

So Ambrose's voice recalled him to the search for truth, even in a Catholic Christian setting. For the young rhetorician had thought Catholics conceived of God as a large, physical man. Only so could humanity be "in his image." What must the Catholic instruction in Thagaste have been like? not to say in Augustine's own household? How could he have had such a crude picture of the Christian faith? Although Augustine was thirty years of age, the reader cannot overlook how elementary for him were certain issues of religious belief.

Into these untouched fields of his mind Ambrose came, drawing together many different strands at once. Here was a masculine authority, not hard as brass, but kind. Here was a father, but of his mother's religion ("he received me like a father"); one not raucous, but reasonable; not superstitious, but thoughtful. Ambrose was an intellectual, who led the popular faith. He was a gentle priest, yet tough. He was a master of rhetoric, who dedicated language to the telling of truth. He was a Catholic Christian, who made sense.

Augustine's venture into the uncertainty of freedom and discovery had borne fruit. Much of that fruitfulness gathered around Ambrose. This teacher-bishop combatted paganism and Manichaean gnosis not only with a specific Christian belief, and not just with a universal, rational philosophy, but with both. His link between those two, as noted above, was the allegorical reading of Scripture. The disclosure of historical tradition as an allegorical language of universal truth elevated the Catholic God stunningly. As religious authority and proponent of dogma, Ambrose was in no way a thin-minded literalist, but brought reasoning power to scriptural interpretation. He proposed allegiance to God with freedom and sophistication of soul. Not only so, he modeled this posture like a father.

Skepticism

Still Augustine was not fully persuaded of Christian truth, but more than ever caught between options.

> I was not won over to the Catholic way, just because learned guardians were able to defend it. . . . For neither could I condemn the Manichaean position I then held. The defenses were equal. So I saw the Catholic view not defeated, but neither was it conqueror. . . . If I could have thought through the notion of a spiritual substance, all that mythic [Manichaean] machinery would have collapsed at once and been thrown out of my soul. I could not. (V, 14, 24–25)

The notion of a spiritual substance (rather than seeing God as bodily stuff) was a missing key, mentally and spiritually.

He found himself in the position of the so-called Academics or Skeptics, a late school in the tradition of Plato's Academy. "Their counsel was uncertainty on every question. They declared the human being could not surely grasp any point of truth" (V, 10, 19). All positions fail; therefore hold to none: "Fluctuating on all positions, I determined to give up my commitment to the Manichaeans. For in a time of such uncertainty, I saw no way to keep faith with that sect" (V, 14, 25).

The Manichaean hold was broken; yet curiously, the discovery of Catholic reasonableness only heightened his isolation: "The defenses were equal." Each view could claim enough to stalemate the other. He became, then, one of the uncommitted, for whom no beliefs are adequate to define oneself. He knew the odd situation of being an acknowledged professional, an officer of the government, a citizen, an heir, a father, while inwardly, anything was possible. His soul lay in open-ended stasis. In a new and complex way, he found himself in the void between discourses, as when a boy.

He very logically sought further help from Ambrose. Yet intimate, personal communication was never possible between the two men. Augustine describes the bishop's unusual combination of accessibility and inaccessibility. No one was denied entry to his house; yet neither was anyone's entry ever announced. When not surrounded by his people in church, Ambrose would be found at home reading silently, imperturbably: "Would anyone dare intrude on someone so intent? We would sit in silence for a long while, and then leave" (VI, 3, 3). Reading silently, rather than aloud, was itself unusual in antiquity. Thus, guidance from Ambrose was all via public presentation. Otherwise, the bishop's mystery of authority sat quietly at the center, surrounded by an electric silence.

Augustine's difficulty focused on being unable to think except in physical, material terms. "When I wished to think of my God, I did not know what to think except a bodily mass." He could not conceive a spiritual substance that had no measurement of size. (See the passage at the head of this chapter.) The problem was not a cloistered, theoretical one but rather involved all his concrete relationships. How does one live and deal when reality is finally a boundless field of force? That contradicted his own most humane moments, but he could not think through it. His mind turned to minglings of Christ and Epicurus. Except for the possibility of life beyond death, the Epicurean calculus, the moderate pursuit of bodily pleasure, made sense to him. (Here again, he struggled with the language of God and the language of everyday striving so discordant in his childhood.) Suppose both Christ and Epicurus were right:

> If we were immortal *and* lived forever by bodily pleasure, without any fear of losing it, why would we not be happy? What else could we ask for? I was ignorant that my very idea itself reached out towards great misery. I was like someone drowned and blind. I could not conceive that the light of honored virtue and beauty . . . was to be embraced *gratis*, freely, for its own sake. . . . And I could not be happy without friends, by my very meaning of happiness— regardless of how much bodily pleasure I had. And certainly I loved these friends *gratis*, freely! and I felt myself loved by them, freely, in return. Oh, look at my twisted approach! (VI, 16, 26)

The practice of living, if God were a sea of atomic impulses, hardly fit with his experience of friendship. He might indeed have seen friendship as a modest, enlightened protest against such an option. He lived therefore at the center of a cancellation of views, one by another. He could think only outwardly, physically, while his inmost self remained restive and detached.

I walked through darkness along a slippery place; I was looking for you outside of myself and did not find the God of my heart. I found myself in the depth of the sea, all my confidence gone. I despaired of finding the truth. (VI, 1, 1)

The Neoplatonist Books

"I walked through darkness . . ." Yet darkness heralds the truth when truth impinges by what it is not. (The Catholics have not shown . . . The Manichaeans have not shown . . . The natural philosophers have not shown . . .) Negatively, a number of viewpoints had been eliminated. Intellectual dissatisfaction implies the reality of truth, otherwise nothing would be lacking in one's present outlook. What is lacking? Why are present views a darkness? Restiveness says there must be something more. Thus the darkness of his motionless life was pregnant, if dangerous. Every statement, "This is not the case," was a step toward the truth not yet seen. So later Catholic theology incorporated the *via negativa*, the negative way toward truth, approaching step by step, laying aside, item by item, what truth is not. Help began when he knew something was wrong.

> You hounded me with inner torments to make me restive, until my inner eye saw you clear, . . . and from day to day you healed the sight of my dark disturbed mind with the stinging oils of wholesome sorrow. (VII, 8, 12)

He lived at the edge of discovery; yet he was blocked.

Then evidently by chance (or by providence) some member of the intellectual circle at Milan gave him some works of the Neoplatonists. The books were Latin translations of the Greek-speaking philosopher, Plotinus, or his follower, Porphyry, or both. Augustine was astonished with what he read. He wrote to a friend only a few months after the discovery:

> Now I have finally come safe into this harbor [of philosophy, the love of wisdom]. And I believe I have found here the pointers to the North Star. For I have often noticed in the sermons of our priest [Ambrose] . . . that when he reflects upon God, he thinks in no way at all of something bodily. Also the human soul is nothing

bodily, for the soul, among all things, is nearest to God. . . . For after only a very little reading in the Platonist books, I compared them (as far as I could) with the authority of those who gave [us] the divine [Scriptures]; and this set me ablaze, so that I wanted to tear loose all my anchors [and fly toward a life committed to wisdom]. (*The Happy Life* I, 4)

For certain rich, full books . . . incredible, yes, incredible! . . . aroused in me—even for me—such an unbelievable fire of excitement. . . . Then what good to me were honors? Or popular ceremonies? Or wanting [to be famous], that empty fame? What soft lures or tough ties to this mortal life [mattered anymore]? (*Against the Skeptics* II, 2, 5)

What did he read there that stirred him so? The above passages offer certain clues. For one thing he associates the books with Ambrose's idea that God is "in no way . . . something bodily." The Neoplatonist books told him how that could be so. It is not fully certain just what sections of those books he read.[2] He did find in them metaphors or paradigms for thinking of God in a new way:

A circle related in its path to a center . . . owes its scope to that center; it has something of the nature of that center. . . . [Just so,] let us consider how it is possible for an identity [like a center] to extend over a universe, [even though we refuse] to distribute that . . . center. That is, we are not to parcel it out among different multiple things. On the contrary, we bring the different multiple things to the unity. . . . A hand may very well control an entire mass, a long plank . . .

There is, we may put it, something that is center.[3] (Plotinus's *Enneads* VI, 8, 18; 4, 7; IV, 3, 17)

When Augustine had thought of God as physical, he had directly thought of the deity as light or electricity. In a flash the Neoplatonists taught him

2. One proposed list of those sections is found in Eugene TeSelle, *Augustine the Theologian* (London: Burns and Oates, 1970), 44–45.
3. Translations from Plotinus follow primarily the translation by S. MacKenna and B. S. Page in *Plotinus: The Six Enneads* (Chicago: Encyclopedia Britannica, 1952), *Great Books of the Western World*, vol. 17.

to think of God *indirectly* by comparison or analogy: God is *like* the power of a principle in math or science. The center of a circle, in principle, always fully controls the curve of the circle. But the center doesn't have to "go there" to the curve, to do its work. Its presence fully governs the curve, while the center itself rests quietly, vanishingly, in its place. God is *like* that.

Augustine reminds us of the child asking the question, "How can God be everywhere, all at the same time?" The answer of the Neoplatonists was not a direct explanation, but a "like" answer: God is like a principle, which is not divisible, but still operates fully everywhere. God is like the principle of gravity fully present and operable everywhere in the universe, without being divided up, without having to "go there." God is like the principle $1+1=2$, which is in two stones or two trees, yet transcends them. Pulverize the stones and burn the trees; $1+1=2$ remains untouched. So God, as principle, is in all things but not attached to those things.

Also, the notion of God as like a principle brought with it another astonishing reorientation. A principle is not physical, but mental. The principle of gravity is a theory whose validity is verified throughout the physical universe, but which is itself mental, an idea. If God is like a principle, then God is best approached not outwardly, among things, but inwardly, by searching out one's own mind.

> Whoever has the strength, . . . arise and withdraw into oneself, forgoing all that is known by the eyes. . . . Withdraw into yourself and look. . . . Seeking [God], seek nothing of [God] outside; within is to be sought what follows upon [that One]; [Godself] do not attempt. . . . [God] is within, at the innermost depth. (*Enneads* I, 6, 8–9; VI, 8, 18)

Consequently, "I entered in and I saw with the eye of my soul . . . above my mind, unchanging light" (VII, 10, 16).

The light of reason, the light of understanding within, gives every person the power to judge. Philosophers disagree on the source of reason's light and on how it informs the mind. Augustine, having read the Neoplatonists, held that the stable, sure standards of judgment are at work from *within* the mind, sorting out the images that pour in through experience. Mathematics was for him a leading example. An architect may conceive three circles interlocking in a certain way on the front of a building. Nature has never provided that architect with just such a picture, not even indeed with one natural, perfect circle as an example. Yet the standards from within the architect's mind provide the perfection of the three circles before the building is even sketched on paper.

Most important, the Neoplatonist light of judgment became a principle that enabled Augustine to understand better Cicero's and Ambrose's hopes for a sound use of language. Contrary to his early experience of empty and separated languages, both Cicero and Ambrose had shown that words and their grammatical structure could state truths valid for any time, any place. Now the Neoplatonists gave him the concepts for better understanding their views. Language is a vast structure of signs that can be critically assessed and guided by an individual's inner standards of what is real and true. On the other hand, that structure of signs can turn against the mind's standards and produce self-serving falsehood. In that case, words become empty tools of aggression. But when guided by the strong inner motive toward accuracy, they become signs of an ordering principle through all things called Wisdom or (later for him, under biblical influence) Word. Language responding to a person's inner motive or truth-seeking becomes a language of praise toward God, the Word, the source of all wisdom.

The Neoplatonist books took Augustine a great step forward in his search for a universal language of praise. Through language, the interior standards applied for Augustine to the most difficult judgments of life, such as those of love, courage, and integrity in human beings. The judgments are more difficult because he knew that moral qualities are defined differently in different societies and cultures (III, 7–9). Still he held that even the different definitions are possible because of a common base of moral reflection in the mind: "I would more easily doubt that I live than doubt that there is truth!" (VII, 10, 16).

What he grasped in Neoplatonism was that principles, unlike corporeal bodies, and even our changeable minds, are stable and sure through all reality. His confidence in a rational world was not unlike Albert Einstein's comment: "That [God] plays dice . . . is something that I cannot believe for a single moment."[4] For Augustine saw the sturdy principles of truth, known from within, as the intellectual light of God in Godself. The beauty of a curve, or of three interlocking circles, grasped from within, is something of God's own radiance. The reliability of mathematics to unlock nature's secrets (as in the philosopher's predicting eclipses) hinted at God's everlastingness: "And you called out to me from far away, 'Yes, I am who I am'"

4. H. Dukas and B. Hoffmann, eds., *Albert Einstein, the Human Side* (Princeton: Princeton University Press, 1979), 68, 143.

(VII, 10, 16). The reliable intellectual light of truth within, assessing experience, Augustine called *illumination*, actively and continuously provided to the mind, and thereby to language, by the God of truth (e.g., *Soliloquies* I, viii, 15).

Darkness and Freedom; God and My Soul

Knowledge by illumination was clear to him, but not knowledge of God in Godself, the source of illumination. Interior standards of judgment were admittedly a kind of clue to God, the one, the center; but God in Godself remained invisible. God was too large, too comprehensive, too all-inclusive, too much beyond, to be seen.

. . . [Godself] do not attempt. (*Enneads* VI, 8, 18)

Within the bright discovery of the Neoplatonist books, much darkness continued. God was assuredly not nothing, but God *was* no-thing; that is, as the basis for all things, God was not any one of those things in particular. How do you conceive of God, the origin, the no-thing?

Also, on the personal side, how do you know what steps to take in life? As long as he had thought of God as a light, material stuff, he had thought of many personal affairs as material and mechanical. The idea of God as physical had fit in with his day-to-day decisions of survival, a desperate utility. Vocation, income, social and professional status, concubinage, marriage: All were matters to be considered, adjusted to, and used as best one could. God also had been outward and bodily, something to be considered, adjusted to, and used as best one could. Only friendship had seemed to him mutual and joyous because freely exchanged. Now the inert heaviness of God and all things had yielded to greater openness.

Then how shall one proceed? What steps shall be taken? In the darkness of God's coming, the Neoplatonist books told him to look within himself for the standards of judgment and decision about truth, about life. The inner standards were not print-outs of what to do; they were guides for free decision. For the first time in his life, Augustine was told to be free, to take free responsibility for who he was.

Every grasp of freedom involves darkness around God, soul, and world. Some things are clear; much is not clear. What is clear is that the person has taken hold of things with a sense of joy and liberation, looking to oneself, before God, for authoritative choices. God is much bigger and more mysterious than had been supposed. Much remains to be discovered, mistakes will occur, but there is confidence that the power for good judgment lies within: "incredible, yes, incredible! . . . such an unbelievable fire of excitement" (*Against the Skeptics* [quoted above]). The darkness of freedom was his own and God's. In human existence much has to be decided that cannot be known for sure. Yet for the first time he began to look to himself, and to God's faithfulness, and to feel like a free, responsible soul, not like a divided, Manichaean object. He was no longer a helpless spectator at his own defeat. He no longer watched an evil substance in himself perform acts that he did not wish or will. ("I rested from myself a little, and my madness was eased into sleep" [VII, 14, 20].) Good and evil lay in his own decision. The God who was like a principle, omnipresent yet undivided, engaged yet free, signaled that Augustine's soul was, somehow like God, a center of engagement, accountability, and free choice.

Conclusion

Augustine's breakthrough in the struggle with evil came with a breakthrough concerning God and the soul. That discovery was, in effect, a discovery that truth *is*. For him to say that "truth is" by no means meant that Augustine claimed to know the whole truth. Rather, he saw that truth is and is knowable, and a long journey leads actually to knowing it. He found himself at last at the gateway of the right journey. His conviction rested upon the discovery of standards or criteria for real knowing present *in* the mind, even before experience. Thus a laboratory technician producing a metal cube follows a sense of perfection more rigorous than measuring devices, indeed, the basis of the measuring devices themselves. Assessing a tree for lumber or giving a blue ribbon to a prize dog is guided by a notion of the ideal tree or dog, even though nature has never quite produced one. Admittedly, the know-how of experience counts heavily in picking a winner; but that know-how could never have accumulated apart from the mind's own driving sense of perfection.

That interior light, or sense of the ideal, tells the difference between things that hold together and those that fall apart. An injured tree or dog cannot measure up to the ideal, is less "real" (i.e., as a fully functioning specimen). Therefore Augustine saw his interior standard as a measure of reality, power, and endurance. The true thing is the real thing. Something that truly measures up to the ideal—a fine coat, a piece of music, an excellent social occasion—is more real and has more force than the mediocre. Ilumination, the test of perfection from within, tells us what is the most nearly real, what can be counted upon. Thus the standards of truth, immaterial and ideal, in themselves, test and evaluate all material nature.

For Augustine, these necessary and enduring standards were the substance of God's own mind, made accessible to our minds interiorly in a continuing act of illumination. The mind of God orders the world universally, like a vast principle of organization, without being "parceled out." By tracing inwardly one's own sense of the ideal, of beauty and perfection, one can approach the very divine mind itself. Such is the free, intellectual grounding of a person in God, over against God the physical field of electricity Augustine had held to before.

In this entire discovery the reader will certainly recognize the long Platonic tradition of thinking, not surprisingly, since the Neoplatonist books gave the insight. Considering the ideal to be the real is a highly familiar option in Western Christianity; yet Ambrose and Augustine were proposing for their situation a revolutionary view. The West often thought in material terms. For substance to be primarily mental or intellectual was a radical notion, conceivably hostile to Christian tradition with its resurrection of the fleshly body.

At the same time, Augustine hardly adopted a thorough and refined Neoplatonist view. Rather, certain linchpin assumptions from Neoplatonism grasped him. One, of course, was interior illumination from God as spiritual substance. Another was this: that statements about the worldin-general are meaningful. (Some present-day philosophies, e.g., logical positivism, hold that general statements about the world—for example, "truth is"—are not meaningful. Only limited statements that can be empirically verified have meaning: "John just entered the house.") If general statements about the world are nevertheless possible, then Augustine's inward drive for the ideal is a telling piece of evidence about that world. That is, if yearning for the ideal versus the transient is not just in my own head, if it links over to sound generalizations about the world and its values, then that yearning makes a valid statement about reality: All things, passing and imperfect, signal and presuppose the ideal beauty of God, for which they yearn.

"If yearning for the ideal as distinct from the transient, is not just in my own head . . .": a large assumption, yet a very clear one for him. When he knew his own mind illumined and guided toward the ideal, and could probe and test the real world by that ideal, it never occurred to him that he might be indulging in fancifulness. All visible things truly implied an intellectual origin *and* goal greater than themselves, seen from the true, ideal light of inward reason. To inquire after the truth about these things therefore presupposed God, the source of this standard of truth. God, the highest good *(summum bonum)*, was not to be proven as the end or result of a long rational inquiry; God was the *presupposition of all* rational inquiry. God was the keeper of the standards of truth about the world. Therefore, in the *Confessions* Augustine cries out that his search for God surely presupposes God already (I, 1, 1).

Also, Augustine considered he was dealing with the real world because he refused to separate theory and practice. The world that he tested by his newfound ideal standards was the world where he had to live, and struggle, and decide. Untrue though that world might be in theory, such speculation was only outrageous fiddling in the situation he had to deal with every day. His metaphysical thought was situated thinking; that is, it arose in the situation of language, behavior, and decision that was given him. (Modern logic purports to have an objective validity within its own coherence. True to his patristic period, Augustine saw logic as part of the character, purpose, and commitment of the logically thinking person.) His revolutionary discovery of ideal substance meant nothing apart from his personal posture within that discovery. His soul was not a divided object (Manichaean), but a free, intellectual entity grappling with the world. To discover spiritual substance was to commit himself to it, in a flash, throughout the depths of who he was. What he discovered, then, was not a theory, but an intellectual person's worship. That is, the truth of reality included a certain honor toward that reality, a worshipful thinking. Not whether he was theoretically mistaken, but how to test his new life, became his question.

The reality of God and reality of soul were ineluctably joined. Recovering his now almost faded wisdom of Cicero, he found a truth that he could love and seek in the practice of life. His intellectual penetration brought with it the perils and chills of the soul's free decisions. He had to walk boldly a shadowy track and risk more pain.

6

Creator, Creation, Evil

(*Confessions* VII, 11–20)

Then with those books of the Platonists in my mind, which called on me to seek out incorporeal truth, I came to behold your "invisible realities, known intellectually through those things which are made" [Romans 1:20] . . . and I perceived [the one] certain [thing] of all to be you! and [I saw you] to be infinite, nevertheless not diffused through finite or infinite spaces; and [I saw] you always to be truly you yourself, the same, never other or otherwise in any part or any motion; and [I saw], truly, all other things *from* you, by this one, single, most definite proof: that they *are*. . . .

And I scrutinized [these] other things lower than you, and I saw them as neither wholly being nor wholly not being; being, indeed, because they are from you; yet not being because they are not WHAT IS. For that truly *is*, which remains [forever] immutable.

And I looked again at [those] other things, and I saw them owing you their being; [indeed, I saw] the whole of all finite things *in* you— not as if in a place—but rather you are holding all things in your hand, your truth! And all things are true to the extent that they *are*, nor is there any falsity whatsoever except when something is thought to be, which is not. (italics added) (VII, 20, 26; 11, 17; 15, 21)

To glimpse God and the soul as he had done was almost immediately to see the wide world, and the order of the world, as good. As Manichaeanism fell away, this new, good world emerged. That is, the world was no longer dualistically divided between good and evil material things, but moved according to one single all-encompassing principle of order. "You are holding all things in your hand, your truth!" To see the world as good meant, in part, then, to see it shaped by a single harmonious ordering; ordering and unifying were the direction of its goodness. A consistency of direction caught up all the world's tumbling and striving. Augustine did see the ordering of the created world as finally unfathomable, known by us only in part. Yet he had total confidence in its goodness.

First, he was reacting to his nine-year Manichaean burden of dealing with the world as evil and contradictory. Still, that is hardly reason enough to believe the world's goodness. Second, he saw the ideal, Neoplatonic standards of truth as beautiful; therefore the world that responds to those standards reflects that beauty. Furthermore, humanity shares intellectually in those same standards. For the mind to pursue mathematics, music and virtue, in its test for the real, was to pursue the beautiful. The world, including the human world, responds to beauty, which is the test of the world's real excellence. To know in life's seeking and striving that the ideal is the real is to seek beauty and thereby disclose the goodness of the world.

As a youngster growing up in his North African home, Augustine had evidently been most sensitive to beauty. He later refers to mountain scenery, to sky and cloud, to the wonder of light or of a human face.[1] Yet the extent to which this enjoyment of beauty tied into his childhood religious experience is doubtful. Surely there was warmth in Monica's descriptions of the Father and of Christ; he later claims a wondrous spiritual beauty in her character. Yet the elements of personal religious faith he chooses to recall for the Confessions have more to do with belief, rite, and frustrated early prayer than with beauty. As a child, did his aesthetic sense of enjoyment respond to nature and not to his religious belief? He loved the name of Christ as Savior, but that stood alien from his early capacity to enjoy the world, in play, in outdoor adventure and exploration, in winning and achievement.

What has been called here his quest to recover his childhood faith at a new level of integrity found partial fulfillment in the Neoplatonist religious vision of the world as beautiful. Here was a faith that found the flashes of beauty in the world, in nature or in friendship, as reflections of an eternal beauty and goodness. The belief *and* enjoyment he knew separately as a boy could unite in his wonder at God's creation.

1. Brown, *Augustine*, 35, gives sample references: e.g., *Confessions* VII, 21, 27; X, 34, 51.

Most scholars agree that in reading the Neoplatonist books he probably encountered very early this passage from Plotinus:

> . . . it would not be sound to condemn this cosmos as less than beautiful, as less than the noblest possible in the corporeal; . . . for it stands a stately whole, complete within itself, . . . the minutest of things tributary to the vast total, the marvellous art shown not merely in the mightiest works . . . , but even amid such littleness as one would think Providence would disdain. . . .
>
> [Even were it less beautiful in detail] it would be absurd to con-demn the whole on the merits of the parts which must be judged only as they enter harmoniously or not into the whole . . . do but survey the cosmos complete and this surely is the pleading you will hear:
>
> "I am made by a God: from that God I came perfect, . . . lacking nothing; for I am the container of all that is, of every plant and animal, of all the kinds of created things, and nations of spirit-beings and lofty souls and humankind happy in their goodness." (Enneads III, 2, 3 and 13)

The relief to him from Manichaean mythology and astrology must have been great. Yet for a twentieth-century turn of mind, the discovery of ideal forms as real, and the goodness of the cosmos as its beauty, seems romantic. Could these notions communicate to him what today's experience calls "real"? Was he a superficial visionary? His experience, during his forty-four-year lifetime after he read Plotinus, included some of the harshest demands and most recalcitrant ugliness laid upon any historical figure. He met all of this, dealt with the difficulties, and yet never wavered in his view of the goodness and beauty of the created order. Indeed, the ideal beauty reflected in the world was for him the tough, white canvas on which he attempted to manage and shape the turbulence that befell him. Such formalism was not an escape, but a governor of turmoil.

Creator, Creation, a Wholeness of Knowledge

Once he had seen the goodness of the world under a single governing order, in which his own mind could participate, it remained to ask more closely how God and this world were related. Clearly, for him, they related as Creator to creation. Evidently he understood this as soon as he read from the Neoplatonists, but with the writing of the *Confessions* some twelve years later (397–399), and in the years that followed, he unified and enlarged his understanding of creation. His pleasure and preoccupation with the wide created order, and the scriptural account of it in Genesis, extended through his career, peaking productively during the years 399 and after.

While Creator-creation are terms that come thoughtlessly to our lips today, they held a careful and particular significance for him. For example, the term "creation" contrasts with "emanation," a flowing out of God's own being by levels, formulating divine mind, divine soul, and finally the material world. In emanation the overflowing appears impersonal with God, while objects emerging far out in the flow have no direct access to God, but only to the level immediately above them. Creation, on the other hand, implies that God directly and deliberately thinks things into being and remains present to them, though not attached to them—a more anthropomorphic and storylike view. Things are then more distinguishable in their own right (not as in an attenuated overflow), even though dependent on God for continuance. Furthermore, they can share in God by their place in God's governance ("in your hand, your truth!").

Plotinus declared for emanation; how then did Augustine arrive at his creation view? Actually, Plotinus blends emanation with creation in the *Enneads*. He cites the flowing out of God, like a radiance; yet God, the One, shows something like free will and personality as well.[2] Things are distantly derived from God; yet God is also omnipresent with them. Probably Augustine read this blend with a Christian predisposition loyal to the creation account in Genesis. One statement of his discovery of the Neoplatonist books, written only a few months afterward, tells that when he read the material, "I beheld there, I declare it, as if returning from a long journey, the religion of my boyhood" (*Against the Skeptics* II, 2, 5).

This statement is probably best interpreted, not that he saw Christianity translated into Neoplatonism, but that he read Plotinus with a favored Christian leaning.

What is there to say, then, about his doctrine of creation? First, creation in popular usage today has given way to an interest in how and when the universe assumed something like its present shape. In other words, what

---

2. *Enneads* VI, 8, esp. 16. Cf. A. H. Armstrong, *St. Augustine and Christian Platonism* (Villanova: Villanova University Press, 1967), 40.

was the sequence of events that produced it all? To the contrary, Augustine had little interest in chronology, a physical sequence in time. Rather, he declares that God created by his Word, by thinking or calling things into being, out of nothing (XI, 5–7). Furthermore, he was not interested in this act as only the first of a long series of happenings, an event now left far behind. His concern, clearly, has no parallel to a "big-bang" scientific theory of the beginnings of the universe, a physical how-and-when occasion. Such an approach cannot, in any case, reach back to an absolute beginning, before which there was actually nothing. Indeed, he had no interest in what went on *before* creation appeared (XI, 10–13). For him, time itself was created along with everything else; therefore, what went on "before" creation is a meaningless question.

Augustine's creational view was therefore not chronological, but onto-logical. That is, he dealt less with a sequence of events and more with the quality and character of how things *are* as creatures, relative to God. The doctrine of creation therefore deals with what it means to be a creature in relation to the Creator at any time, past, present, or future. The beginning means not so much what actually happened first as what stands first in excellence, in the order of all things. What stands first for Augustine is the Creator God, God's Word, and God's Spirit. What derives from God in beauty and goodness, limited but real, are creatures—from the most enlight-ened angelic spirits to formless matter, which almost does not exist at all.

Augustine's clue to seeing creatures as creatures was their fleeting, changing, derivative nature.

> Look! heaven and earth *are;* they cry out that they were made, for they are continually being changed and varied. . . . [For something to manifest in itself] what at one time was not means for that thing to be changed and varied. (italics added) (XI, 4, 6)

For something to change meant clearly to Augustine that it was not eternal. One could conceive, of course, that the very cycling change of nature, the coming and going of all things, the endless round of seasons, is itself eternal, going on forever. This was not Augustine's thought. "Eter-nal" in his thinking inevitably attached to his view of illumination. The ideal standards present to the mind, by which the mind judges things (for example, the standards of mathematics) are eternal, a sharing of the order of God's mind. The intellectual light of those ideal standards never wavers. Only that intellectual light is eternal. Therefore, any natural thing that falls short of those standards at any time (and all do) or changes in any way (and all do) is less than eternal and must at some point not have been.

> Therefore they cry out that they did not make themselves: "We are, because of this: that we were made. Therefore, we were not, before we were, in any way as to be able to be made by ourselves." And the voice of those things speaking is self-evidence! You therefore, Lord, you made these things, you who are beautiful, for they are beautiful, you who are good, for they are good; you who are, for they are. Yet they are not as beautiful, they are not as good, indeed they are not, in the same way as you, their creator, are. Compared to you they are neither beautiful, nor good, nor are! We know these things, thanks be to you—and our knowing is ignorance compared to your knowing. (XI, 4, 6)

Note here that Augustine is not concluding *from* creatures *to* God, nor is he in any simplistic manner concluding from God to creatures. Consider the first of these comments. Popular notions today hold that creation is a means to prove a divine creator. An orderly world must have an intelligent cause; hence, God. This was not Augustine's approach. He by no means thought that the processes of nature demonstrate to a detached mind a rational, beneficent deity. He denied it in the case of the natural philosophers (scientists) and their eclipses, already noted. He declared they could not conclude to God because they lacked "lowliness of heart." That is, to see creatures in relation to their Creator required a moment of humility and honor toward God.

For Augustine to hear creatures cry out that their Creator made them was not a detached, logical inference, but a breathless moment of envisioning God and creatures, together, all at once, in a kind of whole. He calls the testimony by creatures to Creator, "self-evidence." The entire set of relationships is self-evidently real in a single viewing. In other words, God, illumination, and the ideal are *presupposed* in the moment of perceiving creatures as creatures—good, beautiful, and limited, and therefore pointing beyond themselves to a Creator. This whole vision includes an element of honoring God, in relation to whom creatures can be seen, and in relation to whom Augustine was himself a creature, whose "knowing is ignorance compared to your knowing." The cause-effect relation between Creator and creation is seen integrally and intuitively, a fitness of understanding and experience in one enlightened, passionate moment. Apart from this wholeness, Augustine could not grasp *himself* as a creature, keeping a moment of worshipful honor toward the infinite Creator and the Creator's economy.

On the other hand, the Creator does not so dominate that creatures become nothing. Augustine does not by God's inward illumination mentally project creatures outward upon a world-emptiness. Knowledge is not the projection of a mind upon a blank screen. Creatures are real and knowledge of them is real knowledge. Indeed, for Augustine, disciplined knowledge of them is essential within ultimate knowledge of God (a move that distinguishes him from Plotinus, for whom knowledge of God is more nearly direct, not proceeding through disciplined knowledge of the world).[3] Of course, real knowledge is formed by illumination within the mind; but outward objects play their part, received by us through the senses as what Augustine calls *phantasiae*, which yield real knowledge under illumination's scrutiny (*Music* VI, 11, 32).[4] Such knowledge of creatures lies within an illuminated whole, yet sees them individually as they really are. This knowledge also sees the signals of their incompleteness in light of their ideal source, to which they therefore point. True objectivity about creatures is thus encompassed within a single, complete vision of God and world, and of one's own creatureliness before God.

To move into a sphere of knowledge that does not initially include the Creator is never to arrive at that Creator. To see all things in the light of God is to see them as they really are and to include the reality of God from the outset.

Being; the Scale of Being

To see Creator and creatures together in a single viewing meant to see them, despite the gulf of difference between them, as sharing one major commonality, namely, being. That is, knowing how creatures "be" immediately necessitates and presupposes the infinite being of God, "[I saw], truly,

---

3. Cf. *Enneads* I, 6, 9, the withdrawal of the mind into solitude to know God, whereas TeSelle holds that Augustine's approach to God through steps of disciplined knowledge has a root in the approach of the Roman philosopher Varro (*Theologian*, 81).

4. Cf. R. H. Nash, *The Light of the Mind: St. Augustine's Theory of Knowledge* (Lexington: University Press of Kentucky, 1969), 55.

all other things *from* you, by this one, single most definite proof: that they *are.*" The mere being of creatures, changing and transitory as it is, self-evidently relates to the necessary being of God. Yet although both God and creatures "be," and imply the being of one another, an immense difference lies between them. Clearly Augustine's notion of being was not flat and uniform, but rich and varied, requiring different grades of being. All things "be," even God; but some things "be" more than others. Being varies according to richness, fullness, and power. To enter Augustine's field of thought requires entering imaginatively this scale of being.

Augustine expressed the scale by saying of creatures that, in a sense, they both "be" and "not be."

> . . . [these] other things lower than you. . . . I saw them as neither wholly being nor wholly not being; being, indeed, because they are from you; yet not being because they are not WHAT IS.

Any creature is, because it derives from God, who is; but that same creature is not (that is, is not of the fullest, richest possible being) because it was created *ex nihilo*, out of nothing. It has something of the marks of its two parents, God and nothingness, since to be at all is to reflect the great being of God, its source; but to be transitory is to reflect the nothingness from which it came and back to which it returns. All creatures reveal this combination and stand below God on the scale.

Significantly, human language, of such importance to Augustine and his story, is one of these creatures, a special one through whom the ordering of all the others seeks articulation. The life of the human creature, who speaks and writes, expresses even its own positioning and orientation through this one creature, language. Yet language cannot but participate in both the integrity and frailty of the general created order. Language, as a structure of signs, keeps its integrity by responding to the Creator, pursuing and expressing the true ordering of a good world. That expression can invoke general praise and wonder toward the Creator. At the same time, as a creation out of nothing, language is frail. As an instrument of human perversity, it is subject to abuse and may fail to pursue the ideal ordering of the creation. It may become a creature that presents only a broken and distorted view of all creatures, as Augustine knew in childhood. As with the human being itself, language as creature held a peculiar place in the cosmos, its use or abuse wielding great impact on all else.

For among all creatures (and therefore below God) are different levels in the scale of being, measured by the richness of being belonging to any given level. Plants are higher on the scale than stones because they have life, animals higher than plants because they both live and perceive. Humankind and angels are nearest the divine because they have intellects and languages that can share in the eternal character of truth. Every creature is good, and to the extent that it truly is (shows richer being higher on the scale), is increasingly good (IX, 10, 24; cf. City of God XI, 16; XII, 1). Lower on the scale does not mean, however, that a creature shares increasingly in evil—a crucial point that Augustine takes up further on.

Despite the concern for scaling, one powerful distinction among beings overrides all others in Augustine's thought. That is the distinction between God and all other beings, or creatures. All creatures are mutable; God alone is immutable. "For that truly is, which remains [forever] immutable." God is constant in the midst of change. No formal characteristic touched the nature of divinity more closely, for Augustine, than this one. The deity is unquestionably immutable. Truth measures by standards that endure. God is the keeper of truth. Therefore God cannot waver, but must remain consistent, true to God's standards and purposes always. Otherwise, the world has no order or measure, no true or false, no better or worse. Even physical things show the regulation of the Creator, as Augustine repeatedly said, "by measure and number and weight" (Wisdom 11:20), a triad of causal standards kept within the life of the divine Trinity.[5]

Yet is not an immutable, unchanging, unmoving deity impossible to reconcile with the God of grace, covenant, and sacrifice, of the Bible? This question can hardly be treated apart from considering Augustine's view of the living Christ Jesus, the World made flesh, a matter dealt with some steps further on in the story. For the moment, immutability can be thought of as consistency, reliability, faithfulness, raised to the power of universal truth. Nevertheless, he himself struggled with the dilemma of immutability's being accessible in concrete biblical events, as will later appear.

One thing is sure: The stability of eternal, truthful standards in no way, for him, reduced the creation to static quiescence or rigidity. Any belief that incorporates Platonic features suggests to many contemporary readers a visionary view of the world, the dream of an ideal natural or human order. Augustine's was a dynamic, striving world in process, constantly in pursuit of ideal form. The sharp distinction, immutable / mutable, may have indeed posed a problem about God's mobile activity, but on the other hand, it

5. Cf. his Literal Commentary on Genesis IV, 3, 7, and TeSelle, Theologian, 118–19.

opened up the creation to variety, change, turbulence, as much as human sensibility could manage. Mutability means change, change involves time, and Augustine's world of events, natural and human, moved dynamically through time. The massive array of creatures strives in process to fulfill the ideal forms, of which they are expressions, even as they fade and pass from view. That creatures are, but also are specifically this or that, sets the stage for their activity or movement, their actual becoming. The full picture— that they are, that they *are this*, and how they are *becoming* this—is governed by the Three-in-One, Father, Son, and Holy Spirit, from whom, through whom, and in whom they live and move.

All these processes, held together by "your hand, your truth!" showed, for Augustine, a certain independence of operation, not always subject to the direct movement or intervention of God. That is, secondary causes held a place in the Augustinian cosmos. Best known in this matter are his famous "seminal reasons" (*rationes seminales*). Augustine held that when everything was created (the Genesis 2 version) living things were not created straightaway, but rather God created seeds made of water, which in turn developed into specific plants and animals. Such seeds continued to be present in all living reproduction and in what Augustine's ancient world thought must be spontaneous generation (the appearance of maggots in decaying organic matter, for example). What determines whether a watery seed brought forth a rose or a lamb was a rational code implanted by God in the seed, the "seminal reasons," as he called them. His theory was not one of evolution, since each code fixed upon a particular species and did not permit development into something else. At the same time, his seminal reasons did anticipate the present theory of a genetic code carried in the DNA of every living cell.[6] God, for him, is omnipresent to all things; but God does not directly instigate all things. God's Word and Spirit can set up codes by which the divine rational intent can unfold in the processes of nature.

Augustine also held that God's administration of the world used for many given purposes the work of angels, as his lieutenants (*City of God* X, 15). The notion now seems quaint, but Augustine's cosmos was rich and populous with both angels and demons (fallen angels) (*Confessions* X, 42, 67). The present-day reader will do him the greatest justice to think of these as

6. Cf. *Literal . . . Genesis* X, 20, 35ff., and TeSelle, *Theologian*, 217.

powers, like love or beauty, or as principles, like gravity or inertia, reflective of God's mind but not divine in themselves.

Implications, Evaluations

What value does his view of creation hold for people today, granted that so much of its specific furniture has been superseded by scientific disclosure? The importance lies, surely, in the status or level of value he accorded to created things, a well-turned judgment that remains an option today. In brief, he saw creatures as limited, but their identity as good; he saw creatures as secular, but of sacred significance. These combinations continue to be of great worth both to truth and to life. For example, on the limited and secular side, he pulled creatures back from an all-consuming sacredness and superstition. Moonlight is not a gathering of holy particles, identical to feelings of nostalgia within myself (Manichaeanism). Such mythological gnosis is a block, not only to human personal satisfaction, but to rationality. Augustine became part of the wide Western movement originating in the sixth century B.C.E. called the "crisis of myth," the substituting, in place of fanciful, storied explanations, of reasoned investigation. He made the move from astrology to the rudiments of astronomy and became a pillar in the foundations of modern science.

Neoplatonism had freed him from any lingering possibilities of Manichaean gnosis; yet in Neoplatonism itself lay more subtle difficulties concerning the sacred or secular nature of the world. In the complex outlook of Plotinus, God, the One, remained darkly transcendent beyond all. The logic of such a position suggested the One as alone divine, leaving the world as rationally secular and everyday; but it was not so in Plotinus. He saw the world as holy in a secondary way, filled with "created divinities," of which the human soul was one—created eternally.[7] Also, the light of heavenly bodies he saw not as bodily at all, but an incorporeal activity produced by cosmic divinities.[8] The wonder of a semidivine cosmos impressed Augustine, and traces of it remain in his mature position (for example, the

7. *Enneads* VI, 4, 14; cf. V, 1, 2. Cf. Armstrong, *Christian Platonism*, 4–9.
8. *Enneads* II, 1, 4–5, 7; 9, 8; IV, 5, 6–7. Cf. Armstrong, "Plotinus," in *The Cambridge History of Later Greek and Early Medieval Philosophy*, ed. A. H. Armstrong (London: Cambridge University Press, 1967), 257.

human being is destined, in God's kingdom, to become a created "god," not by nature, but by harmony of will with God's will [City of God XIV, 13]). Nevertheless, Augustine could not see creation in so divine a light as Plotinus. All creatures, including angels, humankind, and heavenly bodies, are mutable and temporal, not divine, no matter how profoundly illuminated by divine light. More than in Plotinus, Augustine pressed the line of distinction between the immutable God and the mutable creation.

At the same time, creatures were not so secularized and investigatable as to lose their role of testimony to the Creator. They were part of the single, illuminated view of reality that saw the immense dance of all things, fragile and shining, against the dark, full background of God, their necessary origin. They were simply themselves; yet simply by being, they were part of a chorus of testimony to the divine mind, already sensed within by the human intellect. Augustine did not, in other words, open a logical gap between the complex dynamism of creation and its patterning source in Father, Son, and Holy Spirit. They were held together in reality and intellect by the unifying bond of illumination.

That logical gap did open later in Western thought. Thomas Aquinas took a limited and secondary, but definite step in that direction in the thirteenth century. Thomas held to Augustine's doctrine of creation, including an element of worshipful assent to its vast outlook. Yet aside from that doctrine he proposed a different step regarding temporal things as related to God, a step accessible to autonomous, logical reasoning. Illumination changed, for him, into the work of the autonomous, active intellect of the human mind. That intellect, looking at causes and effects among all things, if faced with the question of God, could independently infer back to a First Cause, which God must be. Envisioning the whole structure of relationships at once became, in part for Thomas, a logical deduction back through things, considered independently.

This secondary move in Thomas became four hundred years later what he never intended: deism's view that the mechanical organization of the universe implied a Maker, whose presence and governance were no longer needed. Beyond deism lay the frequent twentieth-century view that the world is not only distant from its Maker, but by its very being is fallen: To exist is to be flawed. Existence is equivalent to shame or guilt.[9]

9. For a survey description of Aquinas in this regard, and of deism, compare, for example, F. C. Copleston, A History of Philosophy, rev. ed. (London: Barns, Oates and Washburne, 1951), vol. 2, chapters 32, 34; vol. 5, chapter 9. For existence per se as flawed, compare,

Against mythology, gnosis, and pantheism on the one side, and against Thomas's theology of nature, later deism, and existentialism on the other, Augustine's position affirms the divinely significant identity of mortal creatures. He proposed to see the sun and moon, not as gods, and not as hot and cold lifeless material, but as what they are: describable limited creatures that resonate beyond themselves. Relieved of Manichaeanism, Augustine perceptibly cried out, "How much better to love the sun itself, which is at least true to our eyes, than to love the glittering fantasies in those [Manichaean] vessels" (III, 6, 10). The sun and moon are really themselves, with a place in a setting more important than themselves.

The key to Augustine's view of Creator and creature was a liberating distance within a sustaining relationship. Creatures are contingent: They might be, or they might not be. Apart from something greater outside themselves, they would not have come to be. Apart from an underlying scheme that holds them together (for example, what is now called gravity, inertia, atomic structure), they would vanish. They depend on principles that preserve them, even without their knowledge. In the wonder of their form and structure, they hint at the marvel of what it is to *be* at the very fullest, that is, to be God. They can hint in this way because their originator and sustainer leaves self-reflecting traces (Augustine's "marks," *indicia*) in their nature (*The Trinity* XV, 2, 3). To be, in the richest sense, leaves its mark on being in the simplest sense.

At the same time, despite their clear link of being or "is-ness" with God, creatures nevertheless enjoy a liberating distance from the Creator. They boast their own identity and place, even if the price of that separation is transitoriness and mortality. Admittedly, they have identities because of shared being with God; but they have their *own* identities because of their removal from God's overwhelming reality. They boast an integrity that is their own, not simple, ideal unity perhaps, but a harmony of parts that commands respect. It is good to be a star, a worm, a symphony, an ocean, a child, a microbe, a blazing fire, a mountain. (With creatures of rational free will the distance and goodness are of course all the more enhanced.) The Creator steps back a pace, even in the midst of sustaining authority, and lets creatures stand forth, claiming their astonishing array.

These elements of excellence, identity, distance, and mortality combine remarkably in creatures. Distance allows the excellence to step forward in

for example, Erich Heller, *The Disinherited Mind* (Cambridge: Bowes and Bowes, 1952), chapter 7, "The World of Franz Kafka."

its own right, yet guarantees that the identity (in its differentness from God) includes mortality and transitoriness. In such creaturely identity, excellence and mortality seem to contradict, but actually enhance one another. The wonder of a creature actually increases with its vulnerability; the intimation of loss enhances excellence. Thus emerges one of the West's surest aesthetic instincts. To see beauty is important in itself; but to see beauty and know that it is only transient is more richly full of wonder. The superbly beautiful is only the more amazing in its fragility. Admittedly, Augustine affirmed eternity. Yet in his mortal creatures he bequeathed a sense of both goodness and waning temporal passage that showed love for the world, mourned its transitions, and honored God for enabling this special wonder (XIII, 35, 50).

Like tuning an instrument, Augustine assessed the Creator-creature relation with a fine sense for both secular limits and divine significance.

Evil

> Who made me? Is it not my God, who is not simply good, but indeed is Good Itself? How does it come about, then, that I will evil and do not will good? (VII, 3, 5)

What is evil? How did it come to be? The questions of the reality of God, the reality of soul, and the nature of the world had all interlocked with this puzzle of evil. Augustine's personal history had acutely raised the dilemma of evil. In his childhood and youth he had experienced evil as alienation or destruction under the guise of good. The pressure upon him had indeed led him into even a love for evil and thereby for his own self-destruction. The search for intellectual integrity and for redirecting his loves had formed initially (under the stimulus of Cicero) in the loving quest for truth; but this had led him only into Manichaeanism. The bold concern of the Manichaeans for evil had surely attracted him. Yet hearing them led him more deeply into a view of the quasi-materiality of all things, God, evil, and world. The question of evil became snarled in the notion of evil as a corporeal stuff (as the notion of God became similarly snarled). Evil as identifiable stuff meant the splitting of the world, even of the soul (as has been noted) with either passive or violent results. Also, Augustine was distraught later to think that the corporeality of both God and evil meant that the stuff of God suffered damage from the stuff of evil—a shrewd means of putting responsibility of evil on God's limitations rather than taking responsibility for it oneself (VII, 3, 4).

The first great step out of his bewilderment with evil came, as it did with questions of God, soul, and world, through reading the Neoplatonist books. There it appeared that God, like a universal principle, could in no way be pressed upon by some corporeality. Again, like a principle, God is present to all things without being compromised or attached to those things. God is a being, the one, single, infinite (unmeasureable) being, and gives rise to other beings like, but far less than, Godself. All things besides God find themselves on a scale of excellence, from the highest intellectual spirits to the simplest matter (see above).

In relation to the scale of being, the first possibility of accounting for evil arose. Perhaps evil meant less and less good along the scale. If it is better to be a human being than a tree, perhaps to that extent it is an evil thing to be a tree, while in relation to a tree it is even more evil to be a stone. Augustine would have none of this. It is a good thing, each in its own way, to be human, tree, or stone (VII, 12, 18; XIII, 28, 43). His move was an important one, to reject this obvious approach to evil, down the scale, and made matters more philosophically difficult for him, though more fruitful as well. That is, he had to admit that the scale of things declines in goodness, yet account for evil in some other way, indeed, a more perceptive way.

If God and the scale of God's creatures are good, then even the lowest element on the scale, unformed matter, is good. Augustine struggled with the concept of unformed matter, admitting that at first he tried to think of it in ugly, horrid shapes, then realized that these were after all, forms (XII, 6, 6; cf. XII, chapters 3–8 generally). Matter is that potentially something that is almost nothing, described in Scripture as "the earth . . . without form" (Genesis 1:2). Matter is the substratum of things that may, for example, have the form of bread, which when eaten gives way to the form of new flesh and blood in the eater—yet the substratum, the matter, still continues. Augustine derived prime matter from Aristotle, probably through Plotinus, yet finally with his own interpretation. Plotinus saw matter associated with form in things (though not constructively), saw it as a contradictory nothing opposite to the One, the Good, and finally saw it as the principle of evil.[10] Augustine's view of the beauty and goodness of the

10. *Enneads* I, 8, 5 and 9; II, 4, 4–6. Cf. Armstrong, *Cambridge History*, 256–57.

world, unlike Plotinus's, could not picture matter as evil. Matter was instead an essential composite in the scriptural God's good creating. Augustine thus came down clearly on the side of materiality in itself as good, a Christian-biblical note firmly distinct from the Manichaeans, toward whom Plotinus's position took more risk.

Evil, then, is not a decline in creation's scale, nor is it matter. What then is it? And how is it fully eliminated from the scale, which is decreasingly good in removal from God? Augustine begins to resolve both questions in a single passage. In his own Neoplatonic fashion (yet leaving Plotinus) he hits upon his famous response that evil is negative, indeed not anything at all. Only so is the sovereign goodness and unity of the creator unimpaired and the oppressive duality of Mani banished. He handles the declining goodness of creatures on the scale by his idea of plenitude: The whole of creation taken together, including the decline, is superior, overall, to the most excellent creatures, taken alone.

> To you [O God] evil absolutely is not! Not only to you, but also to your universal creation, it is not. For outside creation, nothing exists to break in and corrupt the order you have imposed upon it.
>
> Yet in parts of the creation some things are thought to be evil because they do not harmonize with certain other things. [For example, Augustine might think here of a windstorm that wreaks havoc upon a carefully cultivated vineyard.] Such things nevertheless harmonize with other [features of the created order] and in that respect are good, and thereby in their particular selves are good. Indeed, all such things, not mutually harmonizing with one another, fit in with the lower part of [creation], which we call earth, which has its cloudy and windy sky appropriate to itself. Therefore God forbid that I should now say, "These things should not be."
>
> [I admit] if I were considering these [earthly] things only, I would indeed desire better; but now, even on account of these things alone, I owe you praise, because they show forth that you are to be praised! "From earth, dragons and every abyss, fire, hail, snow, ice, tempestuous wind (all which do your Word), mountains and all hills, fruitful trees and all cedars, beasts and all cattle, snakes and feathered birds; [therefore,] kings of the earth and all peoples, princes and all judges of the earth, young men and virgins, the elders with the younger, let them praise your name. While also, in truth, from the heavens, let them praise you, let them praise you, our God, in the highest

places, all your angels, all your powers, sun and moon, all stars and light, the heavens of heavens and waters which are above the heavens, let them praise your name!" (Psalm 148:7–12, 1–5). No longer, now, was I yearning for better things, because I was thinking about *all* things. Indeed, higher things are better than lower things; nevertheless, with a more sane judgment, I pondered that all things together are better than higher things only. (VII, 13, 19)

In this remarkable passage Augustine commits himself to moves that are fruitful and that yet raise new difficulties. To stand fully clear of Manichaeanism, two matters demanded attention. First, nothing can be outside the province of God and God's creation to function as evil, breaking in. Nothing can be within God's creation that is evil, as such. Whatever evil "is," therefore, it must be nothing. This solves philosophically the substantial nature of evil: it has no substance. At the same time, evil as negative hardly accounts for the active belligerence of evil as encountered in experience. Second, the wide scope of positive creation must all be seen as good, which covers a great deal. Augustine invokes the wild beauty and harmony of the earth, following Psalm 148, roughly corresponding to today's "order of nature." (Note his careful editing of the Psalm, reversing its order and distinguishing nonrational creatures, which manifest that God should be praised, from rational higher creatures, who in fact should praise God.) He keeps Plotinus's beauty of the earth, while rejecting any suggestion in him that materiality is evil. He generously embraces the wonder of the whole physical universe, following scripture. He honors the humblest things, not only the intellectual; he affirms the whole declining order by his principle of plenitude. The difficulty is that he leaves no room for what modernity calls "natural evil," judged of course from the standpoint of human interests. Microbes, viruses, earthquakes, windstorms, fire and flood, natural decay, are all good, and part of a good order. The implication is that humanity must endure what is damaging and destructive of its natural life-purposes. Certainly, to be sure, he believes in the technical arts, defensive against nature: housing, medicine, transportation, agriculture. Yet when natural forces sweep these away and injure humanity, he will not call those forces evil, but see them as within a good order, and good in themselves. This very tough outlook allows no privileged place within the natural whole for human convenience, hopes, needs. Indeed, he suggests that when natural forces seem evil, the fault lies within our own perception.

And having experienced it myself, I felt no surprise that even bread is distasteful to a palate that is not healthy, and light, which is lovely to pure, [sound] eyes, is despicable to sick eyes. Just so, your justice is misery to the unjust, to say nothing of the viper and the vermin, which you made good, suited to the lower parts of your creation— to which the unjust themselves are suited! insofar as they are unlike you; and suited to the higher parts, insofar as they become like you. (VII, 16, 22)

Here personally disagreeable aspects of creation are no flaw in the good creature, but a failure of the human intellect to adjust to the order of the natural whole. Augustine's stern anti-Manichaean view, in and of itself, makes harsh demands on human forbearance. For example, he can affirm, in one specific sense, the notion that whatever is is good.

And it was clear to me that things are good even that are corrupted. . . . Unless they were good things, they would [not] be able to be corrupted . . . [for] what was to be corrupted in them would not be. . . . If they were deprived of every good, they would be absolutely nothing! Therefore, insofar as they are, they are good. Thus the things that are are good, and . . . evil . . . is not a substance because if it were . . . , it would be good . . . And thus I saw . . . that you made all things good. (VII, 12, 18)

Whatever *is* (to the extent that it *really* is) is good. The statement makes sense only in light of Augustine's levels and relative fullness of being. A broken chair is still a chair and good to that extent; reduce it to kindling and it is "good" only for the fire. A "corrupted" chair is no good as a chair, but still good as fuel to make a merry blaze. At whatever level it *is*, it is good at that level; it is no longer good (is "corrupted") at the higher level.

The Source of Evil: A Flaw in the Will

The way is open, then, to focus on evil. Evil is not only nothing; it is the nothing of a lack, a flaw, a breakdown *in* something (which as something is good). It is a negation, a disorderly collapse, a giving way in what would better hold up. It has no status, only inappropriate deterioration. Therefore, no level on the scale of being is evil, nor is natural decay, for transient creatures are good even in their transiency; trees die and fall to make way for younger trees. Indeed, at only one point does the collapse and breakdown truly bring about evil:

> And I asked, "What is injustice, iniquity?" and I did not find a substance, but away *from* the highest substance, you, O God, I found a *perversity of will*, twisted about toward the lowest things and casting out its own visceral, inward parts and outwardly swelling. (italics added) (VII, 16, 22)

The pinpointed source of evil is one kind of flaw and one kind only, namely, a flaw or a breakdown in a rational, free will. No other sort of decline or corruption gives rise to evil but this one. Only a perverse will of angels or of humankind can throw into destructive disorder the good processes that God has created. Only a free will, not out of substance, but out of its own freedom can pursue real damage of God's world. Moreover, the free will does this evil under the guise of happiness and good. The flawed will turns away from God and gathers lower creatures about itself, as if to become its own god in power and prominence. Under the mask of virtue it seeks happiness and rest. Yet actually it is casting out its own inward parts (abusing the power of illumination) and outwardly swelling (inflating itself in material power). Real evil originates in no other way.

Assigning the source of evil to the free will was the final blow at Manichaean gnosis. Nothing as such is evil; the world is not horribly split. Only this strange and perverse turn within the freedom of humanity and angels, self-idolizing pride, can become a source of evil, that is, of absolute disorder. Thus Augustine could look back and see in the pear tree his sixteen-year-old freedom turning to embrace his own destruction. The wonder of accountable freedom, learned from the Neoplatonists, shaped itself into his peculiar view of the will, yearning to love God, but capable of perverse self-preoccupation that can destroy the soul forever. Beyond Manichaean mythology lay the subtlety of real evil, alluring in its promises, its dynamism, and its freedom.

The profundity of evil as "nothing" then appears. A common criticism of this view finds "nothing" too empty for characterizing the destructive aggression of evil. To the contrary, negative in no way means passive, inactive, empty. When evil is understood as a collapsing of the free will into disorder, then aggressive agents of evil come easily to mind, rational creatures who have willfully turned to irrationality in countless cunning ways. In the dramatic mythology of his time Augustine knew of those who, trying to reach God through pride, had resorted to the help of fallen angels in the hope of receiving a vision; but these bright and promising visitors were of course demonic (X, 42, 67). The evil will, eroded by "nothingness," is capable of countless horrid, aggressive scenarios. Furthermore, evil as nothing also rightly means that no one can scrutinize the essence of evil in itself: the dynamic effects of the breakdown can be seen, yes; the thing itself, no. Evil as nothing is all the more disturbing in this active hiddenness. By the time its effects come to view, the evil lack within the will may already be undermining other matters, not yet suspected. Augustine in his evil as "nothing" had come beyond Manichaean passivity into the true challenge of aggressive evil.

With his coming to see evil within the free will as sin, Augustine in principle resolved his struggle with the Manichaeans and moved into the arena where in later years he would confront the view of the British monk, Pelagius, and his associates. There the matter of evil and the will took new complex turns. Also the harsh demand that Christians see natural events as good, mentioned above, required much further dealing in light of the Pelagian issue and its consequences.

Section 2

Salvation . . . (anti-Pelagian)

7

Freedom as Bondage: Original Sin

(*Confessions* VII, 17–21)

Now I had read the platonizing books, and they pressed me into searching out the principles of truth, not just thinking of physical, bodily things. And my mind's eye gazed into your intangible principles [Lord]. They [govern your creation; therefore they] can be understood through created things—but something pushed me back!

I was seeing what I could not deeply contemplate because of my darkness. . . . No question, I was certain about [those principles], but I was weak, unseasoned. I could not enjoy you in your own right.

I gabbled on endlessly like an expert. . . . Now I wanted to seem wise: stuffed with the penalties of my life, with no tears—and now superior!—I was puffed up with knowledge. . . . What a difference there is between presumption and confession, between seeing where to go . . . and finding the way, between catching sight of home and happiness, and actually being there! (VII, 20, 26)

Augustine's mind had accomplished a leap into new understanding through his response to Neoplatonism. Elements of childhood religious teaching had returned to him in a fresh guise and with personal, intellectual integrity. That there should be a single, all-ruling God of the cosmos, compatible with the biblical God of Genesis 1, now appeared to him via the principle of illumination. That God created all things no longer had the flavor of crude superstition but opened into a sensitive reflection on the wonder, yet fading nature, of all creatures, known against the invisible might of their origin.

Likewise the nature of evil had focused for him. What he had understood so fleetingly as a boy, the burden of excessive goals and the self-destructive flight from them, now made a glimmer of sense. At least he saw that evil is not something, a part of substance, but that it is a flaw, a breakdown of order in the will, plus the damaging impact of that flawed will on other things. This fresh insight had vigorously renewed the love of wisdom learned from Cicero, a zeal that had sagged during nine uncertain years of Manichaeanism. That is, the substantial nature of God, the guarantor of evil's nonsubstance, impressed his mind with such clarity that his ardor rose once again to pursue and contemplate the truth. God and the world are real; evil, for all its stubborn intransigence, is not real. This disclosure intensely fired his motivations to love only wisdom alone and to give absolute first place in life to what his intellect showed him was the only reality. In practice, such a loyalty to truth would mean becoming a religious "philosopher," that is, literally, a lover of wisdom, probably a member of a small secluded community of spiritual and intellectual devotion; it would mean accepting baptism in the Catholic Church, to which he now saw no intellectual obstacle; it would mean cultivating his own firm vision and practice of the truth.

His response to these possibilities was one-sided. He yearned passionately for his own vision and practice of truth, both philosophical and Christian, but he planned to gain this through his individual efforts, without commitment to membership in a supportive community. His grasp of the Neoplatonists was slanted toward Christian (what he beheld in those books, by his own account was "that religion . . . implanted in us in our boyhood" [see Chapter 6]). In this connection he cites the importance of having read initially the Neoplatonist books, then afterward looking afresh into the Catholic scriptures (VII, 20, 26). The Neoplatonist reading supported for him a move toward enlightened Catholic baptism and membership. Yet he chose to exercise a philosophical Christian life, alone—or at least without humble dedication to a community of faith. Despite his great ardor, the attempt failed him.

Freedom as Bondage

With Neoplatonism had come the foundation of a personal, accountable freedom. Instead of a mechanically divided self of good and evil stuff Plotinus had pointed him toward a high, free, intellectual center of the person; where Plotinus showed ambiguity about the body, Augustine saw it as created good. He therefore glimpsed the reality of the unified, created person with a single center of intellectual and moral freedom. The standards of illumination at that center were not (as has been said) printouts of what to do in life, but criteria by which to make free decisions. Finding a philosophical home in the Neoplatonist books made him for the first time a consciously free and responsible person, able to take steps of commitment into the future. Not only so, Neoplatonist insight had helped him resolve his intellectual objections to Christian faith. He realized on entirely new foundations God as the one universal principle; creation as dependent on God, yet free; the soul as in touch with truth; and evil as negation or nonbeing. No hindrance to personal integrity really stood between him and Catholic membership any longer. He knew he was free to choose membership and that he had been freed of intellectual impediments for doing so.

Yet he did not act. In one of his early dialogues, written just months after his discovery of the books, he tells that he would have rushed to the philosophical life at once, except that "the counsel of certain men stayed me" (*The Happy Life* I, 4), probably meaning the pragmatic advice that he could not simply abandon his oratorical duties and teaching. As he recalls the matter a dozen years later in the *Confessions* (quoted above): "My mind's eye gazed into your intangible principles . . . but something pushed me back! I was seeing what I could not deeply contemplate, because of my darkness. . . . I was weak, unseasoned." He was *not* habituated to living by inner religious principles. Yet his professional life left him empty and hopeless. His dilemma was hating what easily lay at hand and loving what he could not have. And he knew himself as free. The situation was no one's accountability but his own. How could he respond?

His mind seized upon the notion of a way. His newly discovered principles of truth represented a superior goal for his living, but his anguish lay in the absence of a way, a discipline, a mode of practice, by which to begin moving toward the goal: "What a difference there is . . . between seeing where to go and finding the way, between catching sight of home and happiness, and actually being there!" He knew of course that the Christian Scriptures described a most specific way in concrete narrative terms. He seized upon Paul. (It is difficult to tell, as between the early dialogues and the *Confessions,* just how quickly he turned from Plotinus to a comparative reading of Paul, but it was likely very soon.) In Paul's practical and theological letters to churches Augustine found no lack of a concrete way, offered in stirring imagery. Not only so, he read Paul as he never had before, as if Neoplatonist thought had pulled aside a curtain from the scriptural page. Difficulties with Paul's self-consistency and his relation to the Old Testament melted away with a Neoplatonist interpretive key (VII, 21, 27). (What he probably discovered was that Old Testament law and sacrifice offered Israel a way to God in a fleshly, outward form, which Paul came to know in a superior, spiritual and inward, Neoplatonic form. Of course, the "discovery" may not have been entirely accurate regarding Paul, as his thought is known today.)

Also he found striking additions in Paul not found in the Neoplatonists, not contradiction (as he saw it), but important supplements. Paul added to the Platonizers the grace of God in the humble Christ, God's initiative downward toward humanity rather than human upward striving alone. Augustine was struck by the storylike element in Scripture: tears of confession, the divine sacrifice, Christ's humble heart, the salvation of the people, the city like a bride: "These things stabbed me to the core in amazing ways, when I read [Paul], the least of your apostles, and pondered your works, and was seized with fear" (VII, 21, 27). These are the closing words of Book VII. The story rang true, but as yet it was not his story. It threatened him; he read and was afraid. The Pauline Gospel offered a concrete and imaginative way; yet for him, it was still only a possibility, frightening to contemplate, more frightening if declined.

The problem focused clearly: His new freedom surrounded him with possibilities. Yet the possibilities were too many and too finely balanced for a choice to occur; no one decision could win against the others. On the one hand, vocation and marriage were drawing him. In view of the burden of marriage, even illicit sexuality drew him (VI, 15, 25). The personal dreariness of all this repelled him. The Neoplatonic ideal was drawing him; he loved what he had glimpsed. In view of its remoteness and difficulty the Christian Gospel instead drew him; yet its exacting price terrified him. Let some authority decide for him. To the contrary, his very freedom that posed the problem demanded that he resolve it. Yet that new freedom had become a paralysis. Having to choose was a demand he could not meet. Freedom came to him as bondage.

His very discovery of God, which had set him free, also oddly meant that he had no sure hold on anything—not God, not the church, not himself, but also not the vocation, professional status, or personal ties he had been pursuing to that point. His freedom to choose quickly deteriorated into a dangerous freedom *from* all the options around him. Truly he was free, but the shadowy margin of risk that accompanies any freedom had become a darkness of isolation and uncertainty. His situation had miraculously bettered, only to become worse. His freedom perplexed and frightened him.

Neoplatonic Visions

Early in his account of probing the Neoplatonist books he describes the wonder of reflecting upward toward the One God, the source of his newly realized assurance concerning truth.

> . . . when I first knew you, you took me up that I should see that what I saw *was*, and that I, who was seeing, was not yet! And you beat back the weakness of my sight, radiating on me powerfully, and I shook with love and trembling. (italics added) (VII, 10, 16)

He is wonderfully in touch with his newly found Center, the noncorporeal foundation of the ordering of the world. Love deeply stirs him, as if he were coming home to all he had lost since childhood. He trembles with passion. Later he speaks of the "fragrance" of such a moment.

Yet the excellence of the beloved Light beats him back. He cannot remain. He enlarges this element of loss in another visionary account, along with more detailed mapwork of his ascent:

> So step by step, from bodies into my soul I went; into the soul that senses things through the body, moving inward; into that soul's inward power, which receives exterior things announced by the sense of the body (to this point also animal souls so function) and moving inward returning into the reasoning power that receives for judgment what comes from the bodily senses; and that power, finding itself to be changeable, wavering, raised itself to its own understanding, lifting thought from its usual custom, withdrawing itself from the swarm of conflicting bodily fantasies, to discover the light by which it is bathed, since without any doubt it declared the unchanging preferred to the changing, and hence that power should know the unchanging itself [for without such knowledge,] it could not prefer it, and hence passed through to *that which is*, in the stroke of a trembling glance.

Then truly I saw your invisible things, known through the things which are made.

But I had no strength to fix my sight, my weakness was struck back, I fell to my usual ways. Nothing remained for me but loving the memory and yearning, as if by its fragrance, for what I could not yet feast upon. (italics added) (VII, 17, 23)

Comments on these experiences have varied. Some have expressed unease that a person spiritually at odds with God and himself should succeed in a glimpse of the divine. Others have emphasized the failure of what took place; the attempt at contemplation reached a fruitful point that quickly faded; he attempted what he could not sustain. Others have resisted the notion of failure; for a moment he grasped intellectually the source of truth, a verification of what he had read in the Plotinian books.[1] Possibly the best interpretation is not to choose between the experience as either positive or negative; rather, it was both positive and negative and for the same reason: He gained a glimpse of the divine mind. It was an intellectual moment that saw into the enduring standards of truth in the mind of God; on the other hand, the auspices of the moment were wrong and the situation of the viewer put the good of it into bad account.

More specifically, Augustine rose intellectually to a point of insight where he was not yet prepared, with a full and undivided heart, either to go or to remain. It was indeed good that he had read the books, gained the insight, made the foray. The move was not inappropriate to his intellect, and his intellectual grasp was of high importance. Also, more deeply, it touched his heart ("loving the memory . . . yearning, as if by its fragrance"). At the same time, the move ironically laid bare the deeper division already present within his will, prohibiting him from contemplating God with a full and undivided will. In the disclosure, he knew both God and himself better, and thereby knew himself to be the worse—worse in his whole condition than he had realized. His advance was also his fall.

A Key: Original Sin

This ironic mingling of good and ill echoes what became for him one of the primal paradigms of human existence: the fall and original sin. This

1. For example, cf. P. Courcelle, *Recherches sur les Confessions* . . . (Paris: E. de Boccard, 1950), chapter 4, iii, "Les vaines tentatives d'extases plotiniennes," and responses to it by

paradigm or doctrine has suffered such ill repute in modern times that careful consideration of it in the Augustinian setting is difficult. Nevertheless, original sin serves as an illuminating key for his ecstasy. Furthermore, his experience lends itself to both Plotinian and biblical readings as regards the primal sin. Plotinus held to an original sin and fall of the soul in preexistence, prior to, indeed leading to, its birth as a human being in time. For Plotinus, the original sin (he did not call it that) of the preexistent soul in the intellectual realm is to become preoccupied with the beautiful forms of the material world, rather than always referring that beauty to its source in the One. The result of this unhappy turn and deviation is for the soul itself to fall into the material world through physical birth, ensnarled within time and history. The need of the soul is to return, in spiritual body only, through profound rigor of reflection to intellectual steadiness in the One, beyond time.[2]

Augustine was impressed with Plotinus's idea of the preexistent soul and in 386, having first read him, undoubtedly then understood his ecstatic vision in this light: The ecstasy, even in his fallen earthly condition, was a foretaste of his full return, for which he now yearned and hungered all the more desperately. Augustine continued to allow the possibility of the Plotinian notion of preexistent fall until about 406 c.e. after a period of increasingly substituting biblical categories for Plotinian.[3] Indeed, by the time of the *Confessions* he had burrowed far more deeply into Scripture than was possible in 386, especially reading the so-called Ambrosiaster commentary on Paul. When recording the remembered ecstasy in the *Confessions*, therefore, he undoubtedly knew a level of its biblical, as well as Plotinian, significance as fall and original sin. What was that biblical level?

Augustine provides a clue to the biblical significance of his ecstasy back at the recorded moment of his discovering the Neoplatonist books (VII, 9). There he applies a quotation from Paul (Romans 1:21–22) to conceited, self-elevated teachers: "Although they know God, they do not glorify [this One] as God, or give thanks, but become vain in their thoughts, and their foolish heart is darkened, for declaring themselves wise, they become fools."

A. Pincherle, C. Boyer, H. Marrou in *Augustinus Magister* (Paris: Etudes Augustiniennes, 1954), 1:53–57. Cf. A. Solignac in *Oeuvres* . . . (Paris: Bibliothèque Augustinienne, 1962), 2d ser., 13:691, 701.

2. E.g., *Enneads* IV, 3, 17–18.

3. TeSelle, *Theologian*, 257. But R. J. O'Connell holds that his openness to preexistent fall carried forward until 417–418 and apparently beyond; *The Origin of the Soul in St. Augustine's Later Works* (New York: Fordham University Press, 1987), 14–16 and passim.

(VII, 9, 14). Paul originally wrote this in the past tense, but Augustine remarkably quotes it in the present, as if pointing to certain present company—likely the Neoplatonist philosophers themselves! whom he saw as self-inflated, and whose willingness to accommodate popular pagan rites fits with the animal idolatry Paul next describes (VII, 9, 15; Romans 1:23. Cf. VIII, 2, 3: Victorinus, the translator of the Neoplatonist books Augustine read and surely a self-elevated teacher, participated in animal rites, and so verifies the link of Neoplatonists to self-glorifying idolaters as above). The climactic impact of Augustine's vision ("Then truly I saw your invisible things, known through the things which are made") is directly from the same Pauline passage (Romans 1:20), describing the knowledge of those who then turned proud. And Augustine quotes again, "they know God, they do not glorify . . . God," in VIII, 1, 2, and flatly includes himself (as he was in those days) in that group—a self-glorifying Neoplatonist. Yet is all this self-elevated philosophizing original sin? Yes, if original sin means reaching out for true knowledge of God, but in a destructive way.

The case seems clear, at least in his much later *City of God* XIV, 13 (about 419 c.e.). There he reflects on the Garden of Eden and the original temptation of Adam and Eve by the serpent: Eat the forbidden fruit and then "you shall be as gods" (Genesis 3:5). It would seem that this promise to be as gods must have been for Augustine the core of sin, the egocentric pride of proposing to be like God. Is it not the very original sin of the Garden to decide that one must and will be like the deity? Yet Augustine indicates that the serpent's promise is true! and therefore not in itself the lying deceit. The human being *is* destined to be a "created god"; that is, an angel, *like* God by participating in God's truth and God's characteristics (love, justice, beneficence): "*which they would have been better able to become by adhering to their highest and true Principle through obedience, not by becoming to themselves their own principle through pride*" (italics added) (*City of God* XIV, 13).

The sin of Adam and Eve was not in aspiring to be as gods; that was the goal of their creation. The original sin was the *way* they proceeded to that end. They determined to reach the goal by activating the potential at once, by seizing it out of their own willfulness, rather than keeping a pattern of growth in the wholeness of their being (knowing God, they did not glorify . . . or give thanks . . . became vain . . . fools). They determined to be "as gods" in a precipitous way, leaping to a status where the whole of who they were could not at that moment subsist. The result was that they found themselves tragically divided, having the knowledge of good and evil and therefore the free choice of gods, while at the same time the anxiety of knowing they must die as mortals. Their error was in the way, the *via*, of their procedure.

Note here the difference from Plotinus's fall. For Plotinus, the error was in the goal of choosing downward. For Augustine's biblical reading, the error was the way, the means, of choosing upward. He calls it "becoming . . . their own principle through pride." The *via* they denied (and therefore lost) he calls "adhering . . . through obedience" to God's will for their appropriate development. Further, in the Plotinian fall, the higher intellectual soul oddly remains essentially undamaged, even though dragged into material confusion by the lure of earthly forms.[4] Plotinus sets up, therefore, a dualism in the soul between bodily and spiritual essences that do not merge. In the Augustinian fall, the person as a whole is caught in a division or contradiction *within the will*, with no part unscathed. The agony of divided will means that the personhood of soul-body unity suffers complete damage (see page 118 below).

Note also the correspondence between the situation of Adam and Eve in original sin and fall and the situation of the young Augustine as he recalls and describes it in *Confessions* VII. Adam and Eve's problem was the way; so Augustine recalls that his problem was the lack of a way. "What a difference there is . . . between seeing where to go and finding the way." Augustine gazed upon the source of truth; then without an appropriate way he seized upon godlike status for himself (became vain . . . fool). The similar move by Adam and Eve left them in a state of tragically divided motivation; so Augustine's move disclosed his profound division of will: He yearned to subsist on divine truth; yet he was habituated to other patterns that claimed him (knowing God, they do not glorify God). Also, the fall upward into an illicit "Ye shall be as gods" implies a false superiority of Adam and Eve, knowing as gods, though under sentence of death as mortals. Augustine's reaction to his postecstatic divided state was similarly inflated. He did not redouble his efforts at philosophical discipline; he did not lapse into a simple depression of failure. He projected superiority! "I gabbled on endlessly like an expert. . . . Now I wanted to seem wise: stuffed with the penalties of my life, with no tears—and now superior!—I was puffed up with knowledge."

Remarkably, having discovered the Neoplatonist language of wisdom, and having realized language as a creature able to articulate the beautiful

---

4. E.g., *Enneads* II, 9, 2; III, 6, 5. Cf. Armstrong, *Christian Platonism*, 4, 35–37.

ordering of the creation generally, Augustine fell into the same inflated abuse of language that he had witnessed as a student and young orator, only now he used the very language of *philosophia* to do so! His astonishing progress in understanding was all the more acutely perverted. How did he turn the very concepts of wisdom and truth-seeking into erupting chatter?

The experience of Plotinian ecstasy and his interpretation of it in the *Confessions* twelve years later fit the mode of the biblical original sin and fall: self-glorification precisely *in* the knowledge of godly things; the pursuit of a real good, which because of the manner of pursuit, coincides with the primal evil. Freedom was bondage indeed.

The Incarnation, An Obstacle

As it turned out, the way, the *via*, that he needed was Christ. In his emerging theology Christ was above all the Mediator, God in the flesh, who therefore combined God and creation in himself and linked the two together, to the world's great benefit. As the purely divine Word with the Father, the Mind of God's truth, indeed the light of truth within us, Christ was also the goal of our yearning, as well as the way. Yet in the spring and summer of 386, having feasted upon the Platonizing books, Augustine was already overwhelmed with a sense of goal and desperate for a way toward the goal. He recalls plainly that his search for a way met with no success until he realized and embraced Christ as Mediator (VII, 18, 24). He would later come to see the accessibility of Christ, the way to God, as an out-pouring of singular grace, a universal aid for the mass of humanity.

Yet for the moment all this was closed to him, and for good reason. He had just passed through a personal revolution of thought appropriately *separating* Creator and creation. He no longer looked out upon a Man-ichaean world, in which every object and event was a disguised mythological battle between Light and Dark. In his new reflection, he had loosened the world of creatures from the divine substance; they now had their own significant, secular identity pointing to their Creator, even in their fading mutability. Such a clarification was an achievement in itself, worth long pondering and celebration. Then he realized in Christian doctrine the call to make a single, grand exception to the line separating the Creator from the creation. Here was Christ Jesus, the earthly Lord, who was at once divine, immutable Word and also mortal, mutable human being. His *Confessions* states that at that point he could really make no sense of the assertion.

His hesitation could have included a number of objections grounded fearfully in recent religious agonies: Such an affirmation recalled the hapless Manichaean individual, caught in a mixture of divine spirit and flesh. No Manichaean could bear a doctrine of incarnation; the flesh corrupts. The doctrine recalled pagan polytheism, the walking about of gods on earth in various fleshly guises. No evidence indicates that Augustine actually articulated such objections. He recalls that by the summer of 386 he trusted Catholic doctrine implicitly, wished to be obedient to it. All the more reason that his possible objections should take the form of frustrated puzzlement.

> [At that time] I pictured my Lord Christ as a man of excellent wisdom, whom no one could equal. This was especially true because his wonderful virgin birth showed us how to disdain passing things in order to gain divine immortality. And by his care for us he clearly merited great authority as a teacher. But what was meant by the "Word made flesh," I could not even suspect.
>
> . . . Because the Scriptures are true, I acknowledged the whole human being in Christ, not just a human body, or the body and soul without the mind, but a human being in the true sense—[admittedly] not the Person of Truth. Rather I saw him as preeminent before all others because of a *certain great excellence of human nature, and a more perfect participation in wisdom*. . . . Moreover I confess to have learned [only] somewhat later how in this assertion, that the Word was made flesh, Catholic truth is distinguished from the false teaching of Photinus.[5] (italics added) (VII, 19, 25)

Notice that the notion he had of Christ in the above passage fit precisely with the recently discovered Neoplatonist books, including all of their insights and their problems. Christ was a man, a magnificent teacher, superior to all others in degree of human attainment (not Son of God) because of his superb participation in divine wisdom. His virgin birth did not signal

5. Bishop of Sirmium; he denied Christ's preexistence prior to the Incarnation, affirmed the Virgin Birth, and saw Christ as wise by participation in God's wisdom, rather than being the Person of Truth.

his divine nature; rather, it gave an example to all people to ignore transient things and prepare themselves for the eternal realm. This Christ was an ideal Neoplatonist sage. Indeed, he was clearly what Augustine himself was trying to become in his mystical reflection upward: a steady and informed participant in divine wisdom. Christ was an idealized image of Augustine himself.

This kind of Christ only confirmed Augustine's freedom as bondage. Christ as the excellent example of human nature reminded Augustine of his own freedom and responsibility to become excellent; yet he could not. In the diffusion of his freedom his anxious will felt only abandonment concerning what he should do. Christ Jesus also showed "a more perfect participation in wisdom." Augustine's attempt to imitate that participation led him only into the original sin of seizing upward toward spiritual status, without the growth of his whole person toward that goal. Instead of wise he became only inflated; instead of poised he became only superior. Augustine's expanded, isolated ego, stretched wide by multiple religious and secular impulses, immobilized him. For Christ as a model of human potential disallowed Christ as Lord and carried him further into tragic spiritual expansiveness.

Now his ambivalence in reading Paul becomes more clear. Assuredly, Paul's account of Christ's coming had thundered in his mind. Indeed, he states at the beginning of Book VIII, "The way, the Savior himself, was pleasing." Certainly since childhood he had known an attachment to the name of Christ, fretting that Cicero did not know that name. Now in sophisticated Milan, with so many of his questions answered and Catholic attachments refurbished, the yearning for Christ had increased. Yet he immediately adds, "and to go through his narrow ways was still loathsome." He was attracted by the Way, but repulsed by its actual ways. Christ was an attractive possibility, but not an actual practice of life. The moral dilemma was how to pull his will together to wholeness, to pursue the way of God with all his heart. Further, this moral dilemma attached itself to the one remaining intellectual dilemma that he knew: He could not conceive the Word made flesh; he thought of Christ as what he himself was striving unsuccessfully to be. What he had read in Paul must have struck him a double-sided blow. The drama of what Paul preached, "Christ and him crucified" (1 Corinthians 2:2), penetrated deeply; but if the notion of God *in* Christ, the Incarnation (2 Corinthians 5:19), neither made sense

nor gave moral resource, then the story was unnerving and fearful to consider.

Dubitatio

Therefore, he doubted. He doubted, not in one sense of the word, but in
another: He tells us at the outset of Book VIII that "every doubt" *(dubitatio)*
had dissolved concerning the reality of an Immutable Substance, source of
every other substance in the world. He no longer felt any doubt about the
reality of the Creator and the nature and status of the Creator's mutable
creatures. His intellectual obstacles regarding all of this had fallen away.
Yet in another sense he tells us "I was doubting *(dubitabam)*" (VIII, 1, 2).
That is, he found himself unable to pull himself together to live and practice
the heart's full loyalty to Christ, as he desired. He wanted the goal, but
the requirements of the way chilled and dismayed him. The problem here
was not intellectual (though he did have the intellectual thorn of the Word-
made-flesh still to contend with); but the agony was primarily moral and
emotional. Indeed, the problem was spiritual, in the full, rich meaning of
the word: The sense of whole, heartfelt life, lived well, simply failed him,
more especially failed him as founded on God and truth. This failure as
"doubt" *(dubitatio)* is better translated "wavering." He knew what he
wanted, but he wavered. He concludes VIII, 1, 2 with a familiar New
Testament reference: "Now I had found the good pearl. [Matthew 13:46]
By selling everything that I had, I must make it mine! Yet I was wavering."
    Doubt at this point was far from that tough questioning or independent,
intellectual suspicion that introduces an arduous search for truth.
    Augustine had long exercised that kind of doubt, seeking always at least
a glimmer of sound reason in his quest for personal religious integrity. That
sort of doubt had kept him alert to the truth ever since he sensed at sixteen
that his parents, "as I knew," wanted his education "too much." Augustine's
pilgrimage had thrived on honest, even if at times mistaken, doubt; otherwise, he could never have made the transition from the artificial religious
forms of his childhood to the faith of integrity that he finally found behind
those forms. (Thus twentieth-century theologians have pointed out that
such honest doubt constitutes an indirect testimony to the existence of

truth—since otherwise no motive would exist for doubting—and leads a serious person toward that truth.)[6]

Doubt as personal wavering is another matter. In every sense, he was captive to this *dubitatio*, a halting among various options, some of which he wanted very much, yet others of which he was unwilling to let go. His brilliant public career vied with his yearning for religious integrity. His pride in intellectual self-sufficiency pulled against Christian authority and humility. His impending marriage threatened to exhaust his religious hopes and needs. He had already suffered a painful blow some time before in the dismissal of his concubine, the mother of his son Adeodatus, after thirteen years of monogamous relationship (VI, 15, 25). Church and society considered such dismissal part of a man's moral improvement (as noted above, page 39), since it opened the way to his lawful marriage. Yet Augustine found himself engaged to a girl still two years younger than the legal marital age—and that legal age by Roman law was twelve! Consequently he found himself now cohabitating with a third woman, a woman of convenience, who meant nothing to him by way of companionship or law, a continuing blow to his image of self-mastery. Yet he could not give up this woman, or the vain post of the emperor's panegyrist. Nevertheless he longed for philosophy. He sought the beloved name of Christ in his church and joyous assurance within the Christian communion. Here was *dubitatio* indeed. A single paralyzed ego was struggling to keep the benefits of a complete circle of these attachments, regardless of their mutual contradictions. His head told him that some of these had to go; his heart shrank from letting go of any.

Deep within the frustrated adult still dwelt the small boy of Thagaste, told that he was bright and talented and able to gain anything he wanted (able indeed to justify all parental sacrifice), yet keeping no daily moral and spiritual practice by which to grow toward that goal. He wanted all; he coveted all; he knew no assuring way to move toward any. He had reached the nadir of his isolated fear. A soul praised and acclaimed actually trembled in self-doubt, feeling that no single life-commitment could possibly articulate his full superior potential; yet he oddly felt unworthy to take hold even of such a one. (The situation is not unlike the root of classic paranoia, the attempt to keep all elements of the surrounding environment under one's

6. E.g., Paul Tillich, *The Protestant Era* (Chicago: University of Chicago Press, 1948), xiv–xv.

own conscious and secure control.) Once again, at the end of Book VII he agonizes at the plight of a goal that offers no way.

> It is one thing to see from a wooded mountain top the fatherland of peace, but to find no roadway to it, and to attempt to reach there by an impossible way with fugitives and deserters blockading and intruding all around, under their chief, the lion and the dragon; and another to hold to the way leading there, guarded by the care of the heavenly emperor. (VII, 21, 27)

When there is no way, then the individual remains caught holding all fronts, unwilling to give up the goal, yet unwilling to leave the only summit of vantage in hand, yet still determined to attempt the passage. Augustine's soul tore within its own fabric.

Although their worlds were alien, Augustine's plight of spirit anticipated the dilemma of Franz Kafka at the other end of the Western age: "There is a goal, but there is no way; there is only wavering."[7] Both men's agony rested upon the discovery of the Good (Augustine's God, Kafka's the Law). The gift of the Good, with no process toward the Good, only confirms the soul's torment.

Pelagius versus Augustine

Years later Augustine encountered the work of a British monk named Pelagius. The writings of this man came to his attention as late as about 412 c.e. His discovery of Neoplatonism in Milan occurred in 386, his writing of the Confessions eleven to thirteen years later. Therefore still another thirteen years had passed before he heard of Pelagius, and the world-embracing battle lines were drawn of the Augustinian-Pelagian struggle concerning grace and free will. Yet the major coordinates of Augustine's position against Pelagius were already in place, implicitly within his experience of 386, explicitly within the thought of the Confessions (397–399). A brief survey of Pelagius's position will indicate how inevitable the opposition was.

Since Pelagius came to be counted a heretic, his works are only fragmen-

---

7. Aphorism 26, in *Hochzeitsvorbereitungen*, 42. Cf. Strauss, "Kafka," 206.

tarily preserved. Scholars also do not agree on which of the pieces remaining are authentic.[8] Nevertheless, several points are clear. Pelagius urged primarily the natural goodness (bonum naturae) of the human being, and the natural free choice of will before God, to do righteousness or to sin. Even the capacity for evil is part of this natural goodness, since freedom to do evil means that good is also done freely; and the doing of good is dignifying only if freely chosen. The ability to choose the good, and the actual choosing and doing of it, bring the human spirit to its noblest heights.

To this point, much accords with Augustine's Neoplatonism and his discovery of the free accountability of the rational creature before the Creator. In fact, Pelagius and his associates read certain of Augustine's early anti-Manichaean writings on free will with great pleasure, confident they found in him an ally. On the doctrine of creation Pelagius was most satisfactory to Augustine. Yet at the point of human evil and original sin he was astonished at Pelagius's inadequacy. Evidently, the British monk held that the individual's ability to do good, fundamental to the Pelagian position, can never suffer impairment throughout life, regardless of what that person does. That is, Pelagius saw the substance of human nature always as possibility, the possibility of choosing to do good, regardless of the circumstances. An actual choice of evil he saw as a mere "accident," that is, an accidental or superficial feature of the human substance (Commentary on Romans 7:17). No repeated choices of evil, no matter how frequent, can alter human substance, the possibility of doing well on the next choice. Pelagius's view allowed for entrenched habit, a kind of blind servitude toward sin (Commentary on Romans 7:15). Yet the choice, for example, of a long-term alcoholic not to drink would be at some level free and possible.

Pelagius's argument at this point declared that sin, being negative, was not a substance. A nonsubstance cannot damage a real substance, like free human possibility; therefore one is always free to do well regardless of the past record of wrongdoing. Augustine's apt rejoinder was that not to eat is not a substance; yet not to eat will waste away the substance of the body until it dies. Just so, evil choices will waste away the substance of the soul (Nature and Grace XXI–XXII). Certainly Augustine showed a more dynamic view of the human soul and its well-being than his opponent. A person's

8. For an introduction, cf. Gerald Bonner, Augustine and Modern Research on Pelagianism (Villanova: Villanova University Press, 1972). More recently, cf. B. R. Rees, Pelagius, a Reluctant Heretic (Woodbridge, Suffolk: Boydell, 1988), and The Letters of Pelagius and His Followers (Woodbridge, Suffolk: Boydell, 1991). An excellent survey of content is Brown, Augustine, chapters 29–32.

freedom can indeed suffer from past choices. He found Pelagius's confidence in the static endurance of free choice naive in relation to both Scripture and experience.

Augustine's notion of the free will was far more complex. Initially, in his determination to route the Manichaeans, his discovery of Neoplatonic freedom (and its illumining of Christian free will in the Bible) swept away all other considerations. He had located the nature of evil apart from the Manichaeans' version of it. Nothing as such was evil; the only source of evil was an evil will, which threw good things into an evil disorder. The source of an evil will was the will's freedom. Therefore, he came to say definitively and finally, "Evil is sin, or the penalty for sin" (see page 25 above). The achievement of this view took the burden of evil off any substance whatever, especially the physical and sensuous side of the human being. The human body as created is not evil. No physical hunger or thirst, as such, causes sin (*Nature and Grace* XXV). They may provide the occasion on which the free will chooses to sin by overeating, but that is the will's problem, not the body's. Ever since Augustine, indeed since Paul the Apostle, a prime philosophical element in the West has denied that human evil has its source in the fleshly body or is sensuous in nature. So Augustine later, in his mammoth *City of God*, states that the downward pull of fleshly needs against spiritual aspiration is not the cause, but the *penalty* of sin (XIV, 3). That is, some prior act of evil will predisposes spirit and body against one another.

Thus freedom of choice constituted Augustine's cornerstone against the Manichaeans and in an important sense he never gave it up. At the same time, he became increasingly impressed with the difficulties of rightly exercising freedom and concluded that human freedom is not neutrally disposed in human existence. From 391 to 396 he was writing his lengthy dialogue *Free Choice*. During the same period he was doing intensive biblical study and reading Ambrosiaster, the commentator on Paul mentioned above. The result verified his sense that the will suffers severe difficulty of choice, even in its freedom, and clearly influences the latter part of his *Free Choice*. From Paul and the Ambrosiaster he concluded that Adam and Eve's original sin introduced human death into the world for the first time. "On the day that you eat [from this tree], you shall die" (Genesis 2:17). From their determination to seize directly upon a status as gods came also their mortality, the inevitability of their death. In the age of the Church Fathers, including Augustine, death was the great enemy; no modern view of human death as a natural end existed. To be a human mortal was not natural, not a part of creation and created good. Consequently, for Augustine, original sin diminished the whole human organism, set up an unnatural spirit-flesh antagonism, altered the race "for the worse" (*City of God* XIV, 1). (Augustine of course read the Adam and Eve story literally, which is not essential to seeing in it the difficult tension between human aspiration and human death.) By fallen nature the human being is insecure because threatened with dying; pressure of anxiety then invites the will to capitulate to evil measures of security, hoarding goods and even killing others for safety. The will yields in the midst of personal fragmentation and uncertainty. Then over time custom hardens the addiction to pleasure and safety; prohibition by the Law, "Thou shalt not kill . . . love the Lord thy God," only succeeds in condemning behavior and increasing the desire to transgress (*The Spirit and the Letter* 6, iv).

Augustine saw the result of original sin, mortality, egocentric desire (concupiscence), and habituated custom, as the tragic inability of the will to exercise its freedom of good choice. Reason could know the good; the will could not pull together to follow the good. As he cries out in the *Confessions*, "The soul commands the soul to will . . . yet it is not done!" (VIII, 9, 21). For some ten years after his 386 conversion he considered that the will remained sufficiently free in existence to say yes or no to God's call, or to turn to God and ask for help. After commenting on Romans 9 in 396 (*To Simplicianus*), he determined that even the turning to God was part of the special gift by which God won the will to fruitful action. The appropriate doing of God's law requires delight in and love of that law, which comes only by a special grace. What is done in fear is not done (*The Spirit and the Letter* 26, xiv). For the most part, after 396, he proposed that the fallen will has freedom in God only by special grace, that the will in ordinary existence cannot firm itself up to live by God's truth. Yet if the will cannot exercise its freedom of good choice in the ordinary existing person, in what sense is it free will? It appears not free at all, but bound. Did Augustine betray his own anti-Manichaean cornerstone, free choice of will, in order to fight an anti-Pelagian battle? His position appears caught on contradictory poles: freedom of will and bondage of will.

Augustine: Evil and Freedom

The right response to this dilemma discloses the rich subtlety of the Augustinian view of evil. That is, the bondage gripping the will, in Augustine's view, is not in contradiction with the will's prime nature as free. Rather that bondage, at the same time, helps specify what the real enormity of evil is, as over against the Manichaean and Pelagian versions. For one thing, the binding of the will does not apply to all the freedoms of the person. For example, even in the flawed condition of will, the intellect retains many good qualities and abilities. His self-revelation in the *Confessions* shows that the person is able to reflect on numerous theoretical matters, hold a respectable vocation, treasure significant friendships, and even realize the nature and character of God, despite the will's bondage at the point of integral good. Augustine is impressed with Paul that the Gentiles have the law "written on their hearts" in creation (Romans 2:15), suggesting that they share in the light of truth and are responsive to it in legitimate ways (*The Spirit and the Letter* 43, xxvi ff.). Augustine does not hold to the obliteration of the image of God in sinful humanity even if saving participation in God is lost; otherwise his own enlightened reading of the Neoplatonist books would have been impossible (cf. *City of God* XXII, 24). In his own state of bound will Augustine recalls that he knew "your sweetness [O God] and the beauty of your house, which I loved" (*Confessions* VIII, 1, 2), suggesting that even love of God's very nature is still not sufficient for the soul's true well-being. Nevertheless, the passage shows how much spiritual responsiveness is open even to one who is in the condition of bound will. The soul under original sin still shows a remarkable number of enlightened qualities and moves.

If bondage of will permits pursuit even of high spiritual goods, then it appears that such bondage is trivial; it embraces too many proper and good activities. To the contrary, Augustine viewed the plight of the will with the greatest seriousness and horror. The solution lies in this: Bondage of will does not exclude freedom to pursue higher things because this bondage of the will turns out to be *excessive freedom of the will.* The freedom of the will indeed becomes its own bondage. An excessive number of attachments and pursuits, including the sweetness of God, diffuses the will and paralyzes the human subject. Thus freedom elects too many different passageways and in its stalemate becomes isolated and superficial, in bondage to its restless freedom. Inability to make a decisive move heightens the tension within freedom and becomes a bondage. Yet even in this bondage the will remains free, in that it cannot resign its role to an outside commander. Even to resign would be to choose. Free choice cannot be avoided even in bondage. Thereby lies the self-destructive agony of the bound will. No wonder that the boy Augustine at the pear tree elected to confirm his evil situation by loving it and pursuing it to the end. "I loved . . . I wanted . . . to perish." Caught within its own free situation the will wills to confirm its condition and perish, rather than grapple with its own freedom.

Augustine sensed that the will at its own mercy becomes a kind of necessity. In one clear instance he points out (an argument that he might have used fruitfully more often) that natural necessity need not contradict free determination of will (*Nature and Grace* LIV). The instance he gives is the will to happiness. Everyone *necessarily seeks* happiness; everyone also *freely chooses* happiness. No contradiction exists in these two statements. Clearly, his point applies not only to grace and obedience, but also to sin. The necessity of original sin in no way denies that sin, an enticing addictive, is freely chosen. In other words, freely seeking happiness as necessity may express itself as freely seeking sin as necessity. Then sin becomes the necessary happiness the will chooses, and the sense of bondage deepens.

Under the shadow of death, the natural necessity of sin (freely chosen!) meant that the race had suffered enormous penalty from accumulated evil. (Recall that evil, for him, was either sin or the *penalty* of sin; to be struck down by another is evil, yet not as one's own sin, but rather as the penalty incurred for another's sin.) Therefore, burdened with the accumulated penalty of generations of sin, people come into life beset by ignorance and difficulty: ignorance of how best to choose, and great difficulty in choosing well when the best is clear. Adam and Eve's sin, pride (*superbia*, self-glorification), the short seizure to godlikeness, has been compounded in most of the world by concupiscence (*concupiscentia*), endless desire of all kinds. Indeed, by the years 406–407 (almost ten years after the *Confessions*), Augustine was declaring that humanity is born with a *tradux peccati et mortis* (a transmission of sin and death), that the infant is born guilty of, and corrupted by this original sin, that the result in life is concupiscent desire (*Tractates on John's Gospel* 3, 12, 1).[9] Little wonder that such untamed desires emerged as chaotic freedom, division of will. Pelagius apparently declared that every sin consists of pride. Augustine responded that the *root* of all sin is pride, but that all sins are not done proudly (*Nature and Grace* XXXIII). A world widely damaged commits a plethora of evils in the scramble for self-preservation.

Yet the elements of pride that remain in the situation of evil prove the most haunting. Augustine penetrated far beyond the Manichaean and Pelagian positions to the true fearfulness of evil. He found a genuine, if

9. Cf. TeSelle, *Theologian*, 258.

prideful, aspiration toward the good. Admittedly, evil is negative, a lack or want. Yet that failure insinuates into the will a propensity to dominate in the name of the good, even spiritual good. The good is genuine, but the will has endless desire (concupiscence) and knows no limit in the drive to control and establish that good.

The constructive way to the good becomes lost. The will in its excessive freedom either erodes into inconclusive wavering, deteriorating in its own isolation—or attempts to dominate, taking countless others with it. Augustine now knew that the evil he had tried to understand used the face of good, even the good of spiritual contemplation.

8

The Grace of Christ as Way

(*Confessions* VIII, 1–6)

As Simplicianus told it, [Victorinus] read Holy Scripture and with much intensity scrupulously looked into all Christian writings. Finally, he began to say to Simplicianus, not openly, but secretly and confidentially, "I should tell you that I am now a Christian." And Simplicianus always answered, "I won't believe you or count you a Christian until I see you in Christ's church!" Then Victorinus always made light of his friend: "Ah, then, is it walls that make Christians?" And they often [had this little dialogue] . . .

For Victorinus revered his friends and did not want to offend these [intellectually] superior demon-cultists. He could feel their hostility about to crush down on him from their Babylonian heights—like the Cedars of Lebanon, which the Lord had not yet broken down to contrition.

But afterwards, by reading and yearning he gained strong nourishment. Also, he feared denial by Christ in the presence of the Holy Angels, if he himself were afraid to confess Christ in a human gathering. He felt like a prisoner, a criminal, blushing at the sacraments of the humility of your Word; yet he did not blush at the godless rites of proud demons, which he acknowledged and imitated with his superior air.

So [he reversed]: He treated those vanities shamelessly and came, in shame, before the truth. Suddenly and all unexpectedly, he said to Simplicianus [who told it to me]: "Let's go to the church. I want to be made a Christian." And Simplicianus, abandoning himself to his joy, came on with him. There the church had him drink deeply his first sacraments of instruction. Indeed, not long after, he gave his name to be reborn in baptism, with Rome amazed and the church rejoicing. All the self-important people heard it and were furious. (VIII, 2, 4)

Augustine at Milan in 386 c.e. grasped the evil that beset him and the true good that he desired. He had yet to find his way to conversion and baptism as in the story of Victorinus above. The sequence had been long. Neoplatonist reading had finally shown him the intellectual potential in Catholic teaching and had unburdened his mind of the view that evil is a substance. Yet the results of this entire discovery had been problematic. The high good he had glimpsed had dealt him a blow because of what he called the lack of a way. In view of this lack he moved into a posture much reminiscent of the original sin, at least by his standards in the *City of God*. For though evil was negative, its results were aggressively positive. As a failure within the will, evil identified itself as the original, wrongheaded choice of how to achieve the good. That bad choice was the attempted direct seizure of the good without the time or practice necessary for the whole person to lay hold of that good. The grasping person was pulled in different directions at once in a disastrous drama of "eat your cake and have it, too." This was the original sin: Out of inflated pride Adam and Eve wanted their true godlike destiny fulfilled, instantaneously, on their own terms. They grasped it and pulled themselves apart in the process.

This sundering of the soul expressed the dilemma of freedom—more precisely, of excessive freedom, dissipating the energy of intent in too many ways. This dissipated freedom, intentionality run amuck, immediately produced concupiscence, endless desire in all directions. Concupiscence as restless and circling freedom guaranteed the wasting of energies in a paralysis of the will. Multiple freedoms became a chaotic flow of yearning and therefore, ironically, a bondage. Evil thereby arose as an inevitable function of the free yearning for good. That is, given the human state of anxious mortality, Augustine saw scattered freedom and paralysis of will as inevitable—at the precise point requiring loyalty to God, the one and only true good. Not only was this bondage inevitable at the most crucial level of the soul, it wore the face of good, of godlikeness, and therefore invited even the most moral and spiritual person into its ironic distortions. This bondage was the person's claim upon the good with no actual way *to* the good.

For many years Augustine had sought for an authentic turn in his experience, a turn away from his damaged spiritual circumstances into a fruitful move toward deeper happiness. In the wild stresses of adolescent years he had turned toward Cicero and the love of wisdom. Against the heaviness of moral and religious experience as a boy he had seen in Cicero an adventurous enticement; he had seen there what he would recognize in later years as even the substance of Paul's writings, though in different words. This turning away from evil bondage and heaviness had nevertheless been immediately skewed by involvement with the Manichaeans, who promised only superficially to fulfill Cicero's admonitions.

In 386 discovery of the Neoplatonists constituted a remarkable opportunity to renew the turn. His dialogues written near the time of his first Platonist reading declare that he realized then a release from contentious ambition: "Then what good to me were honors? . . . Or wanting to be famous?" (*Against the Skeptics* II, 2, 5). Evidently the Platonists had released him from his lifelong competitiveness for glory in his empty profession, in favor of philosophy. Yet this renewed turn toward love of philosophy, recalling Cicero, frustrated him once again. His existence was drawn to a stalemate by his conflicting intents. He turned and looked toward philosophy, only to the increase of his despair. Rather than resolving his competing concerns by a new integration, he added only another complicating intensity.

How should he proceed? Evidently by finding a feasible way to the good he had glimpsed. He believed that his only fruitful turn would be within the way of the Catholic church; how could he take hold of that way?

Simplicianus; the Incarnation

He made a useful move; he sought counsel. The very willingness to move outward for help was an encouraging sign, for his desert of waste was the topography of himself. How could he get beyond his own enclosed soul? Certainly he had friends; yet those relationships were heavily controlled by his own powerful leadership. On the other hand, his respect for Ambrose had never produced a real conversation between the two of them. Where his issue of a *way* was most crucial, he had been most isolated. Nevertheless he now made the choice of a counsellor. Simplicianus was an aging priest who had instructed Ambrose when the latter very suddenly had risen from Roman governor to bishop of Milan. Ironically, when Ambrose later died in 397, Simplicianus succeeded him as bishop of the city. Just months prior to this, Simplicianus had taken his own turn writing questions of theology to the newly consecrated bishop of Hippo in North Africa, Augustine. But in 386, the young Augustine turned with his own desperate hope to this respected senior in the church.[1] He went to Simplicianus with the predictable desire to solve the dilemma of the way: "I wanted him, in conferring about my seething restlessness, to propose what mode of life would suit a person affected as I was for walking in your way" (VIII, 1, 1). The question was that of a day-to-day practice that would effectively put religion and philosophy first in life.

Augustine recalls that he told Simplicianus the winding errors of his long search. Simplicianus helpfully built a bridge to his situation by congratulating him on reading the Neoplatonists rather than other philosophers fixed on partial, distorted truths (an echo of Cicero's Hortensius). The link with the Platonizing books was especially fruitful, since the man who had translated the very books Augustine had read, Victorinus, had himself dramatically converted to Catholic Christianity. Simplicianus further offered the story of the proud Victorinus's conversion "in order to exhort me to Christ's humility, hidden from the wise and revealed to little ones" (VIII, 2, 3).

The story (given in part at the head of this chapter) aimed to recall the humility of Christ himself. The naming of humility at this point introduces the most important virtue in the emerging Augustinian theology and ethic, the very opposite of self-inflated pride and concupiscence that had been so laid bare in original sin. That humility is further specifically attached to Christ. In addition, Simplicianus may have spoken to him specifically about the Incarnation, the divine Humility, the Word made flesh, which had proved such an intellectual stumbling block to the young Augustine (VII, 19, 25 above). A slender clue that Simplicianus did so is a distant passage in the City of God (X, 29):

> . . . from the saintly old Simplicianus we used to hear that a certain Platonist was accustomed to say that the beginning [1:1–5] of the holy Gospel . . . according to John ["In the beginning was the Word, and Word was with God . . . etc."] should be written in gold letters and displayed through all the churches in the most prominent places. Yet that God and Master seemed vile to proud ones because "the Word was made flesh and dwelt among us." [1:14]

1. Cf. Brown, Augustine, 93, 103, 106, 153–54.

Augustine's recollection of Simplicianus, Neoplatonism, John's Gospel, and the "proud ones," immediately includes John 1:14, the Incarnation. The passage thereby closely parallels the two sentences in the *Confessions* (VIII, 2, 3, above), in which Simplicianus congratulates Augustine on the choice of Neoplatonism as a philosophy, and urges him to accept the humility of Christ as did the once-proud Victorinus—advice that is only a breath away from telling God's own humility in the Word made flesh.[2]

Another reason to think that Simplicianus helped him with the dilemma of the Incarnation is that nowhere later in the *Confessions* is there an account of this intellectual stumbling-block finding a solution. Yet in every case of an intellectual difficulty in the Christian faith (the substance of God, the nature of evil, the possibility of knowing the truth) Augustine was unable to move forward toward Catholic membership without at least some reasonable light being shed on that difficulty. His progress toward Catholic faith did not, in other words, take the shortcut called *sacrificium intellectus* (the sacrifice of one's understanding of a doctrine simply in order to accept it, because the church demanded it). A critical bridge from the religion of his childhood to its mature version in his adulthood was the bridge of personal, intellectual integrity. Admittedly, whatever he understood intellectually still had to be dealt with morally, personally, and practically (the agony of the *via*, the way). Nevertheless, in every case, some rational enlightenment stood at the bridgehead of effective moral grappling. In 386, he could not yet enjoy God, but he had glimpsed rationally the meaning and nature of God, without which the enjoyment of God would be mere spiritual fancy. A rich interworking of reason and faith became essential to the whole Augustinian theology all along the line. Is it possible that the doctrinal hinge of Christianity, the Incarnation, was the great and puzzling exception to the rest of Augustine's developing theology? Did he receive and appropriate the moral example of Christ's humility as salvaging his practical life and simply overlook the rational contradiction of a God-human, the person of that Christ? Could he affirm his baptismal vows and hold the mental reservation that the Incarnation was unacceptable to the God of truth? Surely not.

---

2. Cf. P. Courcelle, *Recherches sur les Confessions de Saint-Augustin* (Paris: E. De Boccard, 1950), 170, 173; also, his "Saint Augustin 'Photinien' à Milan *(Confessions VII, 19, 25),*" *Ricerche di storia religiosa*, 1 (1954): 63–65, 71.

The Incarnation Accepted

If Simplicianus did bring him to some clarity on the Word made flesh, why does he not explicitly record it so in VIII, 2, 3? Why withhold the wonderful disclosure? To the contrary, he has so dedicated Book VIII to the conversion of his *whole* person to the love of God that he will not risk separating the intellectual element for consideration by itself. That move is typical of the mature Augustinian outlook represented in the *Confessions*. Viable knowledge of the Incarnation, as intellectual insight, is empty apart from acknowledgment of the Incarnation in life. Reason's light on this matter is only part of a whole new engagement of things by the heart, through a life-practice. Augustine could not risk in Book VIII describing a living, formative event (the Incarnation) as another theoretical possibility, all too able to bring on once again a vain superiority (as dominates the close of Book VII). The gulf between Book VII and Book VIII from mere possibility to actualizing in life must remain firm for the sake of his goals of confession and exhortation. Therefore Book VIII offers an account of the whole impact of Christ upon him, the results in his living posture of an encounter both intellectual and practical at once.

There is another reason, most telling of all, to think that Simplicianus effectively taught him the Incarnation. Passages in Augustine's very earliest postconversion works, dialogues written at Cassiciacum only four to six months after his time with Simplicianus, find him articulating and affirming that doctrine. These passages disclose the shape of incarnational teaching as his mind had been able to receive it. They quite reverse the direction of his previous—VII, 19, 25—view of Christ as a man of excellent human nature and a "more perfect participation in wisdom." There the emphasis had been on a man arousing himself to participate "upward" in wisdom, the Neoplatonist sage. By contrast, his early dialogue passages speak of how "the most High God should bring down and submit the authority of the divine intellect all the way to a human body itself" (*Against the Skeptics* III, 19, 42), or "that so great a God for our sake counted it worthy to assume and activate even a body of our kind" (*Order*, II, 5, 16), or of "that authority, . . . which . . . activating a true man, shows him to what extent it has brought itself low for his sake" (*Order* II, 9, 27). Here God is acting to participate downward in bodily human life. This shift from the man participating upward to God participating downward means a reversal of Augustine's conceptual image since the situation of VII, 19, 25. He is thinking of the Incarnation as a divine initiative on humanity's behalf, as distinct from the human initiative of seeking participation in divine truth. He has adopted a mindset that indeed builds upon the Incarnation. The Neoplatonism that he knew did not teach or allow this initiative of the divine Mind specially to assume human flesh; he must have received it from Catholic teaching, most likely from Simplicianus. (Cf. Porphyry's rejection of the Incarnation, *City of God* X, 29.)

Yet the original dilemma of VII, 19, 25, still remains. How could he conceive of a divine initiative downward when the divine is unchanging, immutable? How can an immutable divinity join with a mutable human being? How can the Unchanging One change, take on flesh? Once again, the Cassiciacum passages suggest that he came to hold a dynamic, relational view of immutability, rather than a formalistic, static view. That is, his dialogues declare that one of God's immutable perfections is mercy, and virtually declare that another is humility. Yet if mercy and humility are enduring, unyielding perfections of God, then God's self-lowering in the Incarnation actually confirms the divine immutable perfection. That is, God is immutable in being *ever merciful*, and the humility of the Incarnation seals that fact. God is unchanging in being unchangingly compassionate; God is eternal as eternally steadfast and faithful. Note here the exchange of static, abstract concepts for dynamic, moral, and relational concepts. God is unchanging, but unchanging in love, specially enacted in the Incarnation. Thus the distant God-is-One of the Neoplatonists became enlarged and enriched in the God-is-Love of the New Testament. As in his struggle with Pelagius over human nature, so in his enlargement of Neoplatonism, Augustine proved to be the more dynamic thinker.[3]

Some such process of thought may have been Augustine's if he indeed heard Simplicianus expound to him the Incarnation. In any event, between the spring and fall of 386, he had come to affirm that doctrine. The matter was of high importance because the Incarnation was crucial to Simplicianus's primary point: to show Augustine how a person like himself could walk the church's way; for the church was where the Incarnation continued to be accessible. The Word made flesh was not limited to the first century A.D. The Incarnation was still available in and through the Catholic church, her scriptures, sacraments, rulers, and people. God's active love in the flesh remained still active, still in the concrete flesh of the church.

---

3. Cf. William Mallard, "The Incarnation in Augustine's Conversion," *Recherches Augustiniennes* 15 (1980): 80–98.

Augustine wanted the church's way and now grasped the active Incarnation; these two were one reality of active love. His yearning ardor must have doubled. Furthermore, Victorinus had been a man like himself in many respects, "affected as I was." Victorinus had found his way to the Incarnation, Christ in and through the Church. Perhaps Augustine could as well.

Simplicianus and Victorinus

As Simplicianus told it, Victorinus had been a professor of rhetoric (like the young Augustine), highly acclaimed and successful, a brilliant student of literature and philosophy, a teacher of senators at Rome. Because of his excellence as a teacher, he had merited a statue in the Roman forum. The dark side was that he had revered idols and advocated joining in their worship. He approved even the worship of conquered gods of other peoples, including Anubis, the barking dog. In this, he joined some other of the intellectual elite, including Neoplatonists. They felt that idols provided a mediating experience of the divine for the masses, incapable of sophisticated reflection. Victorinus had defended the practice with all the power of his oratory.

The account of Victorinus's growing conviction of the Christian faith has been quoted above. He was privately convinced, but Simplicianus had continued to urge upon him the necessity of church participation. Victorinus's ready answer had always been, "Ah, then, is it walls that make Christians?" He had feared lowering himself in the eyes of intellectually lofty friends. Eventually, his real convictions had triumphed and he had gone to the church for instruction. Simplicianus gave details of the actual initiation:

> The custom was for those who were to be received into your grace to repeat the profession of faith in a set form from memory, from a prominent place in full sight of the faithful people of Rome. Finally, when the hour came, the priests offered Victorinus the choice of professing more privately, as they did with anyone likely to be too anxious and shy. But Victorinus preferred to profess his healing in full sight of the holy assembly. For it was not healing that he taught when he taught rhetoric; yet he professed it publicly. How much

less should he fear your gentle flock, or uttering your word, when he had no fear speaking his own words to howling swarms of wild men! So when he climbed up to give the confession, all who knew him immediately turned to one another and uttered his name with a clamor of congratulation. And who there did not know him? And the common joy sounded with a pressed intensity through every set of lips: "Victorinus, Victorinus!" As quickly as they resounded with exulting when they saw him, just as quickly they fell silent to hear him. He declared the true faith with brilliant confidence. And they all wanted to seize him and take him into their very hearts. And they did embrace him with their love and joy, for loving and rejoicing were the hands they used to grasp him to themselves. (VIII, 2, 5)

The story is told at length because of the parallel of Victorinus to Augustine himself: rhetorician, orator, philosopher, teacher, high in government recognition and service, prideful and sensitive, leery of commitment, ambivalent in spiritual life. Simplicianus shrewdly told it for the same reason. By letting the story set up a sympathetic bond between Augustine and Victorinus, a zeal for Victorinus's happy outcome, Simplicianus knew that his counselee would identify with the struggle and yearn to repeat Victorinus's choice. "But when your man Simplicianus told me these things about Victorinus, I burned with ardor to imitate him; for this purpose indeed he had told the story" (VIII, 5, 10). Augustine recalls further that during the time of Emperor Julian the Apostate, Christians were forbidden by law to teach literature and oratory; Victorinus had given up that vocation, for which he was so renowned, rather than give up the Christian faith. Augustine yearned to give up his own empty post. He was not yet ready to do so; nevertheless, the Victorinus account immediately contributed. Theologically and spiritually, the story told the surprising character of grace as both a binding and liberating way.

Walls; Grace as the Other

Victorinus had ironically asked, "Is it walls that make Christians?" The answer was yes, as he was later to discover. Walls of stone, no; but, if the imagination can range a bit, the walls that made Christians were the walls of an ordered people's way of life, including their scripture, their worship and sacraments, their authorities, their moral practices, indeed their common humanity itself. The *via*, the way that Augustine sought was a pattern of obedience within an authoritative religion. The walls that made Christians were the boundaries, limits, and rules for walking usefully forward. The metaphor of playing a game (and religious practice has an element of play in it) suggests that the rules of the game, and the lines of the playing field, are the "walls," without which no significant contest takes place. Indeed, without walls and mapwork for living, every place is the same place, every moment is the same moment, and the soul dies stultified.

Both Victorinus and Augustine had been lacking in walls. Successful achievers, they were both excessively free, egocentric, and dominant. Each desperately held together contradictory elements in one life. Victorinus had one world of scholarly reflection and another of cultic frenzy and sham. He manipulated one to the satisfaction of the other; in his rationalizing, these things fit. He defended polytheistic rites and even rituals for gods conquered by Rome, the cult of Osiris, the barking Anubis, as the only link to divine mystery available to the unreflective masses (VIII, 2, 3). Yet how could frenzied orgies serve as links toward rigorous Neoplatonist abstraction? The contradiction weighed upon him. Augustine's inner conflict lay in his distribution of personal goals: religious, intellectual, vocational, marital, even starkly sexual. This overextension left him shrunken and alone at the center. In his anxiety he strove to manage all fronts, knowing he could not. His fear and pain would not let him forgo any of the various satisfactions that he held.

All this was the pride and concupiscence of good men. Both achieved honor as enlightened, religious figures (Augustine as a noted Manichaean, then as an intellectual Catholic catechumen). Each carried an exhausting burden, yearning to be fully and freely committed to the one unifying best hope, yet unable to be relieved of the multiple obligations. Letting go of burdens also meant letting go of accessibility and control, surrendering dominance. Original sin, the short way to godlike powers, exhausted the soul, yet offered wide-ranging influence. Indeed, original sin put one's mark of identity on everything dealt with: job, mistress, wealth, fiancée, friends, oratory, philosophy, divinity. To lay claim to everything encountered is brilliant and exhilarating. To discover that everything finally reflects only oneself is chilling and nauseous. Here was the dilemma of individual expansion: Augustine put his name on everything he touched, but only superficially; all of it together mirrored only his boring heaviness.

Little wonder that he longed for the Other. He longed for the substantial and unyielding Other, a trustworthy authority that would delineate what was his and what was not his, so that he could grapple with what belonged rightly to him. He needed the Other as an authority in whom he felt confidence. He needed the Other as a discipline upon soul-expanding emptiness. Remarkably, in the thorny doctrine of the Incarnation, the teaching he had found inexplicable, lay the Other, who marked off the direction in which he could move and struggle fruitfully.

The Incarnation as Other surprises the usual association with that doctrine, the association of access. The whole genius of the Word made flesh is presumably God-with-us, not the Other, but rather the closeness and likeness of God to ourselves. The likeness is assuredly important, indeed essential. Even in the matter of the Other, likeness is crucial, else the Other could not even be known. Nevertheless, *Confessions* VIII reserves a compelling place for Christ the way, the Incarnate, as Other. Augustine's fearfulness and hesitation in following that way shows his sense of Christ's Otherness.

Yet did not the Other constitute his problem rather than its solution, the Other as the alienation and estrangement of everything in his experience? On the contrary, his sense of alienation arose from too much outward control over things, excessive dominance. Even in his intimate friendships, where he had felt rich mutuality, his leadership had taken the group the way he wanted it to go.

The Other that he met in the Incarnation sharply distinguished itself from this alienation. God was Other, but God had made that terrifying Otherness available, in the Incarnation, in a direct, everyday otherness of discipline and practice. Christ in the Incarnation made himself available as the demanding practice of his church, demanding but promising. Christ was Other, but a most welcome Other, the Other that would confidently challenge in order to reward. The Other of the Incarnation was a way of obedience, but also a mapwork of hope.

Hope in the Other of the Incarnation came even clearer in the matter of language. When Augustine realized and began to yearn for the Incarnation in the church, he grasped an authoritative language of Incarnation that responded to his dilemma concerning language across many years. That language was of course scripture, was "other," strange, rough-hewn, the mystery of the Word made flesh; yet it was simple, accessible, largely in story form, concerning the coming and the doings of the Son of God. Such language was available publicly, cutting wide across intellectual and academic barriers; it told a story of divine activity and humble sacrifice accessible to all. Yet it was clearly also a gateway into an exquisite philosophy of spirit, partly by literal reading, partly by allegory.

Admittedly, this Otherness, scripture and daily practice, frightened him. Yet the Incarnate way was also the promise of an immense relief. His great burden was prideful autonomy, sustaining the mixed life of a sexual compulsive, imperial panegyrist, and spiritual contemplative, all in one; and each of these fell prey to superficiality, hindered by the other two. He invested the scattered energy required to maintain all; exhausted, he still found frustration with each. His burden was heavy, and he carried it with no rest in sight. Yet he would not give it up. He clung to the weight of his own evil by his own insistence and hated it at the same time. By contrast, the hardship of Christ's way promised unprecedented relief. To obey a rule from day to day of what to do, and what not to do, had its sharp edge, but compared to the heaviness he now carried was nothing but relief. To dream of focusing one's energies in a difficult but rewarding direction meant life-giving relief and renewal. With Christ, hardship meant hope. How much more desirable to engage a dozen hard problems than to die a prisoner of one's own scattered soul. His uncommitted person was a burden of bondage, even though he had freely chosen all his different obligations. On the other hand, his committed soul promised the vitality of struggle and achievement, even though under someone else's rule.

The relief of a hard but promising way expressed what would become later Augustine's primary theological preoccupation: the grace of God. Grace came first in a negative and even chilling guise, as the Other. Grace came as a way of life not under his own wayward control. Grace may be described as God in loving, outgoing action. Here the loving action shaped the orderly life of God's people, mapping out a way for Augustine as it had for Victorinus. Grace came as the divine order for life, Incarnate in the church. Grace came as gracious limits, gracious boundaries. He was finding the household of gracious discipline and consistent authorities he had hungered for as a child and adolescent. So Christ's humanity was a historic rule for his people, providing a link to his divinity and his blessing.

Grace came as a concrete plan for renewed progress. Grace came as the cold bath of a healthy and realistic obedience. That is, grace cut back on the burden of Augustine's concupiscence, his compulsion to satisfy all desires. Grace limited his weighty pride, his intellectual short seizure of godlike knowledge. Grace limited his freedom, which had become bondage. Grace showed him a particular, trustworthy, authoritative way—Christ Incarnate in the church—a great promise of intellectual and personal fruitfulness.

Grace offered him boundaries upon his godlike omnipotence ("I can do it all"), in favor of a recognizable, sane identity.

The Christian People

A high point in the story of Victorinus had been his reception at the public baptism, the exulting clamor of the Catholic throng, "Victorinus, Victorinus!" The philosopher-orator had offered his pledge before the entire, gathered congregation. The cry "Victorinus!" acclaimed and sealed his decision. He had decided to leave his pedestal of elite advantage to accept common membership in the Christian body. In matters of soul all were equal before God. The church body claimed him as their own: "And they all wanted to seize him and take him into their very hearts. And they did embrace him with their love and joy, for loving and rejoicing were the hands they used to grasp him to themselves." By accepting public membership in the general body of the Christian people, Victorinus had humbly surrendered his privileged status in Rome's social order. His liberty and protection in the legal hierarchy, as teacher, scholar, and public figure, no longer sheltered him, witness his required resignation from teaching in the wake of his baptism (VIII, 5, 10). It has often been said that equality is not a measure of persons, but a place to meet. Victorinus chose equality before God as a place to meet his fellow members in Christ at a public baptism. He had accepted the surrender of his high-level class standing before the people, and they had greeted him by shouting his name, "Victorinus!" which appropriately means "conqueror": He had conquered himself. He had become, not in talent or usefulness, but in Christ, their equal. Augustine confirms equality in the story of Victorinus by referring it to no less than Paul the Apostle, whose theology of grace became for Augustine a focus of the New Testament.

> [Consider Paul] the least of your apostles himself: . . . Paul, [like a high official], a proconsul, had his pride defeated by [Christ's] warfare, and was put under Christ's easy yoke and *declared a common citizen (provincialis)* of the great King; [then] he loved to be called Paul, rather than [as before] Saul, as a sign of so great a victory. (italics added) (VIII, 4, 9)

At the cross high and low alike accepted common citizenry under God, along with the delight of that citizenry and the common belonging to one another.

Recent scholarship has noted that in the early Christian movement a "mixed style" in literature signaled a new social and class outlook.[4] That is, while ancient literature ordinarily treated serious subject matter only in an elevated style concerned with the doings of the aristocratic and noble, Christian literature treated matters of high seriousness through the affairs of common, ordinary folk. A foremost example is the tragic denial of Christ by his friend Peter, the fisherman, a moment of profound seriousness through the life of a humble man. Elevated leaders like Victorinus and Augustine therefore met a social commonality at the core of the Christian faith, even in connection with the high seriousness of their own conversion and baptism.

The walls of the church that made Christians were therefore not only trustworthy religious authority and discipline; the walls of the church were the people themselves, with their hands outstretched wanting to seize Victorinus and take him to their hearts. How were these people walls? A new prestigious Christian like Victorinus or Augustine met a religious equality in the church that constrained their liberties with others. The brothers and sisters constituted an ethical and moral terrain that could not be violated. At the cross, each one was of equal importance in salvation, regardless of differences in gifts or responsibilities. Augustine was to take his place among these, respected and affirmed, as he must in turn respect and affirm the others. He was simply another human creature in need of the grace of God. Rather than being many different things in isolation he was a particular identity within a close-knit society. Indeed, he was an individual with great abilities and great conflicts needing to be kept in a consistent perspective. The liberties of being completely singular, but also its great burdens, fell away.

With the history of his spectacular personhood had come the temptations to violate the dignity of others. When at the university, he had "defiled . . . the heart's blood of friendship with the stain of concupiscence" (III, 1, 1). He had hardly acknowledged the dignity of womanhood, dismissing the mother of his son, taking another in her place, becoming engaged to still another aged ten. He made his income composing empty imperial

---

4. Cf. E. Auerbach, *Mimesis*, trans. W. R. Trask (Princeton: Princeton University Press, 1953), chapter 2, esp. 40–45.

speeches and teaching others the same, young boys, who "thought of nothing but insane lies and courtroom struggles, for whom weapons for their madness were merchandized out of my mouth" (IX, 2, 2). He grieved to recall that after his conversion he spent twenty more days in this vain manipulation to round out the term. His old wavering life had virtually assured that he would misuse others in the scramble to hold himself together.

Public profession and baptism in the general congregation, becoming a common member, meant a new societal relationship for him that could not transgress others' well-being. Much later he wrote concerning his ethic of love that one must love and enjoy and use others only "in God" (*Christian Doctrine* I, iii–v, xxii–xxxiii). To the modern ear, this sounds stiff, as if laying an artificial piety over every spontaneous relationship. What he meant was rather that no relationship may abuse the dignity of another. Not even love can take the liberty of dominating others. Their prior place is guaranteed within the circle of the grace of God. They can be loved within that prior affirmation of who they are. The hands that reached out to Victorinus were eager hands of welcome, but also hands of restraint. They signaled that he was one of a common body preserving mutuality.

Augustine does not record the scene of his baptism, administered the following Easter, in 387. Was it also a powerfully symbolic, public occasion? Some students have suggested that absence of a description of Augustine's baptism means that the occasion was not of high significance to him. To the contrary, it possibly was much like Victorinus's, which serves in *Confessions* VIII as an example of his great feeling for his own initiation. Exclamations may well have gone around the sanctuary for Augustine as well, when the emperor's brilliant rhetorician appeared to offer his vows. Modesty could have deleted a detailed account and let Victorinus's baptism represent his own in the *Confessions* text. If so, the hands that loved and welcomed the newly baptized Augustine were for him, also, the welcome of a Christian dignity that renewed his concrete relationships with his fellows.

Grace and the Intellectual: The Divine Imbalance

In still one other sense grace came as discipline through the Incarnate One in his church. Grace disciplined Augustine's systematic, intellectual understanding of Christian faith and philosophy. That is, the Incarnation put restraints upon Augustine's ability to discourse at large on God, self, and world. Such restraint appears odd in light of the claim made above that the doctrine of the Incarnation must have had some reasonable light to it before he could accept it. Some reasonable light, yes: he saw that the unchanging God could unite in Christ Jesus with a changeable human being, if God were unchanging love, steadfast mercy. Yet how, for example, that God of unchanging love was understood to be a Trinity, three in one and one in three, was closed to him. Only after much experience as a Christian student and practitioner and years of writing did he hope to understand the doctrine in his *The Trinity* (400–421 c.e.).

On the other hand, when he had first read the Neoplatonist books in the spring of 386, his first flush of enthusiasm caused him to think that he understood a great deal. He recalls that the platonizing philosophy coincided much in substance, if not in words, with the opening of the prologue of John's Gospel: "In the beginning was the Word, and the Word was with God and the Word was God" (VII, 9, 13). Here was a major segment of thought on the eternal Trinity, in particular the relation between the Father and the Son preexisting before creation. As already shown above, Augustine thought that by reflecting back through the nature of truth (the Son) he could glimpse its origin in the One. He attempted this meditation, and though the experience was short-lived he was nevertheless enough encouraged to chatter like an expert (VII, 20, 26). To seize a godlike glimpse of the innermost relation of God, Truth, and world, without living the way of love, only enhanced his egocentricity.

A systematic, coherent insight into God and the world, without the practice of love, became only a systematic, coherent expression of personal vanity. Little wonder that under these circumstances the Incarnation made no rational sense to him (VII, 19, 25), nor did he find any equivalent of incarnational doctrine in the Neoplatonist writings (VII, 9, 14). Yet the Incarnation offered a way of disciplined love that turned the passing insights of personal vanity into a fruitfully growing religious understanding. Such a discipline of love looks only wearisome to the mind that desires instant enlightenment.

The point of the Incarnation was that no philosophical understanding of God and truth really takes root unless one's experiential grasp of the world, which God loves, also takes root. Love of God through the creation offers a harsh route to sublime, eternal truth, since it requires struggling with practical evil, failures of love, and perplexing events. Significantly, Augustine's later *The Trinity* shows progress toward understanding God only through a practical understanding of the material creation, made up of both sinful and blessed loves, and of Christ as Incarnate way. Christian theology is a practical science, even in its most abstruse formulations.

Therefore, a systematic intellectual view of God, even with its moral implications, may lack the depth of moral practice. It may rest satisfied with its own balanced, systematic achievement. To understand God, but not to follow God is intellectual idolatry (although they know God, they do not glorify [this One] as God or give thanks . . . and [they change] even the unchanging glory of your incorruption into idols and various images [VII, 9, 14–15; Romans 1:21, 23]). Against intellectual idolatry and a loveless existence, the Incarnation came as a divine imbalance that threw Augustine into a process of struggle and growth. That is, the Incarnation confronted him concretely and historically as a boundary between himself and God that dissolved personal intellectual self-sufficiency.

A modern writer of fiction has said (in the mouth of one of her characters), "Jesus thrown everything off balance."[5] No image of evil is more telling than the sterile balance of the deteriorating will, self-inflated with just enough spiritual knowledge to be superior. The Incarnation knocked off balance the mind's self-satisfaction and threw Augustine into a way of holistic learning, step by practiced step. By finding grace as way, Augustine discovered what Pelagius could not: that not only can the choice of the good become intellectually and morally self-centered, but that grace harnesses freedom in order, along a narrower path, to make more free.

---

5. Flannery O'Connor, A Good Man Is Hard to Find and Other Stories (New York: Harcourt, Brace and World, 1955), 27, 28.

9

Grace as Call: Christ as Lover

(*Confessions* VIII, 7–12)

From that direction where I had set my face, and yet where I was fearful to cross over, the chaste dignity of Continence appeared, serene, rejoicing (but not dissolute), alluring me with virtue that I should come and not waver, and extending to me pious hands to support and embrace me; and her hands were filled with flocks of good examples: so many young boys and girls, many young people, indeed all ages, grave widows and ancient virgins; and in all of these Continence was in no way sterile, but the fruitful mother of children, and of all the joys of you, her husband, O Lord! And she was mocking me with an exhorting derisiveness, as if she were saying, "Are you not able to do what these young men and young women are doing? Or truly, are these able in themselves? Or not rather in the Lord their God? The Lord their God gave me to them. What is this?—that you stand in yourself [alone] and [therefore] do not stand? Throw yourself on him! Do not be afraid. He will not pull away and let you fall. Throw yourself, be confident. He will receive you. He will make you whole!" . . . The controversy in my heart was simply that of myself against myself. (VIII, 11, 27)

God's move against evil, especially evil as self-glorifying good, was the move of love. Grace as way, the boundary lines of an ordered practice, was only love's leading edge. Therefore grace as way carried also within itself grace as a gift of delight and allure toward God: Grace came as love passionately enjoyed. Only as a source of passionate delight could grace be complete. Grace had come as way within which to move and live; grace then came as eager love for actually following that way, a desire to pursue and possess God. Without this new savor, this fresh delight in God, the steps along the way of practice would have faltered. The walk of the pilgrim was toward a loving, winning Christ, who called the wanderer to a special bliss. Augustine finally became the loving pilgrim.

The subtle and cunning loves of the heart had defined Augustine's journey from the first. At no time had he been devoid of love, but he had loved in scattered, hidden, and conflicting ways. He had loved Monica. He had loved the name and image of Christ, an early seed of religious love. He had loved games and play. In desperation, he had loved the brokenness of language and his own chaos, hurling himself toward nothingness (the pear-tree story). Wondrously, he had loved evil. In another respect, he had loved both good and evil, the highest ideals and the most severe waste; and to love both good and evil at once was itself the worst evil of all. As a successful young professional he had known his loves as empty, destructive and nameless. Still, he had loved his friends dearly. Yet in the death of one (IV, 4–9) he had learned how self-serving even their mutuality had been.

The fruitless tangle of loves demanded redirection and priority. From one point of view his entire theology coalesces in the matter of the direction and redirection of human loves, called out and formed by grace. The *Confessions* therefore offers the core of his theological viewpoint, which continued evolving through a lifelong stream of treatises, dialogues, sermons, and letters. The *Confessions* offers the core because it weaves a narrative of language, religion, evil, and love, and the complex interlacing of these four; and that interlacing follows the directions and attachments of love, both Augustine's and God's.

A major subtheme, not unrelated to love, is that of intellectual integrity, the search for truth. Augustine discovered the redirection of his scattered loves first by waking to an intense desire to find the truth, especially about his personal situation. That yearning to know wisdom, activated by Cicero, stimulated a renewed love for God, though he little understood at the time where this would take him. To turn in hunger and desperation toward the truth at length became for him a turn toward the Neoplatonist light within, which finally became a loving turn toward Christ within the church. His love for truth turned out to be love for Christ, the Word or truth of God. Victorinus, the philosopher, had found and claimed this same Christ as his own.

Nevertheless, though Simplicianus's account of Victorinus had filled him with ardor, Augustine still wavered. Full engagement with the love of Christ was yet to come. His mind and spirit were still not at peace with any single, unified direction; years of inner conflict still troubled him. Grace had come as way, but just what would his way of life look like as a baptized Christian? Victorinus had been a man, "affected as I was." Yet the *Confessions* account of Victorinus says nothing of the particular form his life took after baptism, except that Julian's edict forced him to give up teaching. If Augustine accepted Catholic faith, what would he do? Become a cleric? Remain lay? Become married? Seek philosophical retreat? Moreover, when he adopted a specific role, could he maintain it? Would his heart stay constant?

These questions were not minor ones for him. While many good Catholic Christians could choose among several modes of life, Augustine felt it was not so with him. He did not see the matter of his personal salvation already settled, with the choice of a role as only peripheral. He makes it very clear that the entire relation to God and church could stand or fall with his choice of role within the way, and his perseverance in that role (e.g., VIII, 1, 2). He saw his own salvation, his total well-being, still hanging in the balance.

Marriage and Sexuality

He recalls that his restive unease now focused on one particular area of life, that of marriage and sexuality. For a long time, he had had three enslaving compulsions in life: sexuality, wealth, and ambition. For some time, he had moderated his desire for wealth, hoping only for what would support a life of philosophy (VI, 11, 19). Further, since his discovery of the Neoplatonists, ambition had loosed its hold on him. The sham of his daily job offered him only an empty glory: "The secular career I pursued made me unhappy; indeed, the burden of carrying that obligation was grave indeed when the flaming desire, the old hope for money and renown, had faded" (VIII, 1, 2).

The old childhood desire to win the game and take the prize had shifted to a yearning for philosophy. The statement fits well with his exclamations (already quoted) on finding the Platonizing books: "Then what good to me were honors? Or popular ceremonies? Or wanting to be famous [that empty fame]?" (*Against the Skeptics* II, 2, 5). When he read the Platonizers, he was ready to choose against honors, wealth, and personal acclaim.

Sexuality remained his third question mark, with implications more complex than those of riches or honors. He admits a compulsive need for sexual companionship (VI, 15, 25). Yet restriction of appetite was not alone the problem. As a Catholic Christian, he could marry and have both sexual companionship and religious faith:

> At this point I was still locked into my need for women—not as if the Apostle Paul had forbid me to marry. Yet he did urge something better; he keenly wished that everyone would follow his example [and be celibate]. But I had given in and gone the easier route.
>
> On account of this one obligation, I was caught up in other necessities that left me exhausted and burned out with withering demands. For I found myself subject to other obligations, if I fit in with married life; and certainly I had given and bound myself to marriage. (VIII, 1, 2)

The sequence of the above statement is important. First, he saw no possibility of living apart from relations with the opposite sex. For a baptized Christian, that would mean marriage. Then he faced Paul's admonition (1 Corinthians 7:1–9) that marriage is second-best. Augustine's fiery intensity had difficulty accepting second-best, but he admits to having chosen, thus far, the easier way. The stage appears set for a struggle between the preferred and the mediocre.

Then he shows that matters were worse than the preferred-mediocre option. The obligation to marry was not merely second-best; marriage brought with it other obligations (economic, social, political) that "left me exhausted . . . with withering demands." The whole complex of which marriage was a part, including the class obligation that accompanied marriage, threatened the notion of living the Christian life at all. In his situation, marriage promised to drown any earnest Christian commitments. What today's reader must remember is the complex burden attached to marriage in late Roman antiquity. Could he continue the misery of government oratory in Milan to support a marriage? Furthermore, to marry a person of suitable class meant no real companionship. His chosen fiancée was only ten years of age.

The challenging weight of marriage in that society had the effect of sharpening his choice to a fierce edge: Marry, and risk losing one's own peace entirely, including the Christian life; or choose baptism and philosophic seclusion, and give up sexual companionship forever. Did the promise of grace as discipline necessarily wear so severe a face?

His course was dictated by the inhumane obligations attaching to class and marriage in late Rome. Ironically, Western Christianity owes the renowned conversion of Augustine to the cultural history of Roman institutions in the late fourth and fifth century. The nature of marriage governed the radical decision he faced.[1]

An Option: The Monastic Life

Not only was the choice that faced him harsh and depressing. He also lacked knowledge of the best setting for possible celibacy, that is, knowledge of the monastic movement. Apparently neither the anchorites (isolated desert ascetics), nor the cenobites (monastics living in community) were known to him. He was struggling with the question of whether to give up marriage and sexual relationships in order to survive as a Christian. To have a community devoted to such self-denial—even, as it later turned out, his own informal group of baptized friends—was a life far more encouraging than to face such rigors alone.

Yet he was ignorant that such communities existed. The *Confessions* (VIII, 6, 14) records, astonishingly, that he had been unaware, even of Catholic Christian communities. Monastic expression was so widespread in one form or another that he surely must have recognized some forms of it. The Manichaeans themselves represented a kind of ascetic movement. During the century of Augustine's youth, Athanasius of Alexandria had introduced into the West a Christian ascetic practice that the East had already developed, stirred by the example of the hermit, Antony of Egypt.[2] Ambrose and Jerome had caught the monastic ideal in the West; Ambrose was himself patron of a community of monks outside Milan (VIII, 6, 15). Yet Augustine remembers himself as ignorant of all this.

His ignorance was remarkable. On the other hand, it showed the chaos of his pilgrimage. What would turn out to be his personal solution, Christian monasticism, was readily at hand but he never happened to encounter it. His wide inquiries passed by on another level. The information was very near, yet very far; and had it come sooner, he would likely have rejected it.

As it was, the encounter was by chance (or by providence, as he saw it) and took place within his own house at Milan. The fortuitous nature of

1. Cf. Edward Westermarck, *The History of Human Marriage* (New York: Allerton, 1922), 1:385–87; 2:207, 332, 333, 338. Also, G. Robina Quale, *A History of Marriage Systems* (New York: Greenwood, 1988), 6, 10, 167.

2. Cf. Athanasius of Alexandria, *The Life of Antony* in *Classics of Western Spirituality* (New York: Paulist Press, 1980).

that moment was underscored by the happenstance of a gaming-table in the room where he sat. On the gaming-table lay a book, the letters of Paul. A visitor from Africa, his home country—another ironic touch—visited that day, named Pontitianus, a name that suggests something to do with a bridge (pons). He held a high position at court; Augustine admits no recollection of the original reason for his coming: "I don't know what he wanted of us" (VIII, 6, 14). Again by chance, the visitor picked up the book on the table and was surprised to find it was the letters of Paul, Augustine's apostle of the humble way.

Pontitianus was himself Christian and delighted with Augustine's interest in Paul and the church. He began at once to "build a bridge" that connected the African homeland, Paul, Antony of Egypt, the Catholic way, conversion, Ambrose, and Ambrose's monks outside of Milan—a bridge to Augustine and his personal concerns. The conversation centered on the story of Antony and his astonishing life of ascetic commitment in the desert. Two of Pontitianus's fellow agents at the palace, because of a chance occurrence one afternoon, had made a remarkable commitment to the monastic way after reading Antony's life (VIII, 6, 15).

The surprising conjunction of so many items in Pontitianus's visit left Augustine devastated by the clarity of the choice that lay before him. If he had wondered how he possibly could live a life of Christian celibacy, Pontitianus's account had drawn him a crystal picture of blessed life among the monks. This image of monastic community was a fine-tuning of the church's gracious way, discovered in the story of Victorinus. The church offered to all people disciplined practice and covenant; to many like Augustine, who could not maintain Christian faith and also participate in secular life, the church offered the covenant of monasticism.

The irony of bleak ascetic denial was that it blossomed like a fruitful desert (VIII, 6, 15). He saw that the riches of Roman society were futile, while he saw chastity under the allegorical figure of a fruitful woman, abounding with children: "Continence was in no way sterile, but the fruitful mother of children, and of all the joys of you, her husband, O Lord!" The stage was set for his final contest of decision.

The Will in Conflict

The alternatives were now clear to him: embrace Catholic Christian monasticism, or continue his habitual, self-contradictory life. He found the choice exceedingly painful. The dilemma indeed set up within him the classic struggle of will that has become so associated with his name and his theology. He was acutely unresolved as to what he should do. His will was divided, reaching out in opposing directions; his motives were in conflict. The experience of this state deeply influenced all his later reflection on the human condition.

Several pages of Book VIII examine this matter of the self-conflicting will. Read in sequence, they offer a process in thought with its climax of insight: His own experience of 386 c.e. broadens into wider reflection on human nature in general. The narrative sections that recall his agony of will are VIII, 5, 10–12 (after the Victorinus section); 7, 16–18; 8, 19–20; 9, 21; and 10, 22–24. Between chapters 5 and 7 comes the story of Pontitianus's visit, which serves to focus the subsequent reflection more sharply. Augustine begins this sequence by citing the image of a prisoner:

> . . . when your man Simplicianus told me these things about Victorinus, there on the spot, I was on fire to imitate him. . . . I sighed for his very act, but I was in bondage: not to alien, outward iron, but in bondage to my own iron will. The enemy held my willing, forged of it a chain, and bound me tight. (VIII, 5, 10)

The iron will started out as a free will. Augustine goes on to say that his free will, perversely directed, had become lust (he does not, however, condemn sexuality as such). Lust, he says, became habit, and habit not resisted became necessity. The prisoner found himself chained by the necessities of his own will.

Then he complicates the image by thinking of two wills, not just the one will, or chain. The prisoner's interior will wants to break the chain of habit and be free. This will he calls the new, second, spiritual will; the other he calls the old, first, carnal will. By this move he introduces the theme of the self-conflicting will: the prisoner longs for freedom from the chain of his own habit. Yet he makes the new, freeing will more genuinely himself, the first person "I," while the chain of habit is less oneself and more the hardened product of countless earlier choices: "I was in both [spiritual and carnal wills], but I was more in what I approved in myself than in what I disapproved" (VIII, 5, 11).

He then moves to relate himself to his chain of necessity by fear. "So I feared to be free of all these heavy burdens," a panic over loss of customary meanings, burdensome though they were. Augustine knew well the crushing weight of his expansive, habitual life, yet was terrified to think of going on without it. Fear bound his will-to-be-free to his old will-to-continue.

He next moves to the image of a drowsy sleeper, struggling to rise, which further interiorizes the problem (5, 12). The sweet drowsiness tells the allure of the habitual life as well as its internal power, without giving up the force of the chain figure. The call to rise is the clarity of God's truth as he has now come to see it. The internalizing move enables him to cite Paul on the war within one's own members.

Inserting the Pontitianus story next then leads him to state a new clarity about his will (7, 16–18). The conflict cannot be rationally defended; the right choice is clear, the bad choice indefensible. It is horrible, shaming, to look upon the old will, his old way of life, shorn of any shred of reason to defend it, yet clutching on. He admits that even his sturdy intellectual pilgrimage (Books III–VII) was suspect. He had joined the Manichaeans, not because he was certain of their position, "but with an attitude of preferring it to other positions [including the Catholics'], which I did not look into conscientiously, but fought against with hostility" (VIII, 7, 17).

He had won his right of independent reasoning only by struggle. Now the admission comes that his prized critical inquiries had themselves included an element of self-serving and irrational revolt. Part of his reasoning had served his own voracious hunger for dominance.

In VIII, 7, 18, he uses the new clarity to take one more step inward in the analysis. From the soul trying to awake itself, the drowsy sleeper, he moves to a figure of internal whipping: "Did I spare any blows of judgment, whipping my soul to make it follow me, as I struggled to follow after you?" (VIII, 7, 18). Now the drowsy sleeper in self-conflict has become a full-fledged case of internal flagellation. The figure uses an external mode: a driver beating a poor beast of burden to make it go. Yet the beast is the soul, and Augustine's soul was himself, his own life. He describes a self-relation in torment, a classic image of shame and guilt as aggression turned inward. Significantly, the guilty hammering does not gain results. The soul balks in "speechless dread." When a breakthrough later comes, it is not the result of guilty coercion, but the gift of an open doorway.

Two Wills; The Scattered Will

His interior scrutiny of the will then ponders the nature of so strange a conflict. One might expect a greater gap between, say, soul and body; a broken hand may not obey the command to move. Yet even a feeble limb will obey. Surely the will can more easily obey itself. The will tells itself to follow God. Here the willing is the act itself: To will it is to do it, unlike the case of a broken hand. Yet the will will not obey itself. Why not? He concludes that the will fails to obey its own directives when it is not whole. An individual wills, but not with a full, entire will. In today's language, the person fails of clear and consistent intentionality. Only a part of the moving, working will comes into play, and the act does not get done. "Therefore, it is no monstrosity partly to will a thing, and partly not to will it, but a sickness of the intelligent soul" (VIII, 9, 21). He must conclude, therefore, that "there are two wills, because one of these is not whole, and what is present to one is lacking to the other" (VIII, 9, 21).

He has spiraled back to the notion of two wills (5, 11), but with all the reflective steps inward, the idea looks different now. The image is left behind of a prisoner struggling against a chain. The discourse refines itself toward metaphysics: A human individual can carry a duality of wills.

Immediately he is into dangerous territory. Is he not back on old, discarded Manichaean ground? He no sooner admits the experience of two wills than his mind's eye catches the picture of Mani, nodding gravely, "I told you so." He then launches at once a denial of any Manichaean contamination: "Away with them, O God . . . who declare one good nature and one evil nature, two natures and two minds, when they notice [in an individual] two wills at work deliberating" (VIII, 10, 22).

Not two natures or two substances, argues Augustine. His alternative is straightforward and hammers at the word, "I," to emphasize the unity of the one soul struggling with a self-conflicting will; "I, when I was debating whether I should now serve the Lord, my God (the way I had long proposed to do), *I* was the one who willed to do it, and *I* was the one who willed not to do it; *I* was the one" (italics added) (VIII, 10, 22).

He had learned his lesson well from the Neoplatonist books. The soul is a single, rational, and morally free individual and works out from that individual's center (granted the moving of relationships back and forth). When the will struggles with itself, the conflict is put down to something other than two substances, two individuals. He puts it down to the soul in agony with itself: "I was straining with myself, and I wasted myself [by my own straining], and this wasting away was done by me, [with my doing it] against my own will" (VIII, 10, 22). He has thinned out the more overt poetic images and arrived at the problem within the will. Having cleared his arena for analysis, he then moves to his most fruitful observations (10,

23–24). The argument here against the Manichaeans states that there cannot be two substances making up one individual because clearly the will is
sometimes pulled in *more than two* directions.

His examples are a bit wooden, but the point comes through. A person
may be pulled toward four evil choices at once: lechery, avarice, sloth,
adultery(!) and be stymied as to which to pursue. Such wavering of the will
clearly does not reflect two substances. Then he deepens his argument by
turning to a complex of *good* wills. Again his illustrations are not profound:
reading Paul, meditating on a psalm, discoursing on the Gospel. The will
can be diffused and scattered among a series of "goods."

> Therefore, if all of these equally cause delight at one single time,
> will not the diffusion of wills expand the heart of the individual,
> while the debate goes on where best to take hold? All the options
> are good and struggle with one another until one is chosen, and
> then arises a single, whole will, which before had been divided into
> many. (VIII, 10, 24)

What he shows is that not goodness but *singleness* makes the will good.
For many good things may be willed, and the will remain divided and inert,
and therefore be a wasting, evil will. Indeed, Augustine's own sins were
the sins of a "good" man. The *Confessions* has a popular reputation of
depravity; but Augustine actually fulfilled the role of a good citizen; renowned in his profession, moving through concubinage toward marriage,
supportive of his widowed mother and son, religiously earnest, loved by
friends. Yet inwardly he was wasting. He lacked singleness of will.

Yet what if a will is single, but is singly evil, focused on projects of
domination and destruction? In that case, singleness is surely not goodness.
Augustine would reply that no will can be singly evil, and says so in his
most quoted line: "You have made us for yourself and our heart is restless
until it rests in you" (I, 1, 1). No one can be single of will and be turned
against his or her own created nature and destiny: to rest in God. The evil
will has necessarily turned away from singleness toward duality, or toward
scattered fragmentation. The evil soul is always pulled between its desire
for dominance and its inherent longing for God's truth.

Scattered Will, Excess Freedom, Over-Control

At the end of 10, 24, Augustine comes to the brink of what he implies at the end of Book VII: that the goal without the way results in a divided and therefore evil will. Without using the terms, goal and way, he describes the situation in the final sentences of section 24: "So when eternity above delights us, and the sensuality of passing pleasure grips us below, the same soul wills both the one and the other, but neither with a whole will. Then the soul is dismembered with profound disgust, for it prefers one thing because of the truth, but it does not give up the other, because of daily familiar intimacy" (VIII, 10, 24).

He has come to the climax of his steps inward to the will. The scattered will, thereby the evil will, yearns always for two or more "goods," one of which is always the yearning for God. The division or dissipation is itself the evil, for it wastes and scatters the will and the individual's identity. As he found in VII, 9, 17 and 20, evil can use the face of good, even reflection on good, as a lure to pride and the divided will. Knowing God in the situation of proud diffusion is therefore not a corrective, but only participates in the agony of division.

How easily Augustine could have referred at this point (though he did not) to his abortive attempt at mystical union with God (VII, 17, 23; see also Chapter 7). He had moved inward and upward in longing toward union with the One; but the attempt had only increased the agony of division. Finally, his self-glorification upward was a shadowy figure of the original sin, the primal diffusion of will by Adam and Eve, when their reaching out to be as gods took no account of their human limits and growth, and hurled their wills into conflict. In the closing sentence of 10, 22, he tells that his condition of conflict in the will came to him as a "son of Adam."

Now, also, the topic of the will can be related to the dilemma of over-choice and excessive freedom (Chapter 7). Lunging for the goal of rest in God without a true way; presuming a godlike posture, even of wisdom; suffering a freedom that dissipates for want of gracious boundaries—all these dilemmas that followed his discovery of Neoplatonism were expressions of a scattered will. The isolated Augustine, shocked out of any confident identity, reached out with his will in numerous directions, attempting to retain and control all factors (career, philosophy, Christian baptism, marriage, sexuality), terrified to settle on a single ordering principle while letting others go. Self-expansion and fear suffered in him fragmentation of will.

Augustine's work on the broken or scattered will is an ancient clue to classical paranoia (as suggested above, page 116). When the will is uncertain of its commitments and threatened by isolation, all events take on self-reference, and a nervous attempt to understand and control them follows. The individual reaches out to justify the world, strip bare its dangers, make it safe; but the will of no single person can make the world safe. Rather the all-encompassing will breaks into fragments, reflected in the scattered life. Augustine himself lay on such a rack of opposing tendencies. Everything in his world, his yearning for God and his yearning for familiar security, threatened him with dissipation of will. His isolation, with no intentional contract or way, threatened his ability to function in a rational, daily manner. Most of all, his conflicting loves meant that he could not harmonize his affections into a single love for God, least of all through a monastic life.

The Gathered Will; Christ's Invitation

At first reading Augustine's harsh choice lay between things "above" and things "below" (10, 24). Yet, more carefully considered, even a choice of things above carried its own peculiar threat. To resolve his anguish by willfully choosing God could have been simply another great leap upward, only to fall back to earth. To choose upward could succeed for a while (be a monk with gritted teeth), only to falter and lock the will tighter as a result.

When a breakthrough did come, significantly it did not have the form of a successful mystical vision upward, such as he attempted in VII, 17, 23. The need was not first of all for a good will upward, but for singleness of will. Yet if singleness of will is the will set upon God, what alternative is there to the "good will upward"?

A clue to the alternative follows immediately upon VII, 17, 23, the fading mystical moment. At the opening of VII, 18, 24, he states what was lacking in his upward mystical striving: "I was looking for a way, a way that would nourish my strength until that strength were ready to enjoy you. But I never found that way until I embraced the mediator between God and humanity, the human Christ Jesus . . . the way and truth and life" (VII, 18, 24).

The alternative was for the will to settle itself, not upon God in God's glory, but upon the Incarnation, God-in-Christ. Grace was still the key. If God-in-splendor overextended the will and compounded its dilemma, God-veiled-in-flesh called the will within that will's potential. God Incarnate, near and inviting, offered a specific object, Christ himself in his church, to which scattered loves could gather and attach themselves. Not only so, Augustine found this Christ-in-his-church offering a most delightful and winsome call. His response to that invitation meant a life of monastic discipline, a farewell to marriage and sexual companionship; yet the invitation so embraced his heart that in August 386 he yielded everything to it.

For singleness of aim, the scattered will then found a gathering point. That is, the will needed a focused priority within love, which all other loves could follow. That priority faced not immediately upward to God, or downward to the world, but *horizontally* to a place where God and the world overlapped, to the living Incarnation, the people of God (the church) with Christ as their head. Here was a horizontal gathering point for the will, able to lead the seeker on the long pilgrimage upward to a stable, loving vision of God as Trinity.

The gathered will, then, was simply a priority in love that either sublimated other loves or gave them a fruitful order in which to function. By focusing upon Christ-in-the-church the gathered will attached itself to both flesh and spirit, with no attempt to rend the two apart. Flesh and spirit together meant a religious and ethical order of life now, in this world, under the guidance of the church, her scriptures and sacraments.

Christ's call to that way of life won Augustine's loyalty, from which he never wavered. Yet his inward life, his emotions, never found complete rest. Later in the *Confessions*, reminiscent of Psalms and quoting Paul, he cries out his need of a gathered will, and his hope in "God's right hand," the Incarnate Son of God, for final harmony:

Look at my life: it is distention! But your right hand has undergirded me in my Lord, the Son of man, mediator between you, the one, and us, the many, who are drawn out in many ways about many things. . . . So from my old ways, let me be *gathered up* to follow one. "With the past blotted out, I follow toward the laurels of my high calling": not in things that are going to be and then pass away, but "in things that lie just before me"; not distended, but extended, not by a distention, but "by my intention, I follow" . . .

But now, truly, my years are in groaning. I dissolve in times whose order I do not know; and in tumults of change my thoughts, the intimate vitals of my soul, are torn and scattered: until at length I flow together in you, cleansed and molten in the fire of your love. (italics added) (XI, 29, 39; cf. Philippians 3:13–14)

Christ as Lover

His conversion of August 386, is clear in outline: from a scattered will to a gathered will, from hesitation before Christ as way, to peaceful surrender before Christ's loving invitation. The concrete work of grace as enticing love nevertheless challenges the imagination. What can it mean that Christ came to him as lover? Some things are clear from across his personal history. From childhood he had loved the name of Christ, associated obviously with his mother and with her love for him. Also, reading Cicero had passionately summoned him to embrace the truth and love the wisdom of knowing the truth. Then in Milan with his discovery of Ambrose, he experienced renewed love for the church and for things Catholic (e.g., VI, 5, 7). Also, he had come to a climax of hope in the discovery of the Neoplatonists ("Rich, full books . . . incredible! . . . aroused in me . . . such an unbelievable fire of excitement"). He had compared them with the Scriptures. The Truth that he loved and the biblical Word of God, which he had begun to love, coincided in Christ, compounding his love and longing into one.

The search for truth had followed the guidance of illumination from *within* his own mind. What excited him and gave him a sense of Christ as lover was the approach of truth, the Word of God, from *outside* through Christ Incarnate in the church. The Word of Truth Incarnate was a divine initiative, entering concrete affairs to seek him out, not simply remaining at a lofty removal. Thereby came Christ as lover.

This coming was genuinely Catholic, not a direct anticipation of the Protestant Reformation in future centuries. The Reformation emphasized the direct, personal relationship between Christ and the believer offered through the hearing of the Word of God in Scripture. This hearing occurred, certainly, within the setting of the church and sacraments, but stressed the direct accessibility of Christ to the individual believer.[3] For

3. Cf. Martin Luther, "The Heidelberg Theses (1518)" in *Martin Luther, Selections from His Writings,* ed. John Dillenberger (Garden City, N.Y.: Doubleday, 1961), 501–3, especially Theses 19–21. Also Luther on "faith," in *What Luther Says,* ed. E. M. Plass (St. Louis: Concordia, 1959), 1:466–75, especially nos. 1374, and 1386. Cf. E. Erikson, *Young Man Luther: A Study in Psychoanalysis and History* (New York: Norton, 1958, 1962), 211–14.

Augustine, the Christ who came as lover came embodied in the church, God's people, their worship, and their life together. He experienced not so much a direct, individual relationship with Christ as savior; rather, he joined a company of those who constituted the body of Christ, with Christ himself as their head. His commitment was to the Incarnation continuing within the church. He shared in the life of the Spirit, who touched him personally and joined him to a company who, rather than finding Christ individually, met as one *in* Christ. His intensely inward, personal life, rather than relating directly to the crucified (Luther), moved upward toward a vision of Christ as God's Truth, a vision shared with all the saints. Thus his meeting of Christ in the church blended with his philosophical passion for truth; the meeting did not initiate a continuing individual relationship to Christ, as of person to person.

The Catholic sense of Christ in the church works clearly in the passage concerning the allegorical figure of Continence cited above. Continence is a fruitful mother, the church monastic, with many children by her husband, Christ. Augustine is invited to become one of her company of ascetic children, bearing the fruits of orderly love. Rather than establish an individual relationship with Christ, he is urged to join a family group bonded together by love, all belonging through Continence to her husband and Lord.

The figure of family then yields to one of greater intensity in Christ as lover. Even initially, the Christ of his childhood, of philosophical truth, and of Catholic practice had been for him a figure one could respond to with love. All these had contributed to a complex of feeling that he calls above his "new will," struggling to rise and be free. The winsome call pressed him strongly. At the same time, the anguished need for sexual companionship denied him access; here were feelings that demanded some compensation within the new will, if it was to succeed. Christ had already come as love through the church, through his mother, through the writings of Paul, the figures of Ambrose and Simplicianus, the story of Victorinus, the witness of Pontitianus, through occasions of sacrament and worship, and specifically through the cultic figure of one who humbled himself to bring eternal life to others (I, 11, 17). This loving appeal of Christ intensified itself into the irresistible call of passionate lover. Augustine's agony of sexuality and marriage resolved itself through a spiritualized version of passion in another way. Thus Augustine cries out to Christ, the bridegroom, to exercise his most ardent and joyous claim upon the soul:

> *Age, domine, fac! excita et revoca nos, accende et rape, flagra, dulcesce: amemus, curramus.*

> Go on, Lord, do it! Arouse us and call us back. Set us on fire and
> seize us. Be fragrant. Be sweet. Let us love! Let us run! (VIII, 4, 9)

Even in his intensely personal cry Augustine mutes individualism by the
plural pronouns: "Arouse us," "Let us."

As if in response to such a cry (although not in the immediate context
of the passage), the allegorical figure of fruitful Continence calls upon Augustine to receive Christ himself as a gift: "Throw yourself on him! Do not
be afraid. He will not pull away and let you fall. Throw yourself, be confident. He will receive you. He will make you whole!" This special coming
of Christ for the healing of his people through love later separated Augustine
from the views of his archopponent, Pelagius. In Pelagius's view, no new
creation or rebirth of the soul came to the Christian through the agency
of Christ and the Holy Spirit. Natural free will alone sufficed to follow
biblical instruction, exercise love for God, and win full devotion and salvation (*Nature and Grace*, XI–XII). For Augustine, if the singular impact of
Christ as lover of the soul fell away, the heart of the Gospel vanished and
with it the re-creating power of the Spirit. In the earliest and most moving
of his long series of anti-Pelagian treatises, *The Spirit and the Letter* (412
c.e.), he says:

> . . . besides creation, with the gift of freedom to choose, and besides
> the teaching [on] . . . how to live, humanity receives the Holy
> Spirit, whereby arises in one's soul the delight in and the love of
> God, the supreme and changeless Good. This gift is . . . earnest of
> God's free generosity that one may be kindled afire in heart to cleave
> to one's Creator, [and] kindled in mind to come within the shining
> of the true light.

His following sentences, including a quotation from Romans 5:5, clearly
invoke his own biographical experience as told in the *Confessions*, especially
his need for a way, and for the love actually to follow in that way:

> Free choice alone, if the way of truth is hidden, achieves nothing
> but sin; and when . . . the true way has begun to appear clearly,
> still no doing, no devotion, no good life is there, unless [that true
> way] also is delighted in and loved. And in order that it may be
> loved, "the love of God is shed abroad in our hearts," not by the

free choice whose spring is in ourselves, but "through the Holy Spirit which is given us." (*The Spirit and the Letter* 5 [iii])

Once God-in-Christ had come to him in compelling love, his surrender to a new life simply replaced, if it did not completely abolish, the old agonized division.

The Garden

The deep shift in loyalties took place, by his recollection, in a garden attached to the house that he and Alypius were renting at Milan. Suspension, wavering, hesitation were still the core of his condition. He acknowledges that God was "in your severe mercy doubling the whips of fear and shame." Yet the more a new future pressed in on him, "the more I was struck with terror" to think of the old life gone (VIII, 11, 25).

Significantly, no negative denial resolved the struggle, certainly not violence of the soul against itself. Rather, Augustine cried out for God to end it. "Look at me! Let it be now! Let it be done!" Violence did not resolve the conflict. Neither side of his divided will forcibly blotted out the other. All the whipping and fear did not bring the solution. Rather, a gift was given. He actually threw himself down under a fig tree and sobbed great tears; he continued to cry out something like, "You, Lord, how long? . . . Why not now?"

Then with neither side of the choice a clear victor in his own willing, a third something began to happen. Just as when the first light of dawn comes and is present, and one is not sure when it began, so Augustine found himself doing things that were not part of the previous dark moment. The next events therefore appear arbitrary: He listened to a rhythmic chant from some child next door: "Take up, read; take up, read." He rushed back to Alypius. He opened Paul's letters. He read the section where his eyes first fell, up through an exhortation not to live a frenzied wildness of life, but to "put on Christ." Then "a kind of light of freedom from care poured into my heart, and all darkness of wavering fled" (VIII, 12, 29; cf. Romans 13:11–14).

Such material can clearly be read in more than one way. The question has claimed much attention whether the garden event records historical detail, or whether it is a literary construct.[4] Leaving that debate aside for the moment makes room for two other approaches of a literary sort: (1) reading the garden account as complete in itself, an astonishing, vertical intrusion of grace; (2) reading the account horizontally in the tapestry of a sequential narrative, Confessions I–VIII, and beyond.

Both vertical and horizontal readings are important. The vertical reading separates 12, 28–29, and reads it as testimony to the intersection of God's grace from above. In this regard two things may be said of grace: first, it may not be portrayed directly because grace is not a thing among things, but the basis for all things. Second, since grace is a freely chosen act of God, it cannot be accounted for in a chain of cause and effect; it is not produced by a set of prerequisites. To portray an event in which grace moved, therefore, means to portray secondary items in an arbitrary happening. A cluster of disconnected acts takes place. Suddenly a child chants. Suddenly a man takes this as a message to open the Bible. Verses jump out that would not have spoken with the same power yesterday, or last week, or last year. A light of freedom from care comes within. Such a vertical reading sees the freedom of an act of grace; author and reader honor God's mystery.

Yet the vertical reading alone becomes heavily one-sided. It takes the little cluster of arbitrary events and makes them into a norm for the reader, tries to trace in them a formula for what is clearly free grace. Augustine never attempted to make his moment of conversion in the garden normative for others. The vertical reading alone, setting out to underscore the free mystery of grace, segments the moment to itself and ends up saying, "Grace is like that!" The horizontal reading considers the narrative all the way from Confessions I and includes VIII, 12, 28–29 within it. The act of grace was free and not necessitated; yet it would not have taken place without the struggle with his home and his mother, without the choice and agony of vocation, without the church, the brothers and sisters, the leaders and teachers, the scriptures, the biblical saga of centuries, the sacraments. Nothing necessitates grace. On the other hand, grace does not occur apart from the narrative of grace, the story of a way, in scripture and in the Confessions itself. One characteristic of a narrative is that it can weave freely chosen events into a reasonable, unfolding order without becoming deterministic.

---

4. Compare, for example, Leo Ferrari, The Conversions of St. Augustine, the Saint Augustine Lecture, 1982 (Villanova: The Augustinian Institute, 1984), 50ff. Also, Courcelle, "Le 'Tolle, lege'; fiction littéraire et réalité," in Recherches, 188–202.

Grace is not determined; but on the other hand, grace always includes a landscape, a setting, a geography, that includes all the creation, but also a particular people, a visible way of life, a public set of symbols.

What happened in the garden happened to itself. Yet it had always been happening. It was no foregone conclusion. Yet it was part and parcel of crying for baptism as a child, of rebelling against excessive expectations, of reading Cicero, of questioning the Manichaeans, of hearing Ambrose, of reading the Neoplatonists, of hearing Simplicianus tell Victorinus's story, of hearing Pontitianus tell Antony's. Grace is not seen; but the landscape of grace indeed is seen. The landscape does not necessitate the grace; yet the grace always works through the whole narrative landscape, even surprisingly.

The intersection of the two readings, vertical and horizontal, falls just at the point of the Pauline quotation that Augustine seized upon (Romans 13:13–14). Read vertically, the quotation is an intersection into Augustine's affairs that on this day, at this hour, articulated a movement of grace: "Not in revels and drinking bouts, not in pleasures of bed and lewd acts, not in striving effort and jealous rivalry, but put on the Lord Jesus Christ and do not make forethought for the flesh with inexhaustible desires" (VIII, 12, 29).

Read horizontally, the quotation astonishingly pulls together major themes from the entire story, beginning to end: "revels and drinking bouts," his adolescence, especially the wild year when he was sixteen. "Pleasures of bed and lewd acts . . . striving effort and jealous rivalry" suggest the two foremost problems intertwining through his adult life: how to deal with sexuality and marriage, how to deal with driving ambition. The final phrase of the two verses tells his customary response to his lifelong problems, making "forethought for the flesh with inexhaustible desires." The more his expansive soul plotted to keep his security intact, the more he found himself anxiously desiring. Instead, "put on the Lord Jesus Christ." Despite his intense inner life, the key is finally not to seek Christ within, but to put on the Incarnate one and his singular love, to "put on" the Christian people, their scriptures and their sacraments, as a gracious practice from without. Hedged in by authority that could be trusted and struggled with, Augustine found his raging contradictions within gradually dispersed. The landscape of grace in his own story converges and ties a knot at Romans 13:13–14, read horizontally across the *Confessions*. Salvation is both a gift (vertical) and a process (horizontal).

That quotation, gathering up thirty-two years of personal history, yet peculiarly powerful at one single time and place, articulated the voice of Christ's love that called him, bound him, and freed him. Not only so, that quotation marked the point at which the language of Incarnation finally met and claimed him. His lifelong agony with language found a solution, in language, in a passage from Paul. Chapter 8 has already indicated how in the Incarnation the language of personal religious discipline and the language of academic learning knit together. In the Incarnation, Christ was universal truth, the goal of wisdom, but also Christ was the way *to* the goal through the particular, disciplined language of church, sacraments, and scriptures. The sophisticated language of wisdom must make its first humble move through the singular language of Christ. The world of discourse, complex and simple, was finding healing in the disciplined language of Word made flesh.

What was added in the garden account focusing upon Romans 13:13–14 was an element of energizing delight. He had cried out in prayer (VIII, 4, 9), "Let us love! Let us run!" Somehow the timing of the reading in Romans caused that passage to be a response to his plea. "Put on the Lord Jesus Christ." His wavering ended, and a light of tranquillity poured into his heart, which was now gathered in love of Christ. The language of Incarnation had offered not only a disciplined Way; it offered a compelling nearness in the Word made words. The vitality of God's love had drawn near, and called him winsomely, through Christ, church, sacrament, scripture, and people of God. At last, in these words of God's love he had found the foundation of the language of praise long sought. This language of praise was ordinary words he had always known, but now they came with the twin gifts of integrity and humility that enabled him to use them.

This language of praise and Incarnation had two sides: discipline and call, rule and passion. Love was both ordering and energizing; faith was both public and private. The language of authority, the two-sided language of Incarnation, was the language of love.

The Christ of the Exchange

Following the garden conversion, and more explicitly as the years of his church leadership grew (391, priest at Hippo; 395, bishop), Augustine came to think of the loving Christ as what tradition has called the Christ of the exchange. The idea of exchange Christology became highly popular in

Eastern Christianity, especially so, for example, with Athanasius of Alexandria (d. 373 c.e.), theological architect of the doctrine of the Trinity.[5] The idea of an exchange in Christ stated that the divine Christ became human in order that humanity might become divine. Christ humbled himself, made the divine truth accessible through an earthly story, in order that earthly folk would share in the qualities of God. Thus, for humanity to become divine did not mean to equal or displace God, but to participate, as appropriate for finite humanity, in God's characteristics of love, mercy, and justice. Christ assumed human nature in order that all human nature should show forth the character of God, a human divinity.

Augustine showed glimmers of the exchange motif in Incarnational passages of his early *Dialogues* (Chapter 8 above, page 130), but the theme came to its true prominence in his long series of sermons on the book of Psalms. Did he indeed find Christ the lover in the Psalms of the pre-Christian Hebrew scriptures? Since the Old Testament was for him simply the New Testament concealed in figure, image, and allegory, then the believer searched the beloved Psalter for both the voice and person of Christ, with the assurance of finding him there. For example, in his Good Friday sermon on Psalm 22, Augustine deals with the difficult opening verse, "O God, my god, why have you forsaken me?" (*Expositions in Psalms* 22, 3 [Latin, 21]). Obviously, if Christ is God, the second person of the Trinity, how can he be forsaken by God? How can he forsake himself? Augustine's interpretation is that here the Crucified cries out in the person of his body, the church (He became who we are . . .). The church knows herself separated from God by sin; Christ assumes the church's humanity in love and cries out her cry, taking her suffering up into himself in the hope of healing (. . . that we may become as He is). In a single opening verse, Psalm 22 thus identifies the compassionate Christ, the church, and their mutual suffering.

Christ as lover thus emerges in more rich dark colors in the sermons on Psalms, contrasting with emphasis on tranquil surrender and light, as in the garden. Indeed, some passages play homiletically on the anguish Christ has to pay in rebuff by his people, finally to win them to his love. Such a passage occurs in the sermon on Psalm 100 (Latin, 99) in Augustine's expansion of the simple phrase, "The Lord, he is God." As he climactically urges the people: "The Lord, he himself is God: this one whom you have

---

5. Cf. his *On the Incarnation* (Crestwood: St. Vladimir's Seminary, 1953, 1989), e.g., II, 8–9; III, 13. For Augustine's focus at this point, cf. William Babcock, "The Christ of the Exchange: A Study in the Christology of Augustine's *Enarrationes in Psalmos*" (Ph.D. diss., Yale University, 1972).

crowned with thorns; you have daubed with spit; you have pierced with the lance; you have fixed with nails; you have set guards at the tomb; this one himself is God!" (*Expositions in Psalms* 100 [99], 15). In the intimate, liturgical, household setting with his people Augustine poured out the personal anguish involved in Christ's invitation to his beloved.[6] His powerful oratory, now in the service of scriptural comment, caused wonder at his preaching.

In such a passage as above, Augustine had come to know through the severities of church leadership in North Africa the long pitched struggle of love between God and turbulent humanity. The marked difference between the early and late Augustine was indeed his expectation of immediate growth in grace contrasted with the burdened pastor, wrestling with the long-suffering love and staying power of Christ, not only for himself, but for his people. The way of Christ's beloved, the church, loomed long and torturous ahead.

With this growing sense of continuing struggle, Augustine's two themes of gracious way and call took on a richer and more deeply intertwined meaning. Indeed, the exchange theme, to become human in order to render divine, rested upon the interplay of these two. That Christ was incarnate in his people, their authorities, scriptures, and sacraments, and the language of these, meant that he was veiled within these concrete realities, hidden from minds and spirits in no way ready to grasp him directly. The "flesh" of bread and cup, of scriptural page, of spoken sermon, of bishop, priest, or of simple Christian, in which Christ was Incarnate, presented a humbling veil that the believer could not penetrate except by the long pilgrimage of grace. Christ became present in hiddenness, restraining the worshiper within an order of love as discipline, the long way around.

Yet the very fleshly media that veiled Christ, from another point of view, made him available. Bread and cup, scripture and sermon, presented the visible invitation of Christ to come to him as love, fleshly and accessible. From one side, the Incarnation was boundary; from the other, invitation. Likewise, the language of Incarnation, the Word as words, was both boundary and invitation. As Augustine came to know the lifelong labor of the Christian's growth in love, the counterpoint and mystery of these two, the Lord's veiling and yet his availability, set the horizon of the years of wrestling grace.

In the long pilgrimage of those years (395–430), language came into increasing significance. The Incarnation in the church had become the key to fullness and wholeness in language, as shown above. Yet in the early

---

6. Cf. Babcock, "The Christ of the Exchange," 107–9.

years after his baptism Augustine hoped that language, for the true disciple, could give way increasingly to direct inner contemplation of the Wisdom of God (*The Teacher* 38, 45–46). Even a full ten years after his conversion, he proposed that the Scriptures would not be personally necessary for a Christian who had found true love of God and neighbor, and he urged disciples to move "quickly" through all temporal vehicles (including language) to arrive at a purer vision of truth (*Christian Doctrine* I, xxxiv, xxxix).

Long years as pastor-bishop changed his understanding. Worshipers must continue, again and again, to gather around sacrament, scriptures, proclamation, and all the language of faith, wherein Christ is at once offered and veiled. The way is long in existence before such linguistic sharing can give way to pure inner vision. In effect, despite his Neoplatonist goal, language became for Augustine the Christian's shaping and forming mediator, like the Word made flesh himself, not to be dissolved into direct experience and apprehension. There is a touch of contemporaneity here. The chastened pastor Augustine approximated, on one side of it, a twentieth-century view that language is a medium in which we must live, that no pure experience can dissolve its public contours.[7] For Augustine, this medium of language was a temporary necessity with an eternal goal; for some contemporary thinkers, it is unending. The results in practice recall one another: Language, for Augustine, opened a humble and inviting access to what could be fully known only after long journeying. So with Augustine and other church fathers, the Incarnation celebrated the style called *sermo humilis* (the humble word), the unadorned words of and about Christ, yet passionately declared—a summons to a public, yet hidden mystery of salvation.[8]

He had come far since the discovery that excessive freedom was the severest bondage, was indeed original sin. Adhering to God as love's priority proved a more extended way than he had imagined. At times the stress was more than he could bear.[9] His way could not have continued to open up before him but for the savor and delight he knew in Christ as lover and His passionate invitation to Truth.

---

7. E.g., Martin Heidegger: "Poetry is the establishing of being by means of the word"; "Hölderlin and the Essence of Poetry," in *Existence and Being* (Chicago: Henry Regnery, 1949), 281. Cf. Robert W. Funk, *Language, Hermeneutic, and Word of God* (New York: Harper and Row, 1966), 39.

8. E. Auerbach, *Literary Language and Its Public in Late Latin Antiquity and in the Middle Ages* (New York: Pantheon Books, 1965), 33–43.

9. E.g., *Letter* 95, 3: "O if I had wings like a dove, I would fly away and be at rest" (Psalm 55:6). Cf. Brown, *Augustine*, 243.

Section 3

The City of God . . .
(anti-Donatist, anti-Pagan)

10

Grace Universal:
The World's New Freedom

(*Confessions* IX)

[Monica] and I were standing alone, leaning in at a certain window, overlooking a garden within the house that gave us lodging, there at Ostia on the Tiber. Far from the throngs of people and after the hardship of a long journey, we were refreshing ourselves for the voyage ahead. We were talking together very sweetly . . . asking between us about the present truth, which you are, [O God,] and the quality of the eternal life of the saints, which "neither eye has seen, nor ear has heard, nor has risen in the human heart" [I Corinthians 2:9].

Yet we did open the mouths of our hearts to the lofty flowing of your fountain, "the fountain of life" [Psalm 35:10] . . . so that barely moistened [by that fountain] as our capacity would permit, we might reflect on how so great [a quality of eternal life] could be.

. . . we moved mentally, one level at a time, through the whole bodily reality, even the heavens themselves, where sun and moon and stars shine above the earth; and as we were ascending, always inwardly, in thinking and speaking and wondering at your works, we came into our own minds and passed above them: We touched the region of never-failing fruitfulness, where you feed Israel forever on the food of truth; and life there is the Wisdom, through which all these things are made; . . . and this Wisdom itself is not made, but is just as it was, and so will be always . . .

And while we speak and hunger toward it, we touch that Wisdom, modestly, with the whole thrust of the heart.

Then we sighed and left there the "first fruits of the Spirit" [Romans 8:23], and we returned to the noise of our mouths, where a word both begins and ends. (IX, 10, 23–24)

Since Christ as lover had come to Augustine in and through the church, the final portion of the narrative *Confessions*, Book IX, tells in various ways about the church and his newfound place in it. Not surprisingly, the figure of Monica dominates much of the book (as in the above passage), since his reconciliation with the church introduced a new level of relationship and reconciliation with her. Book IX finds Augustine remembering (in 399 or 400, thirteen years after the events) that he zealously intended a closeness to the Catholic church and her doctrines from the time of the garden conversion (e.g., 5, 13). Undoubtedly, that memory is correct. Although after the conversion he went into private retreat with his household and friends (to Cassiciacum) and did not become a priest until 391, still he moved directly to baptism on his first postconversion Easter (387), and his stay in Rome through most of 388 showed (for example, in *The Morals of the Catholic Church*, I, 1, 2) an intent to work hand-in-hand with the functioning, visible church.[1] His clarity that the church would be his center for both religion and philosophy set the direction for his entire future career (cf. his *True Religion*, written 389–391).

His goal, to live and labor effectively for the Catholic church, fit hand in glove with his newly won Neoplatonist convictions. The Neoplatonists had convinced him of one single source of universal truth. (The discovery fit Cicero's admonition, read at age eighteen, not to pursue this or that sect, but wisdom itself, universally valid; see Chapter 3.) How better could the philosophy of a single universal truth harmonize with religion than with a single worldwide church, drawn without discrimination from all nations and races? For now he had realized that the specific language of Christ, scriptures, and church was an entranceway into a language of universal philosophical truth, including academic rhetoric and dialectic, valid for all people. Augustine came to see in the worldwide unity of the Catholic movement an entranceway into the worldwide unity of wisdom. His vision had some naïveté; yet his intent was just: The love that had come to him

---

1. J. Burnaby, *Amor Dei: A Study of the Religion of St. Augustine* (London: Hodder and Stoughton, 1938), 88. Cf. Brown, *Augustine*, 132.

through grace was available to all nations; therefore, a genuinely Catholic church was the agent of a worldwide, unifying love. Beyond sectarianism lay one truth, one grace, one freedom. People from across the earth (as he knew it) could come to the generosity of God through this one, unified Catholic body (*True Religion*). Universal grace through Christ was the gift of new freedom to the world. *Confessions* IX introduces his zeal for this hope.

Little wonder that he later confronted the sectarian Donatists in his North African homeland as those who denied the essence of grace. They denied the validity of church and sacraments anywhere except in their own provinces. Augustine's integration of philosophical and religious visions meant that no one provincial church could claim a unique hold on the truth; only a worldwide church of great human diversity could represent universal truth. Further, no one provincial church could represent world-unifying love; only a church open to all people could embody unifying love as the key to universal truth.

Strands of the Confessions Story Joined

In order to signal the joining of worldwide truth with religion, the final section of the *Confessions* narrative, Book IX, pulls together all the major strands of the previous eight books into the celebration of a single, inclusive church. Membership in this universal doorway of the spirit, the church, gathers up all the previous themes: the freeing of his bound will, the restoring of broken and empty language, the humility of leaving his oratorical vocation, his baptism, his friendships, his search for rest, his conquest of Manichaeanism, his gaining of intellectual integrity, his struggle to lay hold of the Incarnation, his escape from philosophical pride, his tears of love. Ambrose remains pivotal, as in the preceding account, and also remains strangely distant. Monica receives honor and gratitude, as his entry into the church brings her story to fruition. Further, as the book opens with gratitude for the freeing of his will, so the rest of the book deals, by contrast, with his new captivity of will, his bondage to God in love, through the church's Incarnate Christ as lover.

Inevitably, such a summary links back to the first eight books through an opening statement of the *Confessions'* central theme: the freeing of his will from its bondage to evil.

"O Lord, I am your servant, I am your servant and the son of your handmaid [i.e., perhaps the church, though the suggestion of Monica lies close to the surface, who is called "your handmaid" in II, 3, 7, and IX, 7, 15]. You have broken my chains; I will sacrifice to you the offering [*hostia*, the host] of praise." . . . What evil was not . . . of my own will? . . . The whole [of my salvation] was not to will what I was willing, but rather to will what you were willing. But where, then, was [my will] for those long years of time, and from what deep and secret hiding was my free choice called forth in an instant? . . . [And he recalls then the victorious savor of his new life that won him:] How sweet it suddenly became for me to be deprived of the sweets of folly! (IX, 1, 1; Ps. 116:16–17)

His will was freed from self-centeredness by the public humility of baptism and discipline. His will was freed from burdensome goals, far removed, by the sweet availability of Christ, through church, scripture, sacrament, Spirit. His love no longer sought his own scatteredness or destruction (love of evil), but focused on loving God in God's church, her traditions, and her people. His recorded baptism at Easter, 387 (IX, 6, 14), fulfills his frustrated baptism in childhood (I, 11, 17–18), and recalls the baptism of his dying friend (IV, 4, 8). Indeed, the whole *Confessions* story is the story of his baptism, the Spirit baptizing him throughout the whole of his restless frustration, with the baptismal climax in the garden and his actual baptism that Easter. His friendships since his teen years adorn his story with his power to win others. In this final book (IX) he and his friends now enter the church and monastic life together (IX, 3–4), and where this cannot occur, as with Verecundus, parting is agony. The deaths of two friends, Verecundus and Nebridius, are recorded (IX, 3, 5–6), and stand in contrast to his Manichaean experience of a friend's death (IV, 4, 8). After the garden experience and prior to baptism he retires with household, friends, and pupils to an estate, Cassiciacum, for study and reflection and preparation for Catholic membership. His study there with his associates, captured in what he calls "literary work" (the Cassiciacum *Dialogues*, the *Soliloquies*) had the flavor, he admitted, of the schools (IX, 4, 7). This reflection and writing picks up the long theme of intellectual integrity, while the Cassiciacum "days of rest" (IX, 4, 12) symbolize the profound rest "in you, Lord," for which the intellectual quest and the entire *Confessions* yearns (I, 1, 1).

Book IX introduces the celebrative theme of singing, his fascination with the Psalms and the current hymns of the church, transforming and elevating the long theme of rhetoric and empty language in the previous books. His commentary on Psalm 4 (IX, 4, 8–11) repeatedly contrasts that psalm with the poor substance he had found with the Manichaeans, while he despairs of making clear to them the virtues of the biblical text. As in his biography, he found a victory over the Manichaeans through the Neoplatonists, whose lofty principles he finds echoing through the Psalms. "Oh, in peace! Oh, in That One, the Selfsame! . . . I will take my rest" (IX, 4, 11; Psalm 4:8). The unchanging One of Neoplatonism is the giver of rest and confidence in the Psalms. Yet along with Neoplatonist insights are constraints against the boasting pride to which philosophers fall prey: "the Psalms of David . . . which allow *no inflated spirit* . . . I was on fire to recite them, if I could, across the whole orb of the earth against the haughtiness of human-kind!" (IX, 4, 8). The Psalms, a favorite source of his preaching for years to come, catch up together his entire odyssey from the struggle with the Manichaeans to his grasp of Neoplatonism to his homecoming with the humble Christ.

Finally, the death of Monica with his extensive tribute to her (IX, 8–13) not only completes the saga of her role in the biography, but his grief for her makes comment, by implication, on the amorphous grief felt for his dead friend (IV, 7, 12) and his rejected concubine (VI, 15, 25). Linked to these is his touching account of his son, Adeodatus, his baptism, and early death to follow (IX, 6, 14); the brief account offers the final tragic note in the whole matter of the concubine and his inconclusive relation to her.

The climactic treatment of Monica, his mother, concludes a chapter that honors his mother, the church. Monica, in addition to herself, suggests the presence of the church, her center of loyalty from the first, toward which she inclined Augustine with all her power. The final six chapters of Book IX conclude her personal story while opening the account of Augustine's church life toward his new future.

Certainly, Monica is distinguishable from the church that is now firmly Augustine's own. She recalls the church; yet the church is greater than she. Augustine came to her church, but in his own way. Honoring her and joining the church signaled a successful separation from, and return to, Monica. He challenged the mother and church of his childhood in order to find the deeper truth within both. The separation, even in the new relationship, shows itself in Monica's desire to die (IX, 10, 26; 11, 28): "Son . . . I now take delight in not anything in this life [including presum-ably, her relationship to him]." Augustine stammers his reply, caught be-tween the "rightness" of her preference for heaven and, on the other hand, what such a statement means about her feelings toward him, plus his own sense of impending loss: "What I answered her to these things, I do not adequately recall" (IX, 11, 27). In one true sense, her work had been supremely crowned with happiness (seeing him in the church), and she is ready to go. In another sense, she had been replaced. Her goal for him had become her substitute.

Monica's power of right self-sacrifice endures to the end; her task is over. She dismisses her long desire to be buried in her homeland, next to her husband's body (IX, 11, 28). In effect, she says goodbye. Augustine, now caught up in her church (but which he accepted on his own terms), grieves for her, honors her, yet objectifies her. He requests prayers for her sins and speaks of his parents, not as mother and father, but as those

> through whose flesh you brought me into this life . . . [called] my parents in this transitory light, my brothers [sic] under you, Father, in our Catholic Mother, and my fellow citizens in the eternal Jerusalem. (IX, 13, 37)

Augustine and Monica rediscovered each other, through redirected love, in God; that is, within a horizon larger than themselves.

The Vision at Ostia

The suggestive, yet separable relation between Monica and the church helps in understanding the vision at Ostia. The moment was one of shared, transcendent awareness through a conversation concerning eternal life (see the account of the vision at the head of this chapter). Stopping over at Ostia before the sea voyage, mother and son experienced one quiet day a mutual movement of their minds through many levels of the world and into a Plotinian wonder before the Truth. The moment immediately recalls Augustine's previous such ecstasy (VII, 17, 23), a fragrant moment when he was nevertheless "struck back," to which the occasion at Ostia can be contrasted. Another motif from Books I–VIII, the contemplative ecstasy, thus enters and finds at least partial resolution here. Monica is herself— and also suggests the church. Insofar as she is church, Augustine's glimpse of eternal truth occurs within the church setting; that makes all the difference from the previous ecstasy in Book VII.

Mother and son were standing, leaning in at a certain window that looked upon a garden within the house where they were staying. (The garden also surely suggests the church.) The historical details of this description may well be correct; nevertheless, they fit remarkably into a symbolic occasion as well. Inevitably, the garden must be *within* the house, not only because typical of some Roman houses,[2] but because the garden of the spirit is *within* one's human "house." Spiritual flowering comes from looking within one's own mind, which Augustine and Monica move one another to do. Augustine and Monica were at the house, pausing in their journey, resting. Just so, a pause in the journey through time, removed from outward throngs of sensuous distractions, truly refreshes and lodges the soul, which rests within itself. Only by such rest can the voyage through time later be continued. The Ostian scene as poetic image thus draws the reader into the intellectual movement that took place there, between the two persons.

By speaking "sweetly" about truth and the saints' eternal life they finally sense, above themselves, that Wisdom or Order, or Word, the true standard by which things rise and fall in their imperfection. The creaturely sounds of words were being guided by their inner sense of accuracy and perfection, until that standard itself became the object of their reflection. Congenial to that Wisdom is the truest element in themselves: the free rational judgment of the intellect, which by considering its own powers within can glimpse Wisdom, the source or standard above it that illumines it. The glimpse is therefore intellectual. Yet Augustine speaks of gaining it "with the whole thrust of the heart." The heart plays the crucial role since the Wisdom or Word of God appears only to that intellect directed by the love of the whole person. A moment of loving worship of God's truth turns the intellect inward and upward toward the source of its power. That truth as an enduring standard remains reliable, above time; but then to turn back into time and attempt to speak the truth means wrestling with "the noise of our mouths, where a word both begins and ends"—a good moment to recognize how starkly Augustine saw language, even at its best, as dependent upon inward illumination.

How does this glimpse of That Which Is differ from the one recorded in VII, 17, 23? Each of them knows a moment of ecstasy followed by a difficult return into time. Yet the experience in VII fit into an attitude of intellectual self-importance and prattling on "like an expert," while the experience in

---

2. Cf. Brown, *Augustine,* 26; his characterization of late Roman houses "built from the inside out."

IX emphasizes the hope of recurrence, and of knowing again in the future such spiritual riches. In VII, the negative gains emphasis as much as the positive: "Then truly I saw your invisible things. . . . But I had no strength to fix my sight, my weakness was struck back" (VII, 17, 23); "my mind's eye gazed into your intangible principles . . . but something pushed me back! I was seeing what I could not deeply contemplate, because of my darkness" (VII, 20, 26). The balanced phrasing articulates the two-sided experience: good / bad, gained / lost. In IX, the experience is not divided. The ecstasy, though passing, stands as token or earnest of a future delight now already assured. The glimpse is not of what one falls away from, but of what one is moving toward. Thus, "we were talking together very sweetly, 'forgetting the things that were behind and stretching out toward those that lie before'" (IX, 10, 23; Philippians 3:13). Even in returning to ordinary speech, they do not sense loss so much as postponement, since "we . . . left there the 'first fruits of the Spirit'" (IX, 10, 24; Romans 8:23). The first fruits promise more; they will know in the future an even greater abundance.

What makes the difference? In VII he is isolated, trying self-taught spirituality, subject to a divided will. In IX he relates to the church, whose reality is suggested by Monica. He does not proceed alone. He has to deal with the constraints of the other, in this case, those many others, the church, to whom he belongs, with whom he must work, and who will go with him. Corporate discipline curbs vanity. Yet along with constraint, Monica and the church make the life of truth near and accessible. Language is a veil over the Word, but that veil is also the point at which the Word draws near. A worldwide church and an age-long tradition vivify the promise; all move together confidently toward that future delight. Respect and love for each other signal the deeper love toward which they aspire. Members embody for one another a way by which to go.

Thus as the experience in VII concludes with only a wistful "memory and yearning, as if by . . . fragrance, for what I could not yet feast upon," so the parallel in IX concludes with, in effect, a hopeful program of contemplation, realized in the church, perfected only at the final resurrection. This hopeful program is governed by a conditional "if," repeated throughout the paragraph:

> If the turbulence of the flesh were to fall silent, silent the *phantasiae* of earth and water and air; . . [if] the soul itself should be silent and pass beyond itself . . . and [God] alone should speak, not through these things, but through [Godself] . . . and if this should

continue and all other visions be far removed, is this not, "Enter into the joy of our Lord!"? (IX, 10, 25)

If one will follow the way of the Spirit, finally at the resurrection, joy will be complete. Plotinian ecstasy in the presence of the church leaves one, not divided, but filled with hope.

Insofar as Monica is herself in this account, the moment is her goodbye to Augustine, the announcement of her imminent death. He cannot withhold her from the full wonder of delight, which they together have barely glimpsed. Insofar as Monica recalls the church, the moment is a promise that in the church's company he will himself find his way toward that joy. The sequence returns to the high significance of the way, the *via*, celebrated in Books VII and VIII. Christ is very near as Way for the people because he is incarnate in the worldwide church, open and accessible to all. The grace of his Incarnation remains crucial, echoing the important struggle of Augustine in Books VII and VIII to receive this doctrine into his life. Book IX echoes and verifies the import of the Incarnation in showing that Augustine's two closest friends, Nebridius and Alypius, overcame obstacles and received the doctrine prior to baptism (IX, 3, 6; 4, 7). Surely Augustine must have preceded them in accepting the Word made flesh.

The way made all the difference. Christ Incarnate was himself the way. The church and her language continued to offer his Incarnation. His worldwide church, celebrated throughout Book IX, therefore constituted a way of grace and hope for all people, their liberation from terror and their learning to love. The vision at Ostia stood witness that a Plotinian Augustine had found the church as way.

The Donatists

Some six years later in 393 Augustine, long since returned to North Africa, and now a priest (later a bishop), adopted a stand against a local Christian movement called by their opposition the party of the Donatists.[3] Controversy embroiled him and still does concerning the issue. For Augustine, the Donatist error was clear: This local movement considered themselves the only valid church of Christ. The Donatists not only repudiated the Catholic

3. Brown, *Augustine*, 226.

church (a minority body in Augustine's city of Hippo), but appeared likely to eliminate it, with social leverage on their side. For Augustine, any exclusive sect violated the worldwide grace and love of the Catholic body and could not be permitted to force the Catholics out. The church must be open, offering all the grace of God.

Yet how could Augustine oppose another church in the name of love and grace? The issue finally involved heartbreak and bitterness, while leading at the same time to wide clarification of Augustine's theology of church and sacrament.

Donatist Christianity had been born out of violence and persecution in North Africa and brought elements of that legacy with it into later dealings. The group claimed to be the only valid Christian successors of those martyrs who had stood against Rome's persecution of the church. The last effort to eliminate Christianity had come under Diocletian (303 c.e.). Numerous North African bishops had evidently cooperated with the persecutors, at least to the extent of handing over (traditio) copies of the scriptures and liturgical vessels to Roman officials (thereby becoming traditores, or traitors, to the Christian cause). Others had held firm. The Donatists had assumed the tempting burden of continuing this, the only true church of the martyrs. They saw themselves in direct succession of those whose faith had met the test; their church was pure. By contrast, they saw the Catholic church as universal only by way of compromise, reaching out to include many not clean. Bishops who had been traditores could not, in their view, perform valid sacraments; their falsely ordained successors were now leading Catholic congregations to damnation, since their ordinations were tainted. "Catholic," or whole-church, could only mean the church that kept the whole of the law; and only the martyred or imprisoned Donatist predecessors had done that.[4] The so-called Catholic church was in their view a universal fraud.

The agony of Donatist versus Catholic occurred as a tragedy of transition from the early church of the martyrs to the church of late Roman antiquity, the church of the emperors. The historical error of the Donatists, if indeed they erred, was to press forward one hundred years too long, as though persecution had not ceased. Their point was not without merit. The church had often been at its noblest under persecution; imperial favor easily tempted it to laxity. Yet the Donatists overlooked the fresh possibilities in the new imperial church: to shape the life of the empire and give its people

4. Brown, Augustine, 218.

a new religious meaning to their ordinary lives. Such was the dream of the newly consecrated Bishop Augustine. His was the church of the future, finding opportunity to shape the life of a civilization, not a pure church, but a whole people on pilgrimage.

Not only so, the Donatist movement had declined from the moral courage of martyrs to the ritualistic quibbling of legalists. To perpetuate the glory of the martyr after the age of the martyr has passed is to invite a martyr-complex. Some extremists among the Donatists indeed rushed to their glorious deaths at the hands of Catholics. Yet on the whole, what mattered the most to the Donatists was not so much moral fortitude or fanaticism as belonging to the right religious cultus, free of sacramental taint. North African Christianity placed high value on ritual correctness as a protection from demonic forces. Only a priesthood in direct succession from the heroic confessors provided a cultus of reliable supernatural power. Consequently, the Donatists accepted no baptism performed outside their own circle. Only their own baptism assuredly banished the spirits of evil.

Further, the Donatist movement became identified not only with ritual purity but with certain indigenous social and economic classes. Thus the definition of Donatist Christianity left even further behind the original ideal of fidelity under government persecution. Indeed, certain of the Donatist bishops had been known *traditores* themselves. One of these, elevated to office suddenly by a group of peasants, quarry laborers, and women (indigenous groups least Romanized), had himself handed over liturgical vessels to an imperial agent. Another, the primate or high bishop of Numidia (the North African inland south of Hippo), was suspected of *traditio* by his own clergy.[5] Why were such men Donatist leaders? Evidently more important than personal courage was leadership of the favored ritual and of indigenous, often suppressed classes. The movement, of some hundred years until Augustine's time, had therefore become radically conservative. "Our people, our pure church" could have been a Donatist motto. As a church of remembered martyrs, Donatism was a coiled spring sensitive to any threat or opposition from outside. They were capable of attacking and whitewashing isolated Catholic churches and of torturing and murdering their priests.

The record of violence between Donatist and Catholic grew tragic before Augustine's birth in 354. Constantine (d. 337) had obviously favored the Catholic movement; in 347 an imperial commissioner, Macarius, came to

---

5. W. H. C. Frend, *The Donatist Church: A Movement of Protest in Roman North Africa* (Oxford: Clarendon, 1952), 11, 13, regarding Silvanus and Secundus.

North Africa and made the fateful move of suppressing Donatist activity by fear and coercion. The Catholics thereby struck the first violent blow. Under Julian the Apostate (361–363) the Donatists received official toleration; yet now they would never forget having been suppressed by Rome and their Catholic fellow Christians. By the time Augustine had become priest and bishop at Hippo (391, 395) bitter memories had heightened Donatist suspicion of both Rome and the Catholic church.

Augustine's Theology of Church

The story thus far of the young Augustine, from Cicero, to Mani, to Plotinus, to Ambrose, makes inevitable his favor toward one, universally open church. To avoid partisanship and materialistic, power-hungry strife, to find Wisdom itself, meant finding a universally valid religious philosophy or church. Only then could real unity be pursued: one world of one people under one God. The vision came so clear to him that when he arrived back in North Africa his loyalty to the Catholic ("universal") movement, known in Milan under cosmopolitan circumstances, altered not the slightest. He saw the split-off Donatists in their provincialism as having missed the Gospel completely.

The first, vital mark of the church that Augustine pressed against the Donatists was therefore *catholicity* (wholeness) or universality (*Baptism* II, 9, 14). Only a church present and open in all quarters of the world to all nationalities and races of people could embody the one unifying truth of God. Readers today must recall that the entire civilized world, as Augustine had opportunity in the fifth century to know it, witnessed the flourishing of the Catholic church and its monastic movement. For him, the hour of Ambrose's great church had truly come. He considered that catholicity was being actualized.

Preaching to his people at Hippo, especially from his highly favored book of Psalms, Augustine ardently pressed his views against the Donatist majority in his city. In his Good Friday sermon on Psalm 22 (mentioned above, page 163) he heard the cry of the crucified, "O God, my God, why have you forsaken me?" as Christ identifying with, and giving voice to, his church in her plea for forgiveness. The Donatists have rejected membership in this imperfect pilgrim people, who strive forward with Christ under grace, hoping to see their home country, the City of God. The Donatist posture violates the Psalm and its good news:

> To see Christ brazenly, openly mocked, and by those who cannot even make the excuse "I didn't understand!" As he sits there in glory at his Father's right hand in possession of the whole world, these Donatists have the face to say to him "Here you are, this is your kingdom for you," and in place of the whole world they offer him just Africa! . . . "All the ends of the earth shall remember and be converted to the Lord" [Psalms 22:27]. There you are brothers; that's it; why look to me to answer the Donatists? There is the psalm for you, we have it read today, they have it read today. We should write it up on placards and banners, and go out in procession with it. . . . Is Africa alone redeemed? Here it is in black and white . . . "*all* the ends of the earth"; he said "*all*," my dear schismatic. How are you going to wriggle out of that? You have no way out left, but the way in is always open. (*Sermon on Psalm 22*)[6]

The way in that was open was of course the open door of the Catholic church for any Donatist wishing to return.

Violation of catholicity meant that the Donatists had also violated the second mark of the church that Augustine urged against them, that of *unity* or charity (*Answer to Petilian* II, 78, 172). They boasted their own unity, certainly, but because they could not conceive of worldwide unity, Augustine found them schismatic, splitting the church. Schism meant a violation of Christian love and charity, dividing Christian people from one another, as heresy meant a violation of Christian belief. Since Augustine built his entire theology on renewed and redirected loves, the Donatists' violation of love splitting the church in the name of their own purity scandalized him. The unity of the church in love Augustine saw clearly in classic scriptural passages from his beloved Paul:[7]

If I have prophetic powers, and understand all mysteries and all

---

6. As translated by E. Hill in *An Augustine Reader*, ed. J. J. O'Meara (Garden City, N.Y.: Doubleday, 1973), 238, 247–48.

7. Cf. F. W. Dillistone, "The Anti-Donatist Writings," in *A Companion to the Study of St. Augustine*, ed. R. W. Battenhouse (New York: Oxford University Press, 1955), 186. On the four marks of the church generally and the visible-invisible church, with references, see 186–91. Bible translation, New RSV.

knowledge, and if I have all faith, so as to remove mountains, but do not have love, I am nothing.· (I Corinthians 13:2)

I therefore . . . beg you to lead a life worthy of [your] calling . . . with all humility and gentleness, with patience, bearing with one another in love, making every effort to maintain the unity of the Spirit in the bond of peace. There is one body and one Spirit, just as you were called to the one hope of your calling, one Lord, one faith, one baptism, one God and Father of all . . . (Ephesians 4:1–6)

Right love, for Augustine, fell into two different modes or actions: to use (*uti*), and to enjoy (*frui*) (*Christian Doctrine* I, iii–iv). Love as sheer enjoyment ought to be directed toward God alone, by humanity and angels. All other loves should be a kind of use, that is, loving with a certain high utility; use things in such a way as to see and enjoy God more clearly. Love of fellow human beings is a kind of enjoyment, good and lawful so long as one enjoys them *in* God (*Christian Doctrine* I, xxxiii; see page 139 above). Sin reverses these loves: One uses God and persons in order selfishly to enjoy things.

Since Augustine saw the Donatists as spoilers of love, he evidently saw them as committing this reversal. They loved only themselves and used God and fellow Christians to this end. They therefore had no doctrine of grace (loved and forgiven by God so as to love others), the heartbeat of Augustine's convictions. They needed grace as boundary to constrain their egocentricity and grace as invitation to reconcile them to God and fellow Christians.

A third mark of Augustine's church rejected by the Donatists was that of *apostolicity*, the church's right link to its origins in Christ and his own apostles (*The Unity of the Church* 11, 31). For Augustine, apostolicity was a formal matter not dependent upon the moral and spiritual behavior of present clergy. That is, ordination within any valid church should be traceable in direct succession, from bishop to bishop, all the way back to the apostles and Christ. Visible continuity of church and sacrament through time, since Christ, showed Christ's gift still intact. The Donatists, on the other hand, had shifted valid succession only to their own leaders, and that because of spiritual fidelity under persecution. They limited valid sacraments to a pure church and reviled others because of morally unworthy priests or bishops. Grace, for them, did not cover any baptism or eucharist besmirched by unworthy celebrants, present or past!

Augustine, understanding all sacramental life to be under grace, declared formal, visible succession of bishops enough to guarantee sacramental worth. The sacraments belonged to Christ alone. An apostolic church of grace invited all earnest recipients to trust the sovereignty of Christ in all his sacramental acts. Christ alone rendered sacraments valid and untouchable by human moral failure. Interestingly, Christ therefore validated even Donatist sacraments, despite the leaders' errors or lack of love. Augustine therefore readily accepted Donatist baptism for reentry into the Catholic church. He would not redo what Christ had done already, even through erring priests (*Baptism* I, 12, 18).

The final mark of the church, *holiness*, led to the greatest complexity of issues between Augustine and his opposition. For the Donatists, the issue was straightforward: The holiness of the church was the holiness of its fidelity under persecution. When the time of persecution had passed, that holiness became a matter of the correct ritual descent from the martyrs, or untainted ordination. Augustine saw that ritual correctness could not excuse Donatist behavior, which was often less than holy. For him the holiness of the church was dynamic and complex. Initially and obviously, he urged the holiness of the religion of the heart. Correct management of sacred things outwardly, in order to protect against demons, was not the Gospel. A people whose hearts were touched by grace would struggle and grow a long while before their hearts become entirely true. Holiness in this sense was a matter of growth and perseverance to the end, to the harvest, in the world-wide church (*Answer to Petilian* III, 2, 3).

On the other hand, as already noted, the apostolic sacraments were valid, a guaranteed gift of Christ; the holiness of the church was Christ's sacrament of himself, present, given, and available. Therefore, the church's holiness was already present, a gift. Here was a church that could reach out to all people and invite them to confidence in what Christ had already done for them. Thus Augustine held to what has been called the "real presence" of Christ in the sacraments. Folk coming to the Eucharist, for example, knew inwardly Christ's gift of himself for their sakes, yet shared in a real and powerful work of the Spirit through receiving outwardly the bread and wine.[8] (He did not hold that the actual substance of bread and wine was altered, as became official doctrine in the Middle Ages. Christ's real presence could coincide with the bread and wine without altering their material

8. Cf. F. Van der Meer, *Augustine the Bishop*, trans. B. Battershaw and G. R. Lamb (London: Sheed and Ward, 1961), 371–79. A striking quotation: "What you behold upon the table . . . [in] its outward appearance . . . you see upon your own tables; yet only the appearance is the same, not the power. Similarly, you yourselves have remained what you were. . . . Yet you have been made anew" (p. 374, Codex Guelferbytanus 4096, 7, 1).

composition. His view is not finally defined with full clarity.) "Catholic" meant that Christ had given himself for the world. The church's holiness was the presence of that unshakeable gift.

Yet a dilemma remained between these two ideas of holiness. The growing love in the hearts of the people was the church's holiness; yet that holiness was also Christ's loving presence, given forever. Which was it? the people's process? or Christ's gift? Augustine never wavered on the inviolable presence of Christ's gift in the church. Still, he knew the rough crudity of much of his congregation. He concluded that many who received the valid gift nevertheless were not growing in that grace and in the fruits of the Spirit. He distinguished valid from effective, or "efficacious." Christ's gift of himself was valid; yet only through the people's growth in love did the gift become efficacious and redeeming. Donatist baptism remained valid because Christ's; but it proved not efficacious and redeeming as long as the Donatists violated love toward Catholic brothers and sisters (*Baptism* V, 28, 39).

Augustine therefore came to distinguish a visible and an invisible church. The church visible was that historic continuous company since the apostles, the bearer of Christ's gift. The church invisible was a group *within* that company, their number known only to God, growing in their hearts in love. The invisible, the redeemed, would never be identified until the last day of history when God would disclose who, within the visible church, had actually kept the pilgrimage. In the one holy church Augustine saw himself dealing with two companies of folk, those ultimately redeemed and those ultimately lost, yet never to be sorted out until the end (*Christian Doctrine* III, xxxii). Only thus could he combine two convictions: the worldwide gift of God and the selective processes of the human heart.

Augustine saw the church of grace as embracing the world, even while judging and disciplining the world. His role as pastor was therefore a labor of keeping a dynamic, moving body on its true path, inviting all to the Gospel and disciplining many.

Grace Applied to the Donatists[9]

Clearly, Augustine knew of no theory that permitted toleration of the Donatists. All his hard-won philosophical and religious understanding viewed

9. This section is indebted in various ways to Brown, *Augustine*, chapters 19–21.

them as breeders of misery, square-faced against their fellow Christians. His own conversion had convinced him of a new freedom and joy for people everywhere through grace universal. The Donatist church stood against his every expectation for the church. Yet how do you wage opposition against a rival church in the name of grace, peace, and love? No ideal answer came. Indeed, Augustine's response has clouded his reputation ever since, though its logic was conscientiously clear to him.

As can be expected of an adult convert and relatively new church member, Augustine came to authority at Hippo with the zeal of a reformer. His early appeals for orderly Christian life among his people were persuasive and personal, intended to inspire. He especially resisted feasts to honor the dead (with the Donatists, to honor martyrs). These celebrations were carried over, thinly disguised, from pagan festivals and drunkenness. Curbing such practices meant, of course, that Augustine resisted any cult of the saints (surprising of a Western Catholic father). He did so to eradicate the residue of paganism, to bring his entire people into line with Romans 13:13–15, which had converted him: "Not in revels and drinking bouts . . . but put on . . . Christ."

His earliest persuasive appeals gave way increasingly to impersonal measures. From 393 to 405 he and associated Catholic bishops publicly pressed the error of the Donatist cause; Augustine wrote a popular song against them for his people to chant in the streets. Prior to this aggressive Catholic activity, the Donatists had so established themselves that toleration of them became likely. Mixed marriages between the two churches occurred. Yet to be a Donatist might win favor in a courtship.[10] Augustine saw toleration as simply giving the Donatists a slow and sure victory, since already they were the majority church in Hippo. He could not accept their exclusivity. Oddly, his own sense of the generosity of grace led him to deny their freedom of belief: African Christianity could not exist part Catholic, part Donatist.

He declared that he would never advocate military coercion against them. Yet the sad day came when he accepted this—at another bishop's initiative, who had sought imperial support; then his earlier vow of noncoercion embarrassed him. The Donatists were astonished. They saw themselves as heirs of the martyrs against government oppression. They never dreamed that other Christians, estranged brothers and sisters in the faith, would reinvoke the imperial outrage they all had once suffered. They considered their religious views as of no consequence to Rome.

10. *Sermon* 46, 15. Cf. Brown, *Augustine*, 226–27.

Yet in a twofold irony, the Donatists themselves had suppressed a schism of their own (under Maximian in 395) and had appealed to imperial laws against heresy in doing so! Augustine quickly pointed out the hypocrisy. He justified his own use of coercion as a form of instruction and correction of those requiring religious discipline. Whether morally in error, he sensed the future: The church in the West could never have been culturally significant or effective in the provincial, even tribal mode of the Donatists.

Yet Augustine's position has rankled for centuries. How could one use force to make Christians? The approach contradicted his own recent experience. The savor of Christ's love and that alone had finally won his commitment. The limits of the church's ordered way had been gracious limits, not military steel. The coercion used on him at home and school as a child had been a burden preventing his lively assimilation of the faith. A major item in turning him away from the church during his youth had been the oppressive, far-distant goals of religious and moral behavior, laid upon him with sanctions of coercion and fear. The spark of seeking intellectual and religious integrity had made possible his return to the church at a new, authentic level. Could Christian integrity be gained by heightening coercive pressure? His own experience had shown not.

Indeed, the problem of forced Christian integrity did disturb Augustine. Since his arrival in Hippo in 391, he had seen crowds of pagans push into the church because orthodox Christianity had become the only imperially tolerated and official religion (under Theodosius I in 391). Their motive had been political advantage, with little Christian faith. Now he confronted the further dilution of his Catholic ranks by hordes of sullen Donatists; indeed he opposed coercion up to the last minute, if only for this reason.

Yet dealing with massive, unruly groups forced him to a rude level of discipline and nurture. These people had not tasted the savor of Christ's love; rather, they had tasted the savor of sin. He reverted to the negative lessons of his own childhood. He remembered that under the schoolmaster's rod he had learned much (I, 10, 16), and he turned harsh. A side of him never forgot that life under evil produced violence, that one of the penalties for sin was yet a deeper entanglement in sin (City of God XIV, 13 and 15); the person under grace might be forced to use coercion against evil in a chaotic world.

Was it by chance that around 405, the year of imperial sanctions against the Donatists, he turned theologically to a more stubborn view of original sin? To the notion of original sin as the virtually inevitable short-circuit to godlikeness, he added a biological legacy from parents to child that guaranteed that short-circuit in the new individual.[11] He affirmed the idea (not original with him) that the involuntary physical lust involved in intercourse (as opposed to free rational action alone) tainted the conception of the child, who then entered life biologically turned toward sinful acts (cf. his later *Grace of Christ and Original Sin* II, 37–38). His introduction of biology into original sin flirted with Manichaeanism and some have determined to excise it by appropriating his original sin teaching in a revised form.[12] Did the stubbornness of evil in his dealings at Hippo encourage him to opt for this more drastic version of human fallenness? It may have done so.

Yet his circumstances at Hippo do not alone account for his shift in views and policies. A certain naïveté on his part concerning his own anger and aggression also influenced him. A serious temptation for him throughout life had been ambition and high honor. He tells of his release from that drive, first through the Neoplatonist books, then through the grace of Christ. What he later discovered was that a gift of grace, once given, must continue to be given again and again throughout a process of lifelong cultivation of that gift. Caught up in the vision of grace and faith for the world, he was innocent of his own latent striving for achievement and his implicit anger, motivating a measure of his anti-Donatist program. In his same *Confessions* that records his inner release from such sin (VIII, 1, 2), he in turn admits the continuing struggle with honor and reputation (X, 36, 59).

When official coercion came, he nevertheless took no opportunity by it simply to aggrandize his own position. He had claimed that the only justification for coercion was to instruct and correct an erring people. Whatever his naive strand of competitiveness, he took no satisfaction in conquest, but remained true to his stated justification: He agonized at length with decisions as to which penalties laid upon them would most likely teach the Donatists the errors of their position. He found no peace or joy in the course he had plotted.

From evil in the North African church situation of his childhood he had returned to what seemed unavoidable evil in the same territorial church in his middle adult years. The flood of problems threatened to erode what he had learned at great personal cost about evil, and what he had learned about love. Yet the core of his vision kept its vitality by his characteristic inward nurture. Indeed, his versatile mind and emotions were writing the

11. See Chapter 7, page 122, note 9.
12. Ricoeur, *Symbolism of Evil*, 237, 257–58, 307–8, 311.

Confessions story of his own pilgrimage of love at the same time that he was urging his unrelenting case against the Donatists (397–399).

What he lacked outwardly in relation to the Donatists was a modern state, sympathetic to religion, but establishing none. Thus Donatists and Catholics were not entirely accountable for their mutual situation; the state contributed sharply to the anguish. Rome had allowed in the empire count-less options in religion, but no option as regards loyalty to herself and her official polytheism. Once Rome became a goddess in the pantheon, and the emperor divine and later Christian, laws against "heresy" appeared on the books; even the Donatists invoked them. Behind all the Christian unease with state coercion lay the implicit knowledge that Rome would elect to support one form of Christianity or another. Would this giant, now a Christian empire, be Catholic? Certainly by electing to take to its bosom defined Catholic orthodoxy, Rome virtually decreed that parties within Christianity could not resolve their differences by peaceful persuasion.

Augustine dreamed of a church universally inviting in the name of grace. Instead, he had to wrestle with imperial policy and partisan strife. All his earliest hopes became postponed. Hope had to extend long and far on an unimagined pilgrimage toward what he called the City of God.

11

Grace and Hope: The City of God

(*Confessions* IX)

Not long before [our baptism in 387] the church at Milan had begun a kind of celebration of mutual strength and support: The brothers [and sisters] sang together, their voices and their hearts, with great spirit. Only a year previous, or not much more, Justina, mother of [our] puerile [so-called emperor,] the boy-king Valentinian, had been persecuting your man Ambrose in order to extend her heresy (she had been seduced by the Arians!). The people were devoutly watching and waiting in the church, prepared to die in your service, along with their bishop. There my mother, your handmaid, took her stand in the front ranks caring and watching, and indeed lived on prayer. . . . Then the singing of hymns and psalms [shored up] the people against exhaustion with the strain of their grief; indeed this very event brought about the custom of [congregational] singing, as in the East. From that moment until today, throughout other parts of the world, many have now responded by taking up [this corporate singing,] indeed in almost all your congregations.

Then you revealed through a vision to your memorable presiding priest [Ambrose], where the bodies of your martyrs, Protasius and Gervasius, lay hidden. You had preserved them uncorrupted through all those years in your secret treasure-store. At just the right moment you would bring them forward out of hiding in order to restrain a woman who was mad, even a queen. . . . Indeed the report [of their discovery] spread; then your praises brightened to a fever pitch; then the mind of that enemy woman, though not turned to the sanity of

believing [the faith], was checked from persecuting, in its mad fury.
Thanks be to you, my God! (IX, 7, 15–16)

How indeed was the church to deal with the Roman state, which had
not only become a religion in itself, but then had officially adopted a new,
foreign religion, Christianity, and proceeded to render judgments as to
which form of this religion was true and orthodox? (Constantine had done
so at the Council of Nicea, 325 c.e.) The question of the state and its
religion, combined with Augustine's complex visible and invisible church,
required him to reflect upon the whole nature of society and its historical
destiny. The above passage remarkably anticipates, from its occurrence in
387 and its recollection in 399, a wide spectrum of issues in Augustine's
views of church, state, and history.

Dealing with the State

In light of Ambrose's above encounter with Justina and his own dealing
with the Donatists, how did Augustine come to view the Roman Empire?
Against the Donatists, Augustine had seen the grace of Christ undergirding
the validity of the apostolic church, apart from a particular succession of
martyrs or otherwise morally correct priests. The Catholic, apostolic church
was free by grace to embrace and invite the world, risking imperfection in
the name of Christ's encompassing love.

On the other hand, the embrace could not be so wide that the church
accepted and baptized everything in the culture and in the empire. Less than
a hundred years before, Constantine had appeared so heroic to Christians by
his favor toward them that some saw his empire as approaching the expected
Kingdom of God on earth; the church was simply becoming the state.[1]
Ambrose and Augustine saw it otherwise. The church reached to the empire's widest bounds, but was not to be identified with the empire. Acknowledgment and support of the Roman government did not mean the church
would hand over its authority to the emperor as high priest. (Constantine,
for example, had erected a statue of himself wearing a crown of nails from

1. R. A. Markus, *Saeculum: History and Society in the Theology of St. Augustine* (Cambridge:
Cambridge University Press, 1970), 49–50.

the "true cross"; imperial high priesthood had almost occurred.)[2] The empire's friendly support gave the church a surge of hope for its worldwide coverage; but the church had her own standards. She would not be a department of state.

The *Confessions* passage above shows Augustine sneering at an emperor when he thought appropriate. The young emperor was but a "boy-king," Justina a Jezebel (1 Kings 21, 2 Kings 9). As Elijah had stood against the weak Ahab and his raging queen, Jezebel, so stood Ambrose. Monica is strongly present, her motherhood now caught up in the larger sheltering motherhood of the consoling church. The unusual passage on congregational singing, Augustine's love for it (IX, 6, 14), and the expansion of that singing throughout the world suggests the hope of a worldwide strength and dignity for all people.

The empress-mother is Christian, recalling the empire's choice of that faith as the religious cornerstone of its own vitality. Yet as an Arian Christian, she is prepared to impose her definitions of Christianity—for whatever combined reasons, religious and political—on the bishop of Milan. Ambrose does not see the Roman state as the beast of the Apocalypse as did the author of the book of Revelation (13:11–18). Ambrose himself came to the bishop's office from being governor of the region, with a background of regard for statecraft. Nevertheless, he regarded the bishop's office as higher than the emperor's in religious authority. In 391, just four years later, Theodosius I will make Rome's favor toward Christianity complete; Christianity will become in earnest the only legal imperial religion, with pagan rites proscribed. Yet following even that close tie Theodosius will receive discipline at Ambrose's hands for the slaughter of the people of Thessalonica.[3] The church is ready to stand against the empire when necessary for her own integrity. Ambrose and his people, including Monica, prepare to die should Justina's soldiers rush the church.

Despite the fourth-century close tie between church and empire, the age of martyrs is not necessarily over. Death is welcome before state dominance, even by a nominally Christian state. As if to punctuate the stand, the providential discovery of the pre-Constantinian martyrs' graves, including the bodies of Protasius and Gervasius, links Ambrose back to the heroic days of suffering for Christ against paganism. Augustine's fascination with

---

2. M. A. Huttmann, *The Establishment of Christianity and the Proscription of Paganism* (New York: Columbia University Press, 1914), 110.

3. W. H. C. Frend, *The Rise of Christianity* (Philadelphia: Fortress, 1984), 624–25.

the event is instructive. He claims the religious independence of the church, as in the time of the martyrs. At the same time, the event looks forward to his later preoccupation with the empire and his determination that the government will favor and support Catholic Christianity. Then, less the philosopher and more a leader of Catholic religious life, he will grant credence to cultic miracles and wonders, as in the case here of Protasius and Gervasius.[4] In the story of Ambrose and Justina the best of the pre-Constantinian age of martyrs is combined with the reality of the new tie between church and state in the name of the one Lord Christ.

Augustine therefore received a legacy in which he neither saw the state as a demon to be shunned, nor as the Kingdom of God on earth.[5] Rather, he saw it as a crude order, a tangle of imperfections, a useful instrument of God for lesser though necessary purposes.[6] He welcomed the state's support and protection of the church, as he at length yielded to using imperial coercion against the Donatists. At the same time, he had no illusions about the state and remained determined that in all of her own affairs the church remained supreme. Had he already been converted and baptized at Milan, he would have been watching and singing in the church with Ambrose, against Justina.

The Issue of Religion; The City of God

Despite his fascination with Ambrose's stand against Justina, Augustine did not become a theorist on church and state in a modern sense. All his later reflections on church, state, and the relation between them rose out of considering a prior issue, the issue of right and true religion. Only as he pressed that question did matters of church, state, society, and history, or at least the forerunners of those modern concerns, emerge as major corollaries of his religious views. For him, the initial question regarding human activity was the religious question. All else could only, indeed must, follow and find its place.

As with his personal story in the *Confessions*, so with his later treatment

---

4. Brown, *Augustine*, 413–18.
5. Markus, *Saeculum*, 55.
6. See Rosemary R. Ruether, "Augustine and Christian Political Theology," *Interpretation* 29, no. 3 (July 1975): 252–65.

of wide public affairs; religion, good and bad, stood as the first order of business. Indeed, religion, evil, and love, the large sequential rhythm of topics in the *Confessions*, turns out to be the rhythm of topics in his mighty work, the *City of God*, now universally and historically applied. This epic treatment of true worship since before earthly creation (with the angels) concerns itself with religion gone wrong, the character of evil resulting, and the hope that a reborn people will show forth the gift of loving again, both God and themselves. The twenty-two books of the *City of God* rehearse again on a universal scale the themes of religion, evil, and love found in his early personal life.[7]

Only in 413, twenty-two years after coming to Hippo and eighteen after becoming bishop, did Augustine take up hesitatingly the labor of this vast work, a tracing of the religious issue from its historical roots, both pagan and Christian. Its purpose was straightforward. He wished to show that the pagan religion of Rome was dead, and rightly so, and that in its place the stream of the lovers of God since before creation were emerging as a new Christian city, based in heaven, and increasingly manifest on earth. He treated the primal religious issue nowhere more grandly than in his massive unfolding of Roman religion, Greek reflection, and the Christian Bible in this story of the *City of God*. The plan of the work staggered the readers and even the book binders: Five books pursue the error of pagan religion in pursuit of earthly happiness (Rome); five pursue the same error in pursuit of happiness beyond this earth (Greece); twelve books trace the origins, progress, and destinies (four books each) of two cities or societies, intermingled throughout history, yet to be sorted out and identified on the last day: the Earthly City and the City of God (as traced through the Bible). The Earthly City is made up of those, beginning with the Devil and his angels and on earth Cain, who love self to the contempt of God. The City of God is made up of those, beginning with the obedient angels and on earth Abel, who love God even to the contempt of self (including nevertheless a rightly ordered self-love) (*City of God* XIV, 28; XIX, 14). He aimed, simply, to offer on a grand scale the Christian pattern of salvation. The exhortation of the book was also simple: Seek, yearn for, and love the coming City of God.

The occasion for writing the book, as might be expected, was a moment at which the prime religious issue, pagan versus Christian, came to urgent

---

7. J. J. O'Meara, *Charter of Christendom: The Significance of the City of God* (New York: Macmillan, 1961), 15–16.

focus. The conflict had been building momentum for Augustine ever since his early experience in Hippo of pagan throngs pressed by the empire into joining the church. In the last year of the fourth century the imperial government issued no less than four edicts suppressing paganism, twenty edicts in the last twenty years of that century.[8] Many in the empire were skeptical of Rome's coercion in favor of Christianity. The tangled question came to a head in 410, the fateful year that Alaric the Goth pillaged, burned, and sacked the Eternal City, Rome. The event in itself did not so much demand that Augustine write the City of God, twenty-two books' worth, but took its place in the long accumulating pressure to do so. In fact, the event itself had more practical impact for Augustine on the Donatist question (the government suddenly slackened its sanctions against the Donatists).[9] Nor was his theological response to the disaster so extensive and difficult: he said simply that the city fell as a rebuke and correction from God for the accumulated sins of humanity, church folk included (Sermon 296, 6; City of God I, 10; cf. Letter 111, 2).[10] The real pressure of the event was otherwise: The fall of Rome occasioned the flight of numerous sophisticated and literate pagans from that city to Augustine's old university center, Carthage. The educated, literary case for paganism suddenly strengthened within Augustine's own region. He felt increasingly pressed to reply.[11]

The literary circle that he faced in Carthage supported pagan religion in their profound nostalgia for past Roman glory. These refugees had no part in current pagan expressions of religious decadence: the debauchery of feast days, the decline of ancient municipal myths and rites into popular mystery religions, the esoteric playing with myths and mingling of themes of the Gnostics. They remembered with longing the intricate and beloved ceremonies of even just a generation before, perpetuated by some of the sturdiest of Romans. Such rites recalled Rome's days of finest virtue and success. Decline into popular orgies, transitions into imperial, established Christianity, all struck them as a grievous loss of Rome's religious and political genius. Their sentiments had been represented in late fourth-century Rome by those pressing to retain in the Roman Senate House the traditional Altar of Victory. The crucial altar had been by turns removed and then returned

---

8. O'Meara, Charter of Christendom, 4.
9. Brown, Augustine, 290, 330.
10. See Brown, Augustine, 293.
11. Brown, Augustine, 300–302.

to its place during the fourth century on at least four occasions, a testimony to the religious ambivalence of the period.[12] No ambivalence marked the intellectual pagan refugees Augustine knew to be at Carthage. They affirmed the stately, loved rites of old Rome. Oddly, the practice of these rites was past, now forbidden. They existed only in books, available for reading and discussion, of which Virgil was the Bible. The sentiment of the refugees was locked in a glorified past, a dignified if unyielding conservatism. For all their literary aloofness from current developments, Augustine took their intellectual challenge to Christianity most seriously, with its potential impact upon thoughtful Christian leadership.

Such an impact evidently appeared in questions raised of Augustine by the young imperial commissioner of Carthage, Marcellinus, a strong, disciplined, baptized Christian leader. Marcellinus wanted to know why, if Christianity were the true and right religion, the empire was appearing to decline under a Christian establishment—especially considering the old religion's ancient proven success, and Christianity's troublesome injunction to heads of state (as to all) that they exercise meekness and turn the other cheek.[13] Marcellinus had found himself pressed on whether the New Testament's form of faith could promote a strong empire. He needed theological help.

Augustine at first hoped to reply adequately through two public letters to Marcellinus (*Letters* 137, 138).[14] The problem at length moved him to a greater effort; he began the *City of God* in 413 and spent thirteen years in its completion. The format and style chosen predictably aimed to rebut the elite refugees at Carthage and called, as it were, for a battle of the books. Augustine summoned all his knowledge of Latin classics, remarkably at his fingertips from early memorization, as well as what he knew of Greek philosophy, and of course the Scriptures. The bishop of Hippo, preaching to his congregation from week to week as a pastor, could also mount an intellectual campaign, if called upon to do so.

With detailed and apt references to Roman polytheistic religion, Augustine called into question the glorified origins of pagan practice and showed its recorders, such as Virgil, quietly hinting at disbelief of what they set down. His aim never wavered: to discredit Rome's deities. The one true God had given victory to the Roman people—hardly their own gods!— because of their self-sacrifice aimed at praise, honor, and national glory.

---

12. O'Meara, *Charter of Christendom*, 5.
13. O'Meara, *Charter of Christendom*, 9–10.
14. O'Meara, *Charter of Christendom*, 10–11.

(*City of God* V, 13, 15: "They have received their reward" [Matthew 6:16] notes Augustine, who had surely struggled with love of praise himself.) The Roman gods were not gods, but demons, fallen angels of the Devil, with no hold on providence. No matter how ardently worshiped they had no power to affect Rome's destiny, nor had they brought Rome to her original dominance. One God and one God only reigned over heaven and earth, the God of the Hebrews, now known universally in Christ. Rome's only future lay in the City of God. Religious policy was therefore the empire's most critical issue.

Pessimism and Hope

The most difficult of Christian doctrines for the fugitive sophisticates of Carthage was the Incarnation. No other doctrine was so scandalously parochial. Would God choose an out-of-the-way place, Judea, and a very late, inauspicious year, 29 C.E. (the crucifixion and resurrection) for attempting to save the peoples of all time? Augustine therefore couched his monumental reply, necessarily, in the widest, most universal terms, open to him through the language of the Incarnation as described in chapters above. He traced his two cities from the pre-earthly angels and from the children of Adam and Eve. In his ranging review of the progress of the two cities through history (tracing the course of many peoples, though by no means all national histories [*City of God*, XV–XVIII]), Christ's actual appearance on earth occupies only a few lines (XVIII, 46). The Incarnation appears much more in prophecies of it (XVII–XVIII) and in Porphyry's philosophical rejection of it (X, 29) than in its own occurrence in sequence. The strategy is clearly not to press the scandal of God's coming at a particular, unheralded time and place, but to show the sweeping lines of history, alive with the implicit power of that event. The Incarnation itself occurred in Jesus, but the reality and meaning of the Incarnation have shaped the whole of history, from the beginning on into the future. Let the late Roman skeptic consider the testimony of historical time.

Augustine's work with the sweep of history against the pagan intellectuals led him to propose that he and his contemporaries were living in the "old age of the world."[15] He did not expect the end of time to come soon; many things would yet take place. Yet he saw himself living in the sixth and last

15. Brown, *Augustine*, 296.

great period of history (*City of God* XXII, 30). As a human being suffered agonies and discomfort coming through old age to death, so the world around him showed chaos, disaster, and disorder. The troubles of the empire, the tenacity of a decadent paganism, the violence of Donatist and Catholic, the stubborn sinfulness of self-declared Christians all signaled the world's growing senility. In an elderly world the compounded accumulation of sin was breaking out, and God's retribution against it (letting sin, for example, punish itself by falling into more sin; see page 186 above) befell many. History's long accounts were beginning to fall due.

For Augustine, such evil spawned itself within bad religion. Folk had honored and worshiped demons as if gods, under polytheism. Such gods suffered the same spiritual ills as the people who worshiped them; together they and the people produced increasing pride, concupiscence, and dissipation. The sickness of the old world rooted in wrong religion, in the very gods who some now proposed had given Rome her strength. Adoption of Christianity, the religion of truth, had by no means weakened the state. Erroneous worship, not Christianity, had produced the misery of the times.

In such days of calamity Augustine's people required a foundational sense of identity. Against pagan conservatism, sophisticated and popular, on the one side, and Donatist or Manichaean purist separation on the other, what certainty did they have of their Catholic stand? Their bishop dealt with present calamity and the question of identity by pointing them to the future. They belonged, he told them, not to the tangled city of error, but to an everlasting City, already present, but coming consummately to transform history and time. Their hope in God's coming City remained bright, but they were having to endure the breakdown and death of the old order and pass through those terrors in order to arrive at God's City actualized. The hope for staggered Rome lay in transforming her old vision of universality into the new Christian universality. Her breadth of dominance, ultimately doomed in itself, could pass over into instrumenting the breadth of the new reign of Christ. Thus Rome's conquests would turn out to be a providential shadow of the true Rome of Christ's reign. Rome in her errors and failures would ironically find fulfillment in God's divine society.

Augustine's theme for his book and his proclamation, the *civitas* (bond of citizenship, state, city), played on a category of identity that went deep with every member of the empire. Loyalty to home country could exceed that to parents. *Civitas* caught heartfelt attention.[16] By urging an admittedly biblical theme, *civitas dei* (the City of God [Psalm 46:4]), Augustine deftly

16. Brown, *Augustine*, 287. Also, Ephesians 2:19.

linked an antique Roman loyalty to the Christian Kingdom. He did not rob his hearers and readers of the empire they desperately needed. Pessimistic about world conditions, and therefore not misleading as a realist, Augustine nevertheless made no move to consign the empire to the ash heap. His people could live with the crushing blows, yet keep their Roman *civitas* because they saw it fulfilled, through tribulation, in a higher *civitas*, to which they already belonged. Pessimism still kept faith with hope. Cicero's ideal republic would be, and could be, fulfilled in the fully realized City of God (*City of God* II, 21; XIX, 21, 24).[17] Thus Rome would find herself yielding to, and oddly fulfilled in, a spiritual empire, beyond the dreams of pagan sages.

How were Christian people to live in this mixed situation, in an empire continuing though troubled, and a heavenly city spiritually real but not finished on earth? The citizen of the City of God had to continue as Roman, but love first the heavenly Jerusalem. Christians, in other words, took the stance of *peregrini*, "resident aliens," "sojourning strangers." They remained citizens of the City of God, though mingling daily with the City of Earth. They labored in the world as strangers, watching in their hearts only for Christ's Kingdom. Augustine's proposal at this point remains similar to attitudes of the church in the first three centuries under persecution, in an often hostile empire. As far back as the second century Christians had encouraged one another to "live in the world as strangers."[18] They were in the world, not of the world. In the fifth century the empire was officially Christian; yet with the Donatists once again tolerated in 411, Augustine considered that he himself might well suffer martyrdom. The times were treacherous. Ambrose and his people had prepared themselves to die at the hands of Justina and her nominally Christian emperor son. Just as in that incident, Augustine expected to live in the empire and receive its cooperation; yet should things go badly Christians who loved first the City of God prepared to suffer in the fourth and fifth centuries, just as in the second and third.

The way through the world's old age lay menacing and harsh. In the *City of God* Augustine traced a narrative of hope in its testimony from the foundations of the world. He intellectually documented for his people a sustaining confidence in the long future.

---

17. See Brown, *Augustine*, 312.
18. *Epistle to Diognetus*, 5, in *The Apostolic Fathers; the Apologists of the Second Century*, ed. George Jackson (New York: Appleton and Company, 1882), 132.

Love

As in the *Confessions*, so in the *City of God*, issues of religion and evil found resolution through love. Those who knew sustaining hope were those whose wills had been called by grace, who tasted the new delight of loving God and the things of God. Augustine's discovery of love, personal in the *Confessions*, turns social in the *City of God*. He saw the divine economy as nourishing a vast network of souls, angelic and human, living and dead, bonded in growing love. The church in the love of God is "one single Christ who loves himself" (*Tractates on the Epistles of John* 10, 3).[19] The incarnate action of grace had opened the City of God so that it was no longer largely identified with the line of the Jewish covenant, but touched countless people universally. The surge in church growth, even though motivated by the empire and often superficial, convinced Augustine that grace was working an abundant harvest (especially in the monastic movement). Lovers of the City of God were increasing, even though everywhere mingled with the City of Earth, those who would finally love only themselves. The two cities, two loves, intermingled on earth like wheat and tares (Matthew 13:24–30), only to be disclosed and separated out at the last day. He was convinced that one of intense spiritual insight, like John the Evangelist, author of the fourth Gospel, could have sorted out at a glance the members of the two cities (*Tractates on John's Gospel*, 14, 8, 2–3).[20] Despite the grueling task of attempting to nurture his own congregation, and discouragement with their raucousness, Augustine's own delight in the good City set him into impassioned speech: "[Beloved], when I speak of that [City], and scandals are increasing [all around us], I want never to stop!" (*Expositions in Psalms* 84, 10).[21]

Loving the heavenly City might well have been an exercise in straightforward Neoplatonism: yearning for the hidden, ideal reality behind the shadows of things, one day to be seen by the intellectual eye. What complicated the Christian's love for God's City, however, was biblical love for the created order. The Neoplatonist sage could increasingly withdraw from the material creation. The Catholic Christian, despite resident-alien status, could not deny love for that creation. Augustine himself could not. The

19. See J. N. D. Kelly, *Early Christian Doctrines* (New York: Harper and Brothers, 1958), 413–14.
20. See Brown, *Augustine*, 323.
21. See Brown, *Augustine*, 312.

good of creation joined Christian and non-Christian alike within the same arena of everyday living. Those who loved God and those who did not shared and even cooperated in producing social, legal, economic, and political good of an important kind. Unjust humanity produced such goods for self-centered reasons; Christians, for reasons of service. In any case, the Christian could not disdain the creation, but must exercise created things usefully in love.

Loving both the City of God to come and also the present created order called for a complex posture on a Christian's part. The solution was to love created things in such a way as to use them for God's sake, and for the sake of the coming City (see page 182 above). Creatures are not to be enjoyed simply in and of themselves. Rather, they are to be used in order to build the glory of God and the nurture of his people.

At the same time, Augustine's notion of loving creatures as a "use" was not a shallow utilitarianism. Loving creatures in their usefulness for God and his City moved Augustine to a certain wonder at the creation, an amazement at the beauty and splendor that lay all around humanity's everyday affairs (City of God XXII, 24). He had always had an eye for light and for the effects of light, in the sky, at sea, around his mountainous home. He found astonishment in the heavenly bodies. Most of all, he wondered at human love and intellect gone wrong, remarkable even in their error. For example, he marveled at the love of highway outlaws for one another, such that one would suffer torture rather than betray the whereabouts of his friend (Sermon 169, 14).[22] Likewise, he wondered at the "brilliant . . . ingenuity of philosophers and heretics . . . in defense of [their] errors and false views" (City of God XXII, 24).[23] The crowning quality of life was its capacity to love and be loved. He told his congregation that he could not blame them if they loved the life that lay around them, so long as they would also choose the life they loved (rather than choosing sin and death).[24]

The zealous young convert at Milan, ready to storm heaven's intellectual gates, had given way years later to one much more ready to acknowledge the love of this life's beauty and excellence. One must love and seek the City of God, but in such a way as to reorder, not despise, the loves and beauties that the world offers every day.

22. See Brown, Augustine, 325.
23. See Brown, Augustine, 329.
24. See Brown, Augustine, 325.

Suffering

The ugly no-man's-land separating the loveliness of creation from the consummate love of the City of God was the arena of suffering and death
actualized in the "old age of the world." The Christian believer had to love
and honor the good creation, knowing that it constantly broke down under
the onslaughts of sin, disaster, and death. Only the pilgrimage through
hardship, perseverance under trial, loyalty to the Creator severely tested,
could arrive at the magnificent City, whose excellence and love could never
falter. The pilgrimage had to endure the universal transition, the death of
the aging world for the sake of its being reborn as the beloved New Jerusalem. The journey meant challenge and peril. Augustine even personally
disliked travel;[25] yet for him, the moral-spiritual trek was infinitely more
agonizing than any literal, geographical one could be. Not cheerfulness,
therefore, but anguish and determination marked the church's struggling
way toward the future. The yearning and homesickness for the beloved City
fit the heaviness and pain of keeping on. The peculiar joy that marked the
move forward grew from a hope determined to reach out through suffering.
The faithful people had to pass through death to see the goal of their vision.

Human chaos and violence, individual and political, accounted sufficiently for Augustine's conviction of the world's old age and suffering. Beyond these nevertheless lay natural disasters: "fire, frost, wild beasts" (*City
of God* XI, 22). Emphasis on Augustine's view of evil as moral-ethical evil,
perversity of will, indeed the core of his view, has overshadowed his approach to natural evil, destruction by earthquake, flood, disease, deadly
mishap. He records his scandalized awe at these evils nevertheless in the
City of God. How did his acknowledgment of natural evil fit with his insistence that all evil roots finally in sin? The answer lies in recalling his idea
of original sin and its impact. In original sin humanity short-circuited its
own good, grasping after divine status and missing the disciplined way of
Christ, pulling soul and body into antagonism, and leaving the human
spirit in self-idolizing pride and isolation. For Augustine, as for the Fathers
generally, death came into the world as the mark and penalty of original
sin. The human organism as a whole became diminished, and this damaged
nature was passed on biologically from generation to generation (see page
122 above).

The basis for natural evil thus appears: Nature herself does no evil; but

25. See Brown, *Augustine*, 152. Also, 210, 324.

the human organism, now diminished, cannot deal with natural events which, apart from original sin and its penalties, would have held no terror or damage. Evil lies not in nature, but in humanity's damaged capacity to deal with nature. The flaw is not in the earthquake or the tuberculosis, but in humanity's loss of governance over nature (in paradise) and in the flawed human body, now able to be hurt by these things. Augustine's anti-Manichaean baseline predictably stands forward: "No nature at all is evil" (*City of God* XI, 22). Repulsed by Manichaean dualism and convinced of creation's good, Augustine refused to see the world of nature or any part of it as flawed, fallen, or working evil. Natural disasters were part of God's overall governing order, good in that order's ongoing process, balance, and completeness. The tornado, the lightning, the mosquito, all had their place. Only humankind, at a disadvantage because of the mark of sin, saw these things as evil. Even Augustine himself saw these things as evil; he was appalled at the amount of human tribulation. How could it be justified? The answer seemed clear to him, if regrettable: Weakened by original sin, humanity suffered evil blows from otherwise good, natural events.

Such weakness before nature, plus human-initiated wrong led Augustine to see humanity as a whole suffering a worldwide punishment: "This life itself (if it can be called 'life' and be so universally filled with various evils!) bears witness that all the descendants of mortal humanity have been condemned" (*City of God* XXII, 22).[26] Such a conclusion antagonizes many today. In Augustine's defense, he was insisting that the world must finally make rational sense. As with an abused child who says, "What did I do wrong?" some comfort lies in believing there is a reason for the hurt. The only alternatives to a rational cosmos are statistical chance, fate, or creation itself as fallen (Mani) rather than good. Augustine was struggling to make sense of the mayhem around him.

In addition, he saw the worldwide punishment as backdrop for the Gospel of mercy and compassion. God's response was not only to punish, but to draw near in Christ and join the people in their agony. "My God . . . why have you forsaken me?" (Psalm 22:1) are Christ's words uttered as he identifies with his suffering people and cries out their feelings, on their behalf. Thus worldwide suffering, seen in Christ, appears as the stern love of a disciplining Father. Augustine reverts again to the harshness he knew as a child at school and at home to explain world conditions of his adulthood (*City of God* XXII, 22). Christian people turn the blows to good account,

---

26. See Brown, *Augustine*, 328.

finding in them an opportunity for patience and fidelity. Thus Augustine found the sack of Rome like an olive press: The pressure is harsh, but brings out the good pure oil, as the people of quality come to excellence in hardship (*Sermon* 296, 6).[27] Suffering was worldwide; yet the grace of the suffering Christ invited people worldwide to join him in anguish and redemption, to use suffering as a faithful pilgrimage in his presence, to move toward the beloved City.

Predestination

The most difficult and unyielding element in Augustine's theological work arose in the conflict between the invitation to grace (his own amazing discovery of Christ as lover), and the failure of vast numbers across the empire to respond to that invitation. God's call was exquisitely moving; the antagonism of thousands remained entrenched, even as the church spread across the known world. How could this be? Both within and without the church, violence and fraud persisted. How could universal grace suffer derision? A theological response (that Augustine originally regretted) had been developing in his thought since as early as 396. At that time he had responded to his old teacher and friend, Simplicianus, who had asked him for an interpretation of Romans 9, an account of God's electing grace, in which Paul quotes the passage, "Jacob have I loved, but Esau have I hated" (Malachi 1:2–3). How did Esau fail to find favor with God, and not on any grounds, evidently, except God's arbitrary decision? Augustine's struggle with this passage plus others, in addition to years of experience following, convinced him of a doctrine of predestination, that those who turn to God are chosen by God in advance and given special, added divine help to do so. Those who do not turn to God were not given such special added help. Yet, declared Augustine, there can be no injustice with God (*To Simplicianus* 2, 16 and 22, on Romans 9:10–29). In his response to Simplicianus he had stoutly resisted reaching a predestinarian conclusion since free choice of will had been his cornerstone against the Manichaeans; yet Romans 9 would yield no other conclusion to him. Later his regret turned to ready acceptance; predestination became a working doctrine.

Grace, the keystone of his entire teaching, had led him to predestination.

27. See Brown, *Augustine*, 293.

By grace, God acted to save; natural free choice to obey God (Pelagius) could not save. At the one point of trusting and obeying God, the free will lay in bondage to its excessive freedom (see Chapter 7). The call of grace alone, the compelling love of Christ, could bring the free will to choose a focused commitment. From so firm a conviction of grace without human initiative, only a step remained to predestination. Nevertheless, Augustine argued even in his latest works that predestination by grace did not contradict free will, so important was free will in Scripture and in his case against the Manichaeans (*On Grace and Free Will* II–IV). Indeed, he saw grace as preparing the will to be free, calling it out of bondage to itself and into love. Possibly his best argument for reconciling predestinating grace and free will declares that for one's will to be necessarily turned in a given direction does not deny the will's freely choosing that direction. Thus, a person necessarily wills to be happy; that same person certainly freely chooses to be happy. Grace's necessity is the will's freedom (see page 122 above).

The profound freeing power of grace shaped one side of his predestinarianism. The other side arose from reading Old Testament narratives and the Gospels, and pondering the life he saw around him. That is, the Bible and experience suggested that the number of the redeemed would be small ("For the gate is narrow . . . that leads to life, and there are few who find it" [Matthew 7:14]). He had only to look at the impassioned violence and callousness all around him to wonder how very many could be faithful people. He reckoned in sadness and awe that a vast number had heard no call of compelling grace, but had been left by God accountable for the devices of their own sinful freedom. The race had disobeyed God; some would be salvaged; most would be lost.

How then was grace conceivably universal? What happened to the wide-ranging generosity of God across the world, calling all the nations by Christ's love? Did the universal Gospel shrink to only a few who benefited? In his developing theology across the years Augustine held indeed that the Gospel was open to people universally regardless of nationality or race, and was a clear invitation universally (to an extent never clear under the old Hebrew convenant, nationally oriented). Yet to say that the Gospel was open to all nations did not mean for him that it was equally compelling to all individuals. Error and disaster so entangled the world that the few who were finding their way evidently had known a special movement of God's help in their lives. Grace had elected them; so the Bible and experience evidently indicated. Why had grace not elected and moved the others?

Augustine could not answer, though he saw the terrible indicators that countless numbers had experienced no electing grace. At the same time, he did not dare to identify who were the elect and the nonelect (not even technically the Donatists, since he always urged and accepted their return). The work of God's love was a secret counsel of the heart. Who could say what surprising individuals would finally belong to God? Who could say what Christians, apparently loyal now, would fail to persevere? Who could call in advance the roster of the City of God?

The freedom of grace to work secretly within the heart redeemed, in a measure, his predestinarian view. That is, he never proposed to identify the elect, and form a church only of those elect. He avoided falling back into Manichaeanism: He did not propose to split the world into the known elect and the known nonelect and mount a campaign of one against the other. The basis of God's choice of some and not others remained secret, admittedly a scandal before God's avowed justice. Yet the secret of the choice, hidden from humanity, meant that no individual or group could exercise that choice in God's name. No human agent could consign to outer darkness any person by virtue of publicly accessible traits, as Manichaeans, Donatists, Neoplatonists, Pelagians tended to do. Membership in the visible church by the time of one's death constituted a sign of election; and this net was cast very wide. Admittedly, many in the visible church were not true, or would not persevere; yet many outside would find their way in. Predestination as a secret counsel confessed the mystery of any given human destiny and defied any proud attempt to assume God's judgment seat and assign salvation and damnation on God's behalf. Predestination, that worked through human freedom, guaranteed the freedom of God in God's own saving work.

At one given point, Augustine was more clearly harsh: No unbaptized infant could be saved. His basis lay in original sin, which touched even the newborn (*The Grace of Christ and Original Sin* II, 35–36). Saving grace then necessarily attached to a specific, overt act (water baptism), making an exception to the secret freedom of grace described above. A deep sadness quickly attaches to such an image of loss. A God who loves creation, whose Son died as a universal invitation to hope, may scandalize believers in not succoring the newborn. In the wide field of his theological thought Augustine surely might have had resources to respond differently—and without violating the essence of his original-sin teaching. Any finer solution evidently fell victim to the heated Pelagian controversy. Yet the logic of God's secret justice here stretches to the breaking point.

In part, Augustine's zeal for infant baptism arose from the neglect of that practice in his homeland and of childhood religious nurture generally. He himself as a child had suffered this delay of baptism and nurture to his detriment (I, 11, 17–18; see also Chapter 1). Though he never retreated on the fate of unbaptized infants, recent study has shown that some strands of his theology during his last decade had begun to undermine rigidities usually associated with a predestinarian outlook.[28] Most strikingly, he saw God's interior work of grace as possible from the beginning of time, not only before Jesus, but before Abraham. "What is now called the Christian religion . . . was not lacking from the beginning of humankind" (Retractations I, 12, 3). His theology continued to grow and unfold until his death, here enhancing even more the wide freedom of electing grace.

As with his entire theology of the City of God, predestination is best understood against the background of catastrophe and loss in his world. The churches in his homeland, all the achievements of his leadership, were falling before the Vandal onslaught. Their hostile forces had laid waste to the region when he lay dying in the year 430. A year later Hippo fell. In that setting predestination meant that the faithful, no matter how small or weak, could hold their course in confidence, for God chose them before the foundations of the world, all earthly events to the contrary. Predestination became hope within hopeless circumstances. "If God is for us, who is against us?" (Romans 8:31).

The Empire: A Final Word

Only when the primary religious issue, paganism versus Christianity, the nature of the two cities, and the pilgrimage through time have been considered can Augustine's approach to the state be fully understood, with which this chapter began. In recording the clash between Ambrose and Justina clearly he favored the church's dominance within a cooperation of church and state, or the church's martyrdom for the sake of her freedom should the state turn against her. Yet he was not a theorist of church and state in the modern sense. From what material did he derive his views of the state? Social reality for him fell into two ultimate components, two religious loves (for God and against God) comprising two societies mingled and mixed on

28. See TeSelle, Theologian, 332–35.

earth through time. From two such elemental strands, reflections of heaven and hell, how could a theory of the state derive? What would give substance to this third something, between the two great loves?

The answer to this question of the state is oddly, as with all ultimate answers in Augustine's work, the answer of love. The City of God equals love for God. The City of Earth equals love against God. The state, or the empire, or what Augustine called the *saeculum* (the secular world) also equals a function of love. The modern reader likely responds, "How idealistic! What about justice? Even to say that a state is grounded upon justice is idealistic, much less to say that a state is grounded upon love." To the contrary, to find the state grounded upon justice would be, for Augustine, idealistic and unrealistic beyond all warrant. God alone grounded real justice, and since the empire had hardly perfected its loyalty to the one and only God, assuredly the empire could not represent or exercise true justice (*City of God* XIX, 21). Only the City of God, which under the conditions of history stood forth clearly only in heaven, kept true justice. Since the state did not therefore ground itself upon true justice, Augustine saw it grounded upon love, in this sense: The loves of a people, for bodily security, for protection of goods, for food, for wealth, for tranquillity in home and community, for power and dominance, cause them to bond together for the protection of as many common loves as they can agree upon. The view is not idealistic because the loves are not idealistic. Whatever desires and loves a people have form the character of the state. If they love glory and conquest, as did the early Romans, their virtues and order of affairs will build first upon that love: "A people is the association of a multitude of rational beings bound together by a common agreement as to the objects of their love" (*City of God* XIX, 24).

The loves of course fall subject to sin, since only a very few within any given state have been redirected by grace. The loves that ground the state therefore act mostly as sinful loves, although the loves of those people who happen to be under grace are included, so long as an area of commonality can be found. Because the state must build upon the great tangle of loves, good and evil, among a people, its position remains oddly two-sided. On the one hand, Augustine saw the state as a vast exercise in sin, for the tangle of loves were mostly sinful loves. On the other hand, crucially, Augustine saw the state as a structural check *against* sin, because the bond of the state required the members not to violate those elements their loves held in common: economic order, domestic tranquillity, military security. At this point, the state played a critical role in the providence of God. As a bond against the wayward eruption of sin, the state, by God's ordaining, prevented the overwhelming concupiscence of disorderly loves from endless carnage and violence to humanity. The state was a cauldron of contemptuous loves. The state was also the containment of those contemptuous loves, preventing their seething energy of destruction from running amok. This containment, a form of order imposed against wildness, constituted a rough and imperfect justice exercised by the state. Once the grounding of the state on wayward loves is clear, this crude form of state justice can be admitted—not true justice, but a significant constraint nevertheless (*City of God* XIX, 17).

As the City of God was the new Jerusalem, so Augustine saw the state, the empire, as Babylon, where the Jews had suffered exile and longing for their home. The empire was Babylon in two ways, reflecting the two-sided position of the state: The empire was the whore of Babylon, the City of Earth, the vast projection of tangled, sinful loves. The true, spiritual progress of the City of God on earth could never be enhanced by the state's coercion. Yet the empire was the *saeculum*, the secular world of necessary human business, constraining, keeping order, cooperating with the church.[29] As his view of the state was two-sided, so Augustine spoke in two ways of the City of Earth: At times it was the Devil, his angels, and those destined finally to belong to him. At times it was the state that, as a whole, constituted a wide compromise within love and therefore bore the image of sin and death.[30] Nevertheless Augustine insisted on the providential role of the state and related to it as an essential instrument of socialization.

As might be expected, Augustine's social ethic in keeping with his view of the state was notoriously conservative. No citizen may rebel against the state lest the consequent disorder engulf the world in lust and violence. The history he lived through clearly determined this view. The threat of disruption terrified the people of a waning empire. Enduring an unjust ruler was at least chastisement for the world's harsh sinfulness, whereas governmental overthrow meant indiscriminate carnage. Private property, as well as the state, was a sign of fall and sin. In the original creation, all things were in common. Private rights to property, since a sign of sinfulness, fall subject to the state; the laws of the empire regulated private property by the decision of the ruler. (The state could confiscate Donatist property since their schismatic heresy forfeited their property arrangements.) Au-

---

29. Markus, *Saeculum*, 58–59.
30. O'Meara, *Charter of Christendom*, 48–49.

gustine saw warfare as a horrifying outburst in a sinful world, but saw as folly the hope for cessation of all wars. The best he could propose was his famous just-war theory (again, of course, no ideal justice). A state could take up arms in the just cause of its own defense, or wage offensive war if just reparations had not been paid in connection with previous encounters (*City of God* XIX, 7). Soldiers must obey their government, even when the justice of military action falls into question. The private Christian must never take another's life in personal self-defense. Yet he found himself in the anomalous position of holding that the Christian as soldier in public self-defense under orders took another's life with impunity.

Modern readers see Augustine's social ethic as constrained and pessimistic. His views were nevertheless a response to the decaying political situation he knew all around him. What modern readers forget is that his true social ethic, his bequest to the future in this regard, was growing, not in the state, but within the church, where grace was at work to turn human loyalties to greater decency of life. The church was imperfect and impure; yet within her was developing the true City of God, the order in which redirected loves enabled humanity to work toward just means of relating one to another. Not in the state, but in the church lay the hope for a more nearly just social order, in the centuries that lay ahead.

Section 4

A Trinitarian Theology

12

Grace and Understanding: The Trinity

(*Confessions* I, 1, 1)

Great are you, O Lord, and greatly to be praised. Your power is exceeding, your wisdom finds no measure. And humankind wishes to praise you, [this human] particle of your creation; [this] human-kind that bears the burden of its mortality, that bears the evidence of its sin, and also evidence that you resist the proud—nevertheless [this human] particle of your creation wishes to praise you!

Indeed, you arouse this human creature to take delight in praising you, for you have made us for yourself and our heart is restless until it rests in you.

Give me, O Lord, to know and to understand whether first to call upon you or to praise you, and whether first to know you or to call upon you. For if I do not know you, I may call upon some other, rather than you. Or should you rather be called upon in order to be known? Yet, how will they call upon [you], in whom they have not believed? Or how are they to believe without someone preaching?

And they will praise the Lord who seek him. For the ones seeking find him, and the ones finding praise him. Let me seek you, Lord, calling upon you, and let me call upon you, believing you. For you have been preached to us! My faith calls upon you, O Lord, the faith which you have given me, which you have breathed into me through the humanity of your Son, through the ministry of your preacher. (I, 1, 1)

The end is the beginning. The above quotation, which points in this chapter to one of Augustine's final projects of religious thought, *The Trinity*, stands at the beginning of the *Confessions* and the beginning of this book (Chapter 1). His end, epitomized in his trinitarian thinking, was the *Confessions'* beginning all over again: faith seeking to think toward, and know, and praise God.

In fact, among other things, the *Confessions* story itself is about learning to think. From childhood until his baptism he struggled intensely to understand what was happening to him.

At times, the chaos disallowed making any sense of things. At other times, he made astonishing leaps in his understanding of human thought. He arrived at a conviction that only by grace (God's help to heal and restore) could valid religious reflection finally take place. Grace gave sanity, and sanity sees things as they really are; only then can thought survive.

His great thought-project, *The Trinity*, looks back from further along in his life at human reflective powers energized by grace. In the spirit of the *Confessions*, *The Trinity* praises God that grace has given the doctrine of God as Trinity, and that the doctrine invites a never-ending pilgrimage of understanding.

To trace Augustine's growth in thinking requires first a summary review of certain earlier chapters above on the *Confessions* story, from the viewpoint of a particular topic, namely, three stages in the young Augustine's discoveries concerning human thought: childhood, the young rhetor, and the Catholic Christian.

Childhood: Thinking Under Authority

The *Confessions* pilgrimage included, for the young Augustine, countless obstacles to sound thought. The greatest general obstacle was the division of his childhood experience into two worlds of language, almost unrelated to each other. As has been shown, he could not find consistency in the different orders making demands on him. School was the road to success; yet religious belief was the way to God. Success in his society was hypocritical; yet his parents protected that possible success, even at the expense of his religious nurture. Like every human being he yearned somewhere inside for God ("And humankind wishes to praise you, [this human] particle of your creation"). He drank in deeply the belief his mother taught him. Yet when death almost claimed him, he cried for baptism in vain. He was all too mortal. His sin (disorientation) became adolescent chaos. When he turned school finally into achievement, he turned it into self-inflated pride. Mortality, sin, pride: "[This] humankind that bears the burden of its mortality, that bears the evidence of its sin, and also evidence that you resist the proud—nevertheless . . . wishes to praise you!" In the confusion, he could not think through how the demands laid on him fit together. His world refused to come to order.

His inability to think through his situation hardly involved a lack of data—the facts were abundant and bruising—or a lack of mental quickness. Rather, he could not think through because of the power-struggle that held him. Two worlds competed for him, the world of achievement, and the world of Monica's faith. Both demands were crucial to identity; even Monica herself knew the pull and its dilemmas (I, 11, 17). At the time, neither was pure, the achievement nor the religion—and for one reason. Each in its present form was a system of control representing a vested interest. (A separated world of language, having eloquence, but confused substance, marks out a region of partisan control.) From his parents, all this was with good intent. And his parents' intentions finally won! He became a success, but as bishop, not statesman; and he became religious, but by heartfelt conversion, not external domination. Yet in his early life the power struggle wounded him.

Both sides (father versus mother, earth versus heaven) had authority. If both sides confronted him as authority, then he could think and reflect only *within* those authorities. That is, he had to ponder fulfilling both sides because his life depended on it. The systems of household and society ingrained these in him as the only options. Yet neither side satisfied him. The core of him struggled to deal, or to avoid dealing, and at the same time suffered hurt in his isolation. The core of him wanted something beyond, yet had no idea how to reach it: "For you have made us for yourself and our heart is restless until it rests in you."

He was struggling to think within a circle of authority, within what was *given*. But if the authorities were inadequate, or incomplete, or even false, thinking could not find the sense in it. If faithful authorities say that baptism is of the highest importance, yet withhold it, there must be a reason (I, 11, 17–18). Yet none appears; it doesn't make sense. If childhood cheating and stealing must give way to progress in school, in order to become a statesman, who himself cheats and steals, there must be a reason (I, 10, 16). Yet none appears; it doesn't make sense. If the schoolmaster severely beats me, a child, and my parents laugh, there must be a reason. Ah, here one appears: I didn't study as I should (I, 9, 15). Even so, the abuse continues to wrangle. If one cannot think out how the authority is true, the cause may be that one cannot think well, or has not found the key to understand. Or perhaps the authority is skewed, or even untrue.

The young Augustine came to a chilling discovery that was nevertheless a breakthrough: Evidently the authorities themselves had erred. The first instance was a feeling, not a clear notion: the horrified disbelief at the school beatings. The second was a piece of knowledge, emphasized above (Chapter 2), where he speaks of "my education, which (*as I knew*) my parents wanted too much." He had pierced through household authority into the limitless cold air of the unknown. The parents' goal was a distortion. He had to be true to it; yet he was beyond it. He had independently grasped a truth. The discovery nevertheless pushed him into self-abandonment and destruction: "Look there at my heart . . . hungering . . . toward outer chaos." The authorities he had known were erring. He had no ground to stand on.

A breakdown of known authority brings on an outlook much wider, but perilous. Without a circle of authority, anything becomes possible. Without some givenness within which to ponder how the world works, all options stand open. New liberty becomes a chasm. Yet there is a gain, even if negative. Something important is *not* the case: his parents' infallibility. He has taken hold of a single, independent, freeing thought. Its promise is great if its loss of authorities does not end in disaster.

His first step in learning to think, therefore, was becoming conscious of the circles of authority (home and school) within which he lived. And the moment he became conscious of them, he stepped back from them and saw their limitations. He gained an independence from them without knowing how to use it.

As it turned out—beyond the pear-tree rebellion—he retained the external goals set by the authorities (both home and school), took them into university and career and became an achiever. But his progress did not ring true. Inwardly his heart and mind did not join the great success.

The Young Rhetor: Thinking Universal Truth

When he probed beyond childhood authorities and found a level of independence, he did not secretly turn against all tradition. He did not say privately to himself, "There is no God. We ourselves are all the God there is." That would have been a typically modern Western response. He experienced rather a nameless hungering for God (III, 1, 1). His thinking now undoubtedly belonged to himself; he was free and uncommitted. Yet "I despised . . . being free." His thought was not atheism, but unfulfilled theism. There must be God and an ordering of things by God, but *how shall I find* that God and that ordering? and my place in it?

A great difference lies between the modern temper, "God does not exist, and we must do the best we can," and late antiquity, which presupposed transcendent power, or direction, or reason (the Greek gods of Olympus, the Roman pantheon, mystery religions, astrology, gnosticism, Judaism, Christianity, Platonism, Stoicism), some universal governance—if only humanity could grasp it and relate rightly to it. Augustine, with his age, presupposed the governance, but struggled in the chaotic disordering to find the nature of that governance and the way to it.

To presuppose it, to hunger for it, to lean toward it meant that he was ready when a hint of it came.

His second step in learning to think was to catch a glimpse of universal truth when he read Cicero. He did not immediately understand universal truth or how it might measure and organize things. He glimpsed a vision of it that arose negatively, for Cicero had said to him that truth is *not* the viewpoint of this or that sect or party, but governs everywhere, and is passionately desirable simply as deathless wisdom (III, 4, 8). Beyond the chaos of tongues and views this learned Cicero declared a universal wisdom. The world rests on some consistency. It seems a small thing in contemporary life today to hold that a valid scientific experiment is repeatable anywhere on earth with the same result. Augustine's mind would have gone on full alert at the suggestion. Little wonder his excitement that such reliability might extend all the way to universal truth. In Cicero he saw a learned possibility that God and God's ordering of all things—God's truth—might be real and attainable.

This second step, holding to universal truth, was only a bare beginning. Envisioning the possibility of truth, while exciting, actually invited confusion. (Witness how easily his ideal went astray under the impact of the Manichaeans.) He had to find a key, or likeness, or model of how God governs universally, in truth, all things. The Neoplatonist books gave him such a key and brought the second step to full effectiveness. As shown above (Chapter 5), those exciting books taught him to think of God and God's truth as *like* a principle, as, for example, in math or physics; *like* the center of a circle, which governs the whole circle without expanding or attaching to any part of it. God and God's truth are like that. God is like the principle of gravity, which governs everywhere without having to expand, or parcel itself out to "go" anywhere. The mind inherently grasps principles of ordering—of beauty, of math, of science, of justice—that govern and evaluate everything universally. An architect, needing an equilateral triangle in his drawing, knows what he or she is looking for, though no precise one occurs in nature. The same foundational standards apply everywhere. He had glimpsed an entranceway to universal truth.

Augustine called this discovery learning to think of a "spiritual substance" (V, 14, 25). He had thought of God as a "fleshly" substance, that is, a kind of radio wave that reaches as far as one can imagine. But the principle of gravity does not have to reach; it is already present as a signal of rational ordering; it meets humanity at the level of mind. The way is open to look into the world rationally and think God's thoughts: "yes, incredible . . ." The ultimate substance (the spiritual substance) is not material, but is approached mentally, or intellectually.

This step in learning to think was a flash of insight (stimulated by the Neoplatonists) that shifted to a new model, or analogue, or likeness. He had long known how a principle works (how a ship rudder steers, what reliability is in a friend). Now he elevated that thinking to the nature of God. Now he could fathom what had happened when he questioned the troubling circles of authority at home: He had stepped over into something more deeply, universally true about the human being. It is not fitting to want a child's education "too much." He had sensed the questionable circles of authority—with nothing to guide him on the other side. But now he knew, on that other side, the hope of a whole universal ordering with a right place and role for the human being.

Yet his learning to think was far from over. His new insight caused new difficulties. As he reaped the rewards of his wonderful new discovery (as Chapter 7 discusses), his newly discovered God was not reason enough for him to reform his life! He had gained insight into universal truth—God and his own soul, evil as nonsubstantial, and human responsibility before God—but the inconsistencies of his life remained. He kept the dreary round like a captive. His religious discussions took on new life and excitement, but with the elevation of his own self-importance. "I gabbled . . . like an expert . . . wanted to seem wise . . . now superior! . . . puffed up with knowledge" (VII, 20, 26). He had turned universal truth into his *own* circle of authority, his own linguistic region of prestige and control. He imitated at a new level the language control that had dogged his childhood. Now there was no limit on the insights—artistic, scientific, metaphysical, ethical—he might articulate, yet all as part of his own circle of intellectual power. "Knowing God, they do not glorify [that One] *as* God, but . . . declaring themselves wise, they become fools" (VII, 9, 14; quoting Paul, Romans 1:21–22). The greater his knowledge, the worse his vanity.

To think out the reality of God and God's principles of truth had been a great leap, the unveiling of a rational world. Yet his straight arrow of truth as he followed it mysteriously curved off course. Knowledge can turn to destructive ends if the knower misses the principles of his or her own life. Learning to think had further yet to go.

The Catholic Christian: Authority Rediscovered

Oddly, the discovery of universal principles of truth was not the full freedom and resolution that it promised. He found himself confronting a third stage: learning to think within the Catholic Christian circle of authority. Yet he had left that authority behind with his mother and his hometown. Surely it would be a retreat, a step backward to return. For important reasons, he decided it was not.

His own failures while a self-styled philosopher, reflecting on universal truth, were clear to him. He had already begun the slide downward: One newly discovers God and then assumes an authority that should belong only to God! Next, God's ethical and moral principles suffer because the thinker does not exemplify them. Then beyond these, the thinker may use new principles for some utility that damages part of the world (technology can do this), or may slant knowledge to serve vested interests (e.g., biased research). Finally, forlornly, one may falsify data for personal gain.

Augustine needed some daily practice of life, disciplined dealings with others, that would mark him as a lover of truth. He could not know the truth without the humility of truth. Truth is vast; the individual, small. But how could he know humility when a mind like his made intellectual progress in great leaps and declared the results for all to hear? Humility required acknowledged limits, and those limits finally appeared as a circle of authority, in this case Christian authority. Yet how is one to think within a limited circle of authority, where questions may not be honored, and practices not be challenged? Would Augustine not find himself within a language-world of regional, private control for the sake of someone's institutional power? Would he not be giving up universal truth, won at so great a cost of seeking and striving? Should he sacrifice his ranging intellect for the acceptance of revealed doctrine? Should he revert to an adult version of his original childhood bondage? Should he become a Catholic Christian?

Modern readers may find the ancient church surprising at this point. Prescribed ritual and ethical Christian practice did not block truth, but opened it. If a seeker was to know God's love for all creation, and respect for the dignity of every creature, in creation's full harmony, then the seeker must begin by his or her own very small practice of love, respect, and self-restraint. Otherwise, the true order of things could never open to the mind. Apart from love doubtless the seeker could learn to predict eclipses (V, 3, 4) and other purely physical phenomena. But the valued *significance* of sun, moon, atmosphere, ozone, vegetation, the total environment, including humankind in its right role and proportion, could never appear without this beginning discipline of love and self-restraint. Knowledge for the ancient church was rich and wide, including in a single fabric what the modern world calls the scientific, the ethical, and the aesthetic. Knowledge of physical phenomena apart from knowledge of God was not only a bare abstraction; it was probably perverse. Worst of all was actually to know God, but "not glorify [that One] *as* God" and, declaring oneself wise, become a fool. So Augustine paraded a seemingly rich, full understanding as a badge only of vanity and pompous authority. Then expertise becomes a downfall and self-inflation distorts claimed knowledge (VII, 20, 26). Augustine had to find a practice of life and mind that would *acknowledge* God if he was to come to a valid knowledge *of* God. He sought out Simplicianus for this purpose: that "he would show me a fit mode of life for someone like me to walk in your way [O God]" (VIII, 1, 1). Augustine's final, renowned conversion in the garden (VIII, 12, 29) was a conversion to Christian monasticism, dedicated humility. Only so could he learn truly to think God's thoughts.

Nevertheless, what about the intellect and its freedom? What about understanding? Granted a spiritual posture of humility at the base of knowing God's vast righteousness and God's creation, what about the mind's freedom to think critically? The church asked not only for a respectful, modest way of life (to see all things in their right worth), but also for the acceptance of doctrines, statements of belief, many that did not make ordinary sense. Should the intellect simply resign at this point? What about the right of the intellect to question all assertions? What about issues regarding the sacraments? the Incarnation? the Trinity? Must he simply believe these without objection?

As it turned out, belief was not a matter of giving up the right to think, but setting out on a journey of such thinking with something given to think about. Belief produced far greater confidence in coming to know God in the future, than purely individual reason or autonomous judgment could produce now. Belief was a communal act, not an isolated lunge to make something true. It linked to a community of the past (my tradition) as well as of the present and the future. Therefore, belief was trust, across boundaries, toward others and their teachings, where one could no longer privately control and manipulate. (Far from capitulating to someone's private language control, belief took Augustine out of his *own* private language control.) His childhood yearning for a household of trusted boundaries at length found a home in the believing Christian community.

Also, belief within this community already had glimpses of rational meaning. Belief leaned toward understanding, whereas the Manichaeans' "science" had deteriorated into mythology. Ambrose taught that the creation of humankind "in God's image" hardly meant that God had a humanlike body, hair, and teeth (VI, 3, 4; cf. Genesis 1:27)! Humanity rather bears the image of God in the free, rational mind. Belief in the Scriptures did not exclude, but rather promoted nurturing, rational interpretation. Belief in the Incarnation did not mean that the eternally unchanging God came suddenly to earth and walked about (VII, 19, 25). Rather, God's love, in God's mercy and humility, took special opportunity to communicate with the world (see Chapter 8). No doctrine failed to have at least glimmers of rational understanding in it. And the leadership that asked for belief in such authority was itself so reasonable and humane! Ambrose "received me like a father" (V, 13, 23). Simplicianus gave him the most thoughtful attention (VIII, 2–5). To live the life of such a community meant both to think and to become humane oneself. One would know God as one became more like God. Thought and life became inseparable. The God of Abraham, the God of Moses, would yet turn out to be the God of universal truth. To think within such a circle of authority was to think with humility, increasing insight, and total personal growth. Augustine's great burden of needing immediate certainty about all issues of thought eased and slipped away (VI, 4, 6).

The Trinity

Near the end of *Confessions* I, 1, 1, he says: "My faith calls upon you, O Lord, the faith which you have given me, which you have breathed into me through the humanity of your Son, through the ministry of your preacher." This compelling first section of the book, summing up so much of its whole meaning, ends with this gentle turn toward, as it were, God as Trinity: Lord (Father), breathed (Spirit), and Son. This hinted reference suggests the Triune God as both foundation and goal of all his seeking, the God from whom he came and to whom he yearns to return. It is not surprising that shortly after completing the *Confessions* he began a major work, *The Trinity*, that would occupy him, from time to time, for about twenty years (400–421 C.E.).

He told in it of belief seeking understanding, as he had projected in *Confessions* I. His entire discovery of thinking within Catholic Christian authority unfolds within the fifteen books of *The Trinity*. His purpose is to begin with the received, orthodox, Christian doctrine of the Trinity and come to understand it as a valid teaching on God—the universally, philosophically true God. A large order.

The prospects were not encouraging. The doctrine seemed to defy ordinary logic. It declares one God, yet in three persons, Father, Son, and Holy Spirit. Perhaps that means that each of the persons is somehow a "part" of God, and all of them taken together add up to one, complete God. No, the doctrine insists that *each* of the persons, for example, the Holy Spirit, is in its own right the full, true God. Yet the three taken together are not three Gods, but just One (*Trinity* I, 4, 7–6, 9). How can faithful people understand this?

The doctrine grew out of a peculiar history over generations. One strand was monotheism, profound loyalty to the one God. The other most important strand was the Christ-story, Jesus as God present to the world in a human being. Does this addition still keep monotheism, or does it imply two gods? Worship of the Holy Spirit, God's breath as immediate life-giver, raised the question as to three possible Gods. Can such a localized, Mid-Eastern account, peculiar to a particular people in history, point to the one, worldwide universal God of all truth?

Despite difficulties, Augustine sets out firmly. In the section to be considered here (Books IX–XV) he begins, "We . . . seek a trinity . . . which is God" (IX, 1, 1). The seeking may not have a conclusive result—in this life. Therefore, "seek [God's] face forevermore" (Psalm 105:4). Passionate commitment to the search, and yet its humbling awesomeness, lead him to say,

> Let us then seek as if we were about to find, and find as if we were about to seek.

Then he declares what it means to think within the circle of Christian authority:

> Let us doubt without unbelief concerning the things to be be-
> lieved; . . .

That is, ask of the Three-in-One, "How can this be?" without ceasing to
believe in it, and,

> Let us affirm without rashness concerning things to be understood.

Believe in the Three-in-One, not arrogantly, but humbly, while dedicated
to the long search for understanding.

> In the first statement, hold fast to authority; in the second, seek out
> truth (IX, 1, 1).

He holds together authoritative belief and truth universal. His passion for
both authority and reason goes back almost thirty years (prior to the *Confessions*) to his very earliest dialogues following his conversion (386 C.E.
[*Against the Skeptics* III, 20, 43]).

His approach to the journey is to find already known models or images
in everyday experience that suggest, in some way, a three-in-one and one-
in-three. To grasp such a model may suggest how God, in a vastly more
elevated manner, can be Three-in-One. Not surprisingly, his chosen model
is the human mind. For God created the human being in God's own image;
therefore the human mind should be in God's own image of three-in-one.
Yet how is the mind, in fact, a three-in-one?

Suppose, he says, a mind that loves itself (IX, 2, 2). In any love situation,
three elements appear: the lover, the beloved, and the love between them.
A mind that loves itself offers not only these three, but a strong oneness,
since only a single mind is involved; therefore, the three are in one. But
there is at least one major flaw. The mind that loves and the mind that *is*
loved are the same; therefore, only a two-in-one occurs, mind and love.

Someone asks: why choose something so difficult—a mind that loves
itself—when even Saint Patrick is said to have chosen a three-leaved sham-
rock? Augustine wants to come as close as possible to the triune image of
God; humanity and the human mind were made in that image. Therefore,
he chooses mind.

Undaunted, he shifts the model to a mind that *knows and* loves itself, apparently a more adequate image (IX, 3, 3). During the remainder of seven books, he continues to attempt improvements, shifting the model some ten times, with the last proposal really subdividing into two (XIV, 2, 4; 12, 15). The following diagram selects only two of the proposals as he moves them forward (a third will appear in the next section).

1. The mind (X, 10, 13)   as memory, understanding, and
                                           will.

2. Elements in the mind's activ-   form of the object seen, image of
   ity of physical sight: (X, 12,   the form impressed on the sense,
   19; XI, 2, 5)   and will, applying the image to
                                           the object and retaining it.

The mind as memory, understanding, and will is an attractive model of three-in-one, since each of the three can be thought of as really the whole mind in operation; yet all three taken together are certainly only one mind. Since nothing outside the mind is involved here (looking out on a river or a mountain), about which one might make a mistake, one cannot doubt for a moment one's own interior mind and its remembering, understanding, and willing.[1] Yet the price of this certainty is that the model is too purely interior, and the three begin to collapse into one another and into a simple unity. Augustine admits that it is difficult to discern between the mind's memory of itself and its understanding of itself. Therefore, a good model of the Trinity is not available by simply turning within. A correction for this is looking for a trinity in the mind turned outward.

Augustine sees a kind of trinity in the outward experience of seeing, for example, a horse. The mind wills the image of the horse gained through the eyes back to the horse itself, to grasp and to know that the horse is there. The three elements involved here certainly do not collapse into one another, but are highly diverse: the form of the horse, its image in one's

---

1. The point is roughly similar to the famous "I think, therefore I am" of René Descartes some twelve hundred years later. Augustine's near formulation is, "Even if one doubts, one lives" (etiam si dubitat, vivit) (Trinity X, 10, 14). Yet the two thinkers draw entirely different conclusions from the one insight. Descartes sees in his own undeniable self-consciousness a beginning point for all philosophy. Augustine sees only another failing model of the Trinity because the consciousness closes in on itself, collapsing into oneness, lacking outward movement or threeness. Cf. David S. Pacini, "Freedom, Self-Relatedness, and God," doctoral dissertation, Harvard University, 1979, chapter 2, "Augustine of Hippo: The Divine Form and Mind."

sense-perception, and that image willed back to the horse itself and retained in one's attention. All this constitutes, "See the horse!" The unity of the three is clear: Each is only a different location or direction of the same, single horse-image. Yet one is in an outward body; one, in a human interior sense; and one moves between.

A reader may feel that this see-the-horse model is hardly a striking vision of God. Augustine points out that this outward seeing does offer a kind of trinity, but not an image of God (XII, 4, 4). A model of the image of God must include the mind within itself, contemplating interiorly. For it is the mind itself, he holds, that is made in God's image. Yet his most telling statement is this: "When, within the [nature of the mind] we seek the Trinity, we seek it in the *whole* mind, not separating rational action in temporal things from the contemplation of eternal things" (XII, 4, 4; italics added). In the course of the treatise he has evidently made a most important decision: not to seek a model of the Trinity within the human mind by going only deeper and deeper into the mind's interiority. Under the influence of the Neoplatonists he might have done that. Rather, in Christian belief, the mind appropriately goes, not only inward, but outward to passing material events (the creation is good), *if* it does so well—that is, if it keeps outward things in perspective and does not slip into building its own self-centered material kingdom.

Inwardness alone might be a life of isolated asceticism. The mind comes closer and closer to a triune image of God when it is a *whole* mind, incorporating knowledge and experience of the outward swirl of events with the self-containment of contemplation. Again, a large order. Yet God is such: both outgoing and self-contained. God as Three implies involvement in creation. God as One implies drawing that creation closer and closer into harmonious unity with Godself. The mind that is more and more deeply in the trinitarian image keeps its poise, not only in the material world of rocks and trees and windstorms, but in the human world of the clash of wills—where all will to be happy, but so many *do* what makes them unhappy (XIII, 3, 6; 6, 9). How can the mind keep such poise, to know passing things and deal with them, and yet maintain contemplation of God?

The Trinity: A Formation of Life

By now the quest for trinitarian images within the mind is obviously more than an innocent description of the mind's structure. The search for more adequate images means the wrestling of the mind to *be* a more adequate image of God, to go on a pilgrimage of understanding the Trinity by becoming more and more in the *likeness* of that Trinity. Therefore, the search for understanding, far from being only an intellectual analysis, turns out to be a spiritual and moral formation. For faith to seek understanding therefore means growing in the wholeness of one's spirit. The way is long and difficult, for the seeker walks a narrow strand, looking inward for contemplation without complete withdrawal, reaching outward to the rush of material events without falling into chaos. How can one keep so taxing a commitment?

3. The mind under the impact of the Incarnation of Christ (XIII, 9, 12; 19, 24; 20, 26. XIV, 12, 15) as remembering, knowing, and loving God and the things of faith.

The grace of God specially enables the strenuous journey, and in a specific manner. In the above image proposal, anticipated on page 224, Augustine invokes Christ Incarnate, the Word made flesh, who responds exactly to both inward and outward needs of the pilgrim seeker. Christ was the Incarnate Word of God. If the fleshly world is unsettling, seize upon Christ, whose Word of truth illumines the mind and offers there poise, sound judgment, and even wisdom, in the midst of all material things. (He invites inward.) Yet Christ the Word was in the flesh. If the intellectual life withdraws and knows only its own interiority, seize upon Christ, whose flesh will not betray, but rather, through humility, offer the whole creation as God's gift. (He invites outward.) Concerning outward things he brings knowledge; concerning inward things he brings wisdom (XIII, 19, 24; Colossians 2:2–3).

Certainly the Incarnation brings the climax in Augustine's account of faith and understanding. What models of the Trinity now appear? The mind that receives the Incarnation (by authority!) now knows the things of faith, that is, the scriptural story from creation through Abraham, Moses, the prophets, to Jesus, the apostles; also, the preaching, the sacraments, the community of faith. The mind holds these items in memory, studies and ponders them, and loves them. In memory, knowledge, and love of these things a kind of Trinity appears, though Augustine will not allow that it is yet an image of God (XIII, 20, 26; XIV, 2, 4). It is rather an ordering and cleansing of the soul from chaos and disorientation.

The image of God occurs only in the heightening of the interior mind as the outward story of faith begins to bear fruit in inward contemplation. That is, the image of the Trinity in the human mind begins to come clear, not when the mind remembers, knows, and loves Jesus' resurrection; and not when the mind remembers, knows, and loves itself (even under the impact of that resurrection); but when the mind in a breathtaking turn upward remembers, knows, and loves God (XIV, 12, 15). To find a true model of the Trinity in one's mind is finally to see the Trinity, the source and goal of all, above one's mind.

Someone objects. Augustine could have admitted this turn toward God far back at the beginning: "To see the Trinity look upward, worship God!" and saved the long recital. To the contrary, only a mind that has struggled with the world and with itself, and has discovered in the Incarnation that God struggles with the world and within us; and has come to know that, despite all, the creation is good; and can enjoy itself in this knowledge ("a mind that . . . loves itself"): only that mind can turn and become like the Trinity in contemplating the Trinity. The worshiper takes with him or her the total of outward and inward experience into worship's uplifted mind. The narrow trail of long seeking finds reward.

Augustine admits, even toward the end of fifteen books, that the journey has only begun. "Such knowledge is too wonderful for me, it is high; I cannot attain unto it" (XV, 7, 13; Psalm 139:6). And he cries out in prayer at the very end, "Free me, my God, from that multitude of speech which I suffer within my soul, miserable in your sight . . . !" (XV, 28, 51). Even the language of Incarnation will have to fall silent, finally, in the passionate embrace of truth.

What, then, of understanding? "I . . . have desired to see with the understanding what I have believed" (XV, 28, 51). And he implores God to help him to continue to seek, and not falter out of weariness (after twenty-one years of intermittent writing). Though he has made certain discoveries, seeking does not end: "Let us . . . find as if we were about to seek" (IX, 1, 1). He does not claim the understanding he had hoped for.

The treatise ends with his understanding of the Trinity unfulfilled. Does his belief in authority therefore stand unjustified and shamed? His purpose had been to think within a circle of authority that would ultimately liberate his understanding; he would come to understand what at first he had believed. Now, after many years he says only, "Such knowledge is too wonderful for me; it is high . . ." He admits clearly that his model of memory, understanding, and will in the mind, even a worshiping mind, falls short (XV, 7, 11). The Creator resides far beyond.

Has he come to understanding in any sense? A clue may lie in his recapitulation of the entire treatise (XV, 3, 4–5), especially in one notation concerning Book VIII, which immediately preceded the journey of the images:

> I pointed out [in Book VIII] that a nature, not only truly incorporeal but also immutable, which is God, may be understood (insofar as that is possible!) . . . through love, which in Holy Scripture is called "God" [I John 4:16] . . .
>
> [There] a trinity, in some manner . . . begins to appear: namely, as one who loves, and one who is loved, and the love [itself]. (XV, 3, 5; cf. IX, 2, 2)

Perhaps the long journey of the images (Books IX–XIV) is in part an elaboration of this proposal from Book VIII. The human mind seeks an image of the Trinity in itself by its formation in love. For the trinitarian doctrine of a Parent God, who goes out to a Child, sharing a Life-Bond between them forever, certainly describes a God who is love. Then understanding itself must seek a love-formation.

"Let us love. Let us run" (Confessions VIII, 4, 9). The seeking mind passionately yearns for this God and for God's consummate embrace. The longing began all the way back with the discovery of Cicero: "How I felt myself on fire, my God . . . to turn back . . . toward you!" (Chapter 3). On the brink of conversion he pleaded with God to seize him: "Be fragrant, be sweet" (Chapter 9). God had given birth to love in him. What was he to do? What was his journey?

Love unfailingly asks a long commitment. As a monastic he had to intensify his interior devotion to God without isolating himself in secluded joy, for the Trinity does not isolate itself from the world. Yet he had to engage world, time, events, without being seduced or broken by them, for the Trinity never wavers despite its groaning engagement with creation. The pilgrimage of love demanded wider and wider embrace with a deeper and deeper foundation.

Where had his learning to think taken him? What had he come to understand? He had come to understand something of love. No theoretical analysis of the Trinity could ever understand God, but only one's formation in the image of God's life. If grace, through belief and authority, gave understanding (and it did), the understanding had to be wisdom regarding love (and it was). Yet did the philosophical God of universal truth that he sought in his understanding turn out to be the Triune God of faith? The answer can only be another question: Does love turn out to be the universal truth?

His book fell eons away from penetrating God-in-Godself, but it recorded his grappling to learn something of formation. To know as God knows, one must love as God loves. To find is only to begin to seek.

Conclusion

The *Confessions* narrative is the story of a conversion: a conversion that took place in a garden; a conversion that took place from the time Augustine read Cicero (age eighteen) until he was baptized, Easter, 387 (age thirty-two); a conversion that took place across his whole life. The story was not just of having arrived at a certain point, but of the long way around to get there.

Conversion means, literally "turning." The climax of his great turn includes the act of receiving to his heart the Incarnation, after long struggles without benefit of that deep gift. This sequence—extended struggle, Incarnation, new beginning—put its shape on everything he later wrote. He was a conversion thinker.

In the *Confessions* itself seven books have to do with his pursuing Roman professional ideals, then adopting a version of Greek philosophical enlightenment, both unsatisfactory. His turn to the Incarnation comes only in Book VIII, at the point of a new beginning for him. His *City of God* spends ten books on the goals of Roman and Greek life and thought (as does *Confessions* I–VII), then turns to the impact of the Incarnation across the history of the City of God, God's new beginning for the world. His *Trinity* spends four books (IX–XII) on the philosophical wrestling of a mind, inward and outward, with models of trinitarian form; only in XIII does the Incarnation emerge to give new scope and energy to the search. In anti-Pelagian writings (e.g., *The Spirit and the Letter*, *Nature and Grace*) struggles with natural free will in religion give way to the wonder of Incarnate grace and the renewal of the heart.

Just so, his life was a wrestling with cultural forms until, at length, his turn to the Incarnation opened his new way: "Late, late, have I loved you, O Beauty, ancient and new" (X, 27, 38). Such conversion etches deep into thought. It was a prism through which he saw God, world, himself, history. His *City of God* finds the history of the world (as available to him) following something of the same religious course as his own personal life portrayed in the *Confessions*. Even his description of the angels at creation shows them "converting," turning first to gaze at one day's work in creation (evening) and then turning upward, in wonder, to God's illumination (morning) (*Literal Commentary on Genesis* IV, 24, 41; Genesis 1:5).

Such a shared pattern among different works shows that the range of his religious thought finds an introduction, at least roughly, through his *Confessions* narrative. Yet the shared pattern raises more urgent issues.

A contemporary critic may say that Augustine's using his conversion as a key for understanding everything else, even world history, is distressingly biased and nonobjective. Has his powerful ego simply stamped itself across reality, calling up a mighty drama of God, angels, creation, peoples, empires all composed out of eccentric events that happened to him, individually? Hardly. For one thing, his individuality first formed itself out of many of these same mighty forces. Even in his home of origin, two worlds, the pagan (Patricius) and the Christian (Monica), struggled under one roof. Life grounded his individuality on the mighty forces he went on to describe. They were real; he was speaking of what he really knew.

Yet more important: Rather than forcing his own image on reality, he held that his particular experience, alienated, restless, had at length found a meaning, a home, in creation. An ordering of the world is there, if only humanity can find its place within that ordering. His conversion was the discovery of the meaning of his restlessness and the beginning of its resolution. His conversion was the discovery within the world's ordering of a fruitful place for his life. Far from reading the universe through his preestablished views, he found his views a gift from the nature of things, from how the universe really works. His conversion taught him truth. He had glimpsed the one true world, beyond the persistent two-world divisions practiced everywhere by humanity (see "Introduction" above).

All this was long ago. Yet humanity still ponders restlessness. In the West, the earlier twentieth-century version of restlessness was alienation within history and time, loss of authenticity, corrupt institutions, collapse into war and massive human death. Now, in addition, the question is nature. Is humankind a destructive agent within the natural created world, destined only to disrupt sublime processes and earn a miserable end? The long strand of memory from Augustine declares that an order of grace impinges upon the world. Humanity may yet continue to turn, and seek it, and find it.

Further Reading

Augustine (Select works in chronological order)

The Happy Life, Against the Skeptics, Order (The Cassiciacum Dialogues). Trans. L. Schopp, D. J. Kavanaugh, R. P. Russell. In *The Fathers of the Church* series. Vol. 1. New York: Cima, 1948. (386)

The Soliloquies. Trans. J. H. S. Burleigh. In *Augustine: Earlier Writings.* In the *Library of Christian Classics* (Ichthus Edition). Philadelphia: Westminster, 1953. (386)

The Catholic and Manichaean Ways of Life. (Also translated as *The Morals of the Catholic Church . . .*). Trans. D. A. and I. J. Gallagher. In the *Fathers of the Church* series. Vol. 56. Washington, D.C.: The Catholic University of America Press, 1966. (388)

The Teacher. Trans. J. H. S. Burleigh. In *Augustine: Earlier Writings.* In the *Library of Christian Classics* (Ichthus edition). Philadelphia: Westminster, 1953. (389)

Free Will. Trans. J. H. S. Burleigh. In *Augustine: Earlier Writings.* In the *Library of Christian Classics* (Ichthus edition). Philadelphia: Westminster, 1953. (388–395)

True Religion. Trans. J. H. S. Burleigh. In *Augustine: Earlier Writings.* In the *Library of Christian Classics* (Ichthus edition). Philadelphia: Westminster, 1953. (390)

Expositions of Psalms. In *A Library of the Fathers.* 6 vols. Oxford: John Henry Parker, 1850. (392–420)

Christian Doctrine. Trans. D. W. Robertson, Jr. New York: Liberal Arts, 1958. (396, finished 427)

To Simplicianus—On Various Questions. Book 1. Trans. J. H. S. Burleigh. In *Augustine: Earlier Writings.* In the *Library of Christian Classics* (Ichthus edition). Philadelphia: Westminster, 1953. (396)

Confessions. (For different translations, see above, pages xiii–xiv, "A Note on the *Confessions.*") (397–399)

The Trinity. Trans. E. Hill. In *The Works of St. Augustine, a Translation for the 21st Century.* Part 1. Vol. 5. Brooklyn: New City Press, 1991. (400–421)

Baptism, against the Donatists. Trans. J. R. King. In the *Nicene Post-Nicene Fathers* series. 1st series. Vol. 4. New York: Charles Scribner's Sons, 1909. (400–401)

Answer to the Letters of Petilian. Trans. J. R. King. In the *Nicene Post-Nicene Fathers* series. 1st series. Vol. 4. New York: Charles Scribner's Sons, 1909. (401–405)

The Literal Meaning of Genesis. (Also translated as *Genesis according to the Letter.*) Trans. J. H. Taylor. In the *Ancient Christian Writers* series. Nos. 41–42. New York: Newman, 1982. (402–415)

Tractates on the Gospel of John. Trans. J. W. Rettig. In the *Fathers of the Church* series. Vols. 78–79, 88. Washington, D.C.: The Catholic University of America Press, 1988– . (406–407, 418–421)

The Spirit and the Letter. Trans. J. Burnaby. In the *Library of Christian Classics.* Vol. 8. Philadelphia: Westminster, 1955. (412)

The City of God. Trans. H. Bettenson. New York: Penguin Books, 1972. (413–426)

Nature and Grace. Ed. W. J. Oates. In *Basic Writings of St. Augustine.* Vol. 1. New York: Random House, 1948. (415)

The Grace of Christ and Original Sin. Book 2. Trans. P. Holmes. In *An Augustine Reader,* ed. J. J. O'Meara. Garden City, N.Y.: Image Books, 1973. (418)

The Enchiridion on Faith, Hope, and Love. Trans. J. F. Shaw. Chicago: Gateway Edition, 1961. (423)

Grace and Free Will. Ed. W. J. Oates. In *Basic Writings of St. Augustine.* Vol. 1. New York: Random House, 1948. (427)

Retractations. Trans. M. I. Bogan. In the *Fathers of the Church* series. Vol. 60. Washington, D.C.: The Catholic University of America Press, 1968. (427)

Other Ancient Sources

Athanasius of Alexandria. Trans. anon. *The Incarnation.* Crestwood: St. Vladimir's Seminary, 1953, 1989.

———. *The Life of Antony.* Trans. R. C. Gregg. In *Classics of Western Spirituality.* New York: Paulist Press, 1980.

Pelagius. *Commentaries on Paul* (fragments). In D. W. Johnson. "Purging the Poison: The Revision of Pelagius' Pauline Commentaries . . ." Ph.D. diss., Princeton Theological Seminary, 1990.

———. *Commentary on St. Paul's Epistle to the Romans.* Trans. T. DeBruyn. Oxford: Clarendon Press, 1993.

———. *Letters.* Trans. B. R. Rees. In *The Letters of Pelagius and His Followers.* Bury St. Edmunds: Boydell Press, 1991.

Plotinus. *The Six Enneads.* Trans. S. MacKenna and B. S. Page. In *Great Books of the Western World.* Vol. 17. Chicago: Encyclopaedia Britannica, 1952.

Contemporary Works

Armstrong, A. H., ed. *The Cambridge History of Later Greek and Early Medieval Philosophy.* London: Cambridge University Press, 1967.

———. *St. Augustine and Christian Platonism.* Villanova: Villanova University Press, 1967.

Auerbach, Erich. *Literary Language and Its Public in Late Latin Antiquity and in the Middle Ages.* New York: Pantheon, 1965.

———. *Mimesis*. Trans. W. R. Trask. Princeton: Princeton University Press, 1953.

Babcock, William. "The Christ of the Exchange: A Study in the Christology of Augustine's *Enarrationes in Psalmos.*" Ph.D. diss., Yale University, 1972.

———, ed. *The Ethics of St. Augustine*. Atlanta: Scholars Press, 1991.

Battenhouse, R. W., ed. *A Companion to the Study of St. Augustine*. New York: Oxford University Press, 1955.

Bondi, Roberta C. *To Love as God Loves: Conversations with the Early Church.* Philadelphia: Fortress, 1987.

Bonner, Gerald. *St. Augustine of Hippo: Life and Controversies*. New York: AMS, 1985.

Brown, Peter. *Augustine of Hippo: a Biography*. Berkeley and Los Angeles: University of California Press, 1969.

Burnaby, John. *Amor Dei: A Study of the Religion of St. Augustine*. London: Hodder and Stoughton, 1938.

Capps, D., and J. E. Dittes, eds. *The Hunger of the Heart: Reflections on the Confessions of Augustine*. Purdue University: Society for the Social and Scientific Study of Religion, 1990.

Deane, H. A. *The Political and Social Ideas of St. Augustine*. New York: Columbia University Press, 1963.

Ferrari, Leo. *The Conversions of St. Augustine*. Villanova: Augustinian Institute, 1984.

Frend, W. H. C. *The Donatist Church: A Movement of Protest in Roman North Africa*. Oxford: Clarendon, 1952.

———. *The Rise of Christianity*. Philadelphia: Fortress, 1984.

Geisler, N. L., ed. *What Augustine Says*. Grand Rapids, Mich.: Baker Book House, 1982.

Jonas, Hans. *The Gnostic Religion*. 2d ed., revised. Boston: Beacon, 1963.

Kelly, J. N. D. *Early Christian Doctrines*. New York: Harper and Brothers, 1958.

Lawless, George. *Augustine of Hippo and His Monastic Rule*. New York: Oxford University Press, 1987.

Mallard, William. "The Incarnation in Augustine's Conversion." *Recherches Augustiniennes*. Paris: Etudes Augustiniennes, 1980. 15:80–98.

Markus, R. A. *Saeculum: History and Society in the Theology of St. Augustine*. Cambridge: Cambridge University Press, 1970.

Marrou, Henri. *St. Augustine and His Influence Through the Ages*. Trans. P. Hepburne-Scott. London: Longmans, Green, 1957.

McWilliam, Joanne. *Augustine: From Rhetor to Theologian*. Waterloo: Wilfrid Laurier University Press, 1992.

Miles, M. R. *Desire and Delight: A New Reading of Augustine's Confessions*. New York: Crossroad, 1992.

Nash, R. H. *The Light of the Mind: St. Augustine's Theory of Knowledge*. Lexington: University Press of Kentucky, 1969.

O'Connell, R. J. *The Origin of the Soul in St. Augustine's Later Works*. New York: Fordham University Press, 1987.

———. *St. Augustine's Confessions*. Cambridge: Harvard University Press, 1969.

O'Meara, J. J., ed. *An Augustine Reader*. Garden City, N.Y.: Doubleday, 1973.

———. *Charter of Christendom: The Significance of the City of God*. New York: Macmillan, 1961.

———. *The Young Augustine*. London: Longmans, Green, 1954.

Pacini, David S. "Freedom, Self-Relatedness, and God." Chapter 2. Ph.D. diss., Harvard University, 1979.

Rees, B. R. *Pelagius, a Reluctant Heretic*. Woodbridge, Suffolk: Boydell, 1988.

Ricoeur, Paul. *The Symbolism of Evil*. New York: Harper and Row, 1967.

Ruether, Rosemary R. "Augustine and Christian Political Theology." *Interpretation* 29, no. 3 (July 1975): 252–65.

Starnes, Colin. *Augustine's Conversion: A Guide to the Argument of Confessions I–IX.* Waterloo: Wilfrid Laurier University Press, 1990.

Strauss, W. A. "Franz Kafka." *Centennial Review* 5, no. 2 (spring 1961).

Tillich, Paul. *A History of Christian Thought.* Vol. 1, sec. II. New York: Simon and Schuster, 1972.

Van der Meer, F. *Augustine the Bishop.* Trans. B. Battershaw and G. R. Lamb. London: Sheed and Ward, 1961.

Index of Citations

Scripture

Confessions

For Augustine's other works cited, see Index of Topics: Augustine, writings.

Index of Topics